Poetic Inquiry
as Social Justice
and Political Response

Edited by

Sandra L. Faulkner
Bowling Green State University

and

Abigail Cloud
Bowling Green State University

Series in Literary Studies

VERNON PRESS

www.vernonpress.com

In the Americas:
Vernon Press
1000 N West Street,
Suite 1200, Wilmington,
Delaware 19801
United States

In the rest of the world:
Vernon Press
C/Sancti Espiritu 17,
Malaga, 29006
Spain

Series in Literary Studies

Library of Congress Control Number: 2019939877

ISBN: 978-1-62273-834-2

Also available:

978-1-62273-649-2 [Hardback]; 978-1-62273-752-9 [PDF, E-Book]

Cover design by Vernon Press. Cover image: Poetic Inquiry by Sandra L. Faulkner.

Table of Contents

Foreword

This volume presents refereed work from the 6th International Symposium on Poetic Inquiry (ISPI) and the 17th annual Winter Wheat: The *Mid-American Review* Festival of Writing held at Bowling Green State University in 2017. The ISPI symposium is a biennial gathering of international poets, researchers, students, and community members interested in the use of poetry and poetic inquiry as a research method, methodology, and/or approach (see below for a history of all the gatherings). This informal community of poets and researchers meets in person, online, and on the page to engage in the fun and difficult conversations about what poetry can do in our qualitative work and practices.[1] Winter Wheat is a festival consisting of generative workshops and readings that celebrates writers and readers, produced by internationally distributed literary journal *Mid-American Review* and hosted on the campus of Bowling Green State University.[2] In early November 2017, the conferences co-convened with the theme *Poetry as/in/for Social Justice*; participants at the symposium considered how poetic inquiry can be used to interrogate social structures, cultural norms, and discourses that create inequalities and social injustice and how poetry can act as response and political voice.

For this volume, we invited manuscripts and poetry from the symposium that engage with poetry's potential for connectivity, political power, and evocation through methodological, theoretical, performative, and empirical work. The poet-researchers consider questions of how poetry and poetic inquiry can be a response to political and social events, be used as a pedagogical tool to critique inequitable social structures, and speak to our local identities and politics. This volume represents a growing body of work on the use of poetry as/in/for qualitative research (see below for a list of ISPI publications).[3] Specifically, *Poetic Inquiry as Social Justice and Political Response* speaks to the use of poetry in critical qualitative research and practice focused on social justice. Other ISPI volumes and journals have focused on the range of poetic inquiry from the use of literature-voiced poems (VOX THEORIA) to researcher-voiced poems (VOX AUTOBIOGRAPHIA) to participant-voiced poems (VOX PARTICIPARE);[4] poetry as a way of knowing, being, and telling;[5] poetic inquiry in the fields of healthcare and education;[6] poetic inquiry as reflection and renewal;[7] poetic inquiry as social justice;[8] and the connection between poetry and the natural world through an examination of the ecological scope of poetic inquirers.[9]

In this collection, poetry is a response, a call to action, agitation, and a frame for future social justice work. The authors answer a question posed in previous ISPI gatherings: "What spaces can poetry create for dialogue about critical awareness, social justice, and re-visioning of social, cultural, and political worlds?"[10] This collection adds to the growing body of poetic inquiry through the demonstration of poetry as political action, response, and reflective practice. We hope this collection inspires you to write and engage with political poetry to realize the power of poetry as political action, response, and reflective practice.

We dedicate this volume to Carl Leggo—friend, poet, mentor, teacher, and champion of Poetic Inquiry.

Gatherings of the International Symposium on Poetic Inquiry

2007   Vancouver, British Columbia, Canada
        Hosted by Monica Prendergast and Carl Leggo (University of
        British Columbia's Centre for Cross-Faculty Inquiry & Faculty of
        Education)

2009   Charlottetown, Prince Edward Island, Canada
        Hosted by Suzanne Thomas (Centre for Education Research,
        Faculty of Education, University of Prince Edward Island) and
        Ardra Cole (Centre for Arts-Informed Research, Ontario Institute
        for Studies in Education, University of Toronto)

2011   Bournemouth University, Bournemouth, England
        Hosted by Kate Galvin and Les Todres (Bournemouth University,
        Dorset, UK)

2013   Avmor Gallery in Old Montreal, Quebec, Canada
        Hosted by Lynn Butler-Kisber (McGill University), Mary Stewart
        (LEARN Quebec), and John J. Guiney Yallop (Acadia University)

2015   University of British Columbia Botanical Gardens, Vancouver,
        British Columbia, Canada
        Hosted by Pauline Sameshima (Lakehead University), Alexandra
        Fidyk (University of Alberta), Kedrick James (University of
        British Columbia), and Carl Leggo (University of British
        Columbia)

2017   Bowling Green State University, Bowling Green, Ohio, USA
        Co-convened with the Annual Winter Wheat: The *Mid-American
        Review* Festival of Writing
        Hosted by Sandra L. Faulkner and Abigail Cloud (Bowling Green
        State University, School of Cultural and Critical Studies, The
        Department of English, and *Mid-American Review*)

Publications from the International Symposium on Poetic Inquiry 1-6

2009   *Poetic Inquiry: Vibrant Voices in the Social Sciences.* Edited by
        Monica Prendergast, Carl Leggo, and Pauline Sameshima, Sense.

2009   Poetic Inquiry, *Educational Insights 3(3).* Guest Editors: Monica
        Prendergast, Carl Leggo, and Pauline Sameshima.

2012   *The Art of Poetic Inquiry.* Edited by Suzanne Thomas, Ardra Cole,
        and Sheila Stewart, Backalong Books.

2014   The Practices of Poetic Inquiry. *in education 20(2).* Guest Editors:
        John J. Guiney Yallop, Sean Wiebe, and Sandra L. Faulkner.

2016   *Poetic Inquiry II: Seeing, Caring, Understanding.* Edited by
        Kathleen Galvin and Monica Prendergast, Sense.

2017   *Inquiries of Reflection and Renewal.* Edited by Lynn Butler-Kisber,
        John J. Guiney Yallop, Mary Stewart, and Sean Wiebe, MacIntyre
        Purcell.

2017   *Poetic Inquiry: Enchantments of Place.* Edited by Pauline
        Sameshima, Alexandra Fidyk, Kedrick James, and Carl Leggo,
        Vernon Press.

2018   Poetry and Social Justice. *Art/Research International: A
        Transdisciplinary Journal, 3(1).* Guest Editor: Sandra L. Faulkner.

2019   *Poetic Inquiry as Social Justice and Political Response.* Edited by
        Sandra L. Faulkner and Abigail Cloud, Vernon Press.

Notes

1. http://www.poeticinquiry.ca/

2. https://casit.bgsu.edu/midamericanreview/winter-wheat-about/

3. Faulkner, 2019.

4. Prendergast, Leggo, and Sameshima, *Poetic Inquiry: Vibrant Voices.*

5. Thomas, Cole, and Stewart, *The Art of Poetic Inquiry.*

6. Galvin and Prendergast, "The Practices of Poetic Inquiry."

7. Butler-Kisber, Guiney Yallop, Stewart, and Wiebe, *Poetic Inquiries of Reflection and Renewal.*

8. Faulkner, *Poetry and Social Justice.*

9. Sameshima, Fidyk, James, and Leggo, *Poetic Inquiry III: Enchantments.*

10. Sameshima, Fidyk, James, and Leggo, *Poetic Inquiry III: Enchantments,* 18.

Bibliography

Butler-Kisber, Lynn, John J. Guiney Yallop, Mary Stewart, and Sean Wiebe, editors. *Poetic Inquiries of Reflection and Renewal: poetry as research.* Nova Scotia: MacIntyre Purcell, 2017.

Faulkner, Sandra L., editor. *Poetry and Social Justice Special Issue Art/Research International: A Transdisciplinary Journal,* 3, no. 1 (2018).

Faulkner, Sandra L. *Poetic Inquiry: Craft, Method, and Practice,* 2nd ed. New York: Routledge, 2019.

Galvin, Kathleen, and Monica Prendergast, editors. *Poetic Inquiry II: Seeing, Caring, Understanding: Using Poetry as and for Inquiry.* Rotterdam, The Netherlands: Sense, 2016.

Prendergast, Monica, Carl Leggo, and Pauline Sameshima, editors. *Poetic Inquiry: Vibrant Voices in the Social Sciences.* Rotterdam: Sense/Brill Publishers, 2009.

Sameshima, Pauline, Alexandra Fidyk, Kedrick James, and Carl Leggo, editors. *Poetic Inquiry III: Enchantments of Place.* Wilmington, DE: Vernon Press, 2017.

Thomas, Suzanne, Ardra Cole, and Sheila Stewart, editors. *The Art of Poetic Inquiry.* Nova Scotia: Backalong Books, 2012.

Poetic Inquiry as Social Justice and Political Response

Sandra L. Faulkner,
Bowling Green State University

"Poetry matters because it can waken us to realities that fall into the realm of the political."[1]

Many social researchers use poetry in their work to re-present the human experience in a more approachable, powerful, emotionally poignant, and accurate form than prose research reports allow.[2] Scholar poets use poetry as a form of research representation, as data analysis, as a research tool, and as a research methodology. As Norman Denzin notes, "the poet makes the world visible in new and different ways, in ways ordinary social science writing does not allow. The poet is accessible, visible, and present in the text, in ways that traditional writing forms discourage."[3] Poetic inquiry includes, "the use of poetry crafted from research endeavors, either before project analysis, as a project analysis, and/or poetry that is part of or that constitutes an entire research project."[4] Though a fixed definition of poetic inquiry does not exist, poetic inquiry describes, "a method of turning research interviews, transcripts, observations, personal experience, and reflections into poems or poetic forms."[5]

One reason scholars use poetry in their work is the power of poetry as a means to engage a political voice. Poetic inquiry can be an active response to social issues, a political commentary, and a call to action:

> The poetic inquiry movement offers a contribution to a developing body of evidence that is not merely a third person perspective, as in conventional evidence, but is also intimate with first and second person perspectives and is thus a fertile pathway to ethical, caring, and empathic work. In reading or listening to a poem we are bearing witness to the other, to the person writing the poem, or to the situation that is the subject of the poem and this is a fundamental part of caring work.[6]

Poetic inquiry represents engaged social science.[7] Writing and performing poetry can be political activity; many scholars and poets turn to poetry as a way to make sense of, critique, and respond to current events. For example, poets write poetry in response to events in the news for *Rattle*'s online magazine *Poets Respond*,[®8] and other online journals like *Writers Resist*[9] and *Rise Up Review*.[10] The response offers a way to critique power structures, offer alternative views, and advocate for social justice. Burford uses poetry in his research on the neoliberal university as a kind of political practice that "enables inhabitants of the university to reflect on a diverse array of political phenomena—from the structuring frame of heteronormativity to the wide scale marketization of universities across the globe."[11] Reale uses poetic inquiry in her work with refugees from Sicily and Africa as a form of social activism.[12] She writes her research as poetry because she is "interested in presenting my research in ways that are easily relatable, understood, and accessible. [She] was not interested in presenting [her] research in a jargon-filled and sterile way, able only to be interpreted by the chosen few."[13] Poets and researchers can use poetry to engage audiences and activate poetry's political potential.[14]

Poetry can help us shape lives in ways that we want to live; we create and tell stories that advocate for social justice and change. Rita Dove considers poetry to work through poets' use of empathy and reader's recognition of themselves and their worlds in verse: "Poets … are sensitive to their surroundings in the world where they live. So, speaking out is almost unavoidable. That can sustain people, because if someone reads a poet's description of an experience for which they had no words before, it again offers the reassurance of telling them that they are not alone."[15] Ivan Brady writes of how poetic methods are steeped in an author's self-awareness; "poets write *in* and *with* the facts and frameworks of what they see in themselves *in relation to* Others in particular landscapes, emotional, and social situations."[16] Poetic inquiry as political activism works because it makes the personal political. Faulkner tells us how this works: "Poetry taps into the universal through radical subjectivity. The poet's use of personal experience creates something larger from the particular; the concrete specifics become universal when the audience relates to, embodies, and/or experiences the work as if it were their own words."[17]

This volume addresses poetry's role as a creative art that is vital in the inquiry process and presentation, a method of engaging in important social issues.[18] The pieces in this collection engage with poetry's potential for connectivity, political power, and evocation through methodological, theoretical, performative, and empirical work. The poets reveal inequitable social conditions in education, immigration, politics, and their local communities; they use poetry to question inequality and show how poetry can be a personal and political response. The political task of poetry is "making way for new worlds and words."[19] Some poets, like Rita Dove and Naomi Shihab Nye, argue that art, and poetry in particular, are important to deny tyranny in all forms.[20] Poetic inquirers, such as Monica Prendergast, consider poetic inquiry an important tool for social change and social justice.

> I am interested in social poetry as the core mandate for critical poetic inquirers whose work is in support of equity, human rights, and justice worldwide. Critical poetic inquiry invites us to engage as active witnesses within our research sites, as witnesses standing beside participants in their search for justice, recognition, healing, a better life.[21]

The authors in this volume use poetic inquiry as a way to reflect on power inequities, to make their personal experience part of the critique, and to realize the potential power in poetry as political discourse.

Notes

1. Orr, "The Politics of Poetry," 416.

2. Faulkner, "Poetic Inquiry: Craft, Method, and Practice."

3. Denzin, *Interpretive Autoethnography*, 86.

4. Faulkner, "Poetic Inquiry," 210.

5. Faulkner, *Poetic Inquiry: Craft, Method, and Practice*.

6. Galvin and Prendergast, 2016, xv.

7. Faulkner, "Poetry Is Politics."

8. https://www.rattle.com/respond/

9. http://www.writersresist.com/

10. http://www.riseupreview.com/index.html

11. Burford, "Sketching Possibilities," 238.

12. Reale, "Living One Day."

13. Reale, "We Never Thought," 110.

14. Orr, "The Politics of Poetry."

15. Masciotra, "Rita Dove."

16. Brady, Foreword, xiv

17. Faulkner, "Poetic Inquiry," 210.

18. Faulkner, "Poetic Inquiry."

19. Fisher, "Outside the Republic," 984.

20. Masciotra, "Rita Dove."

21. Prendergast, "Surrender," 683.

Bibliography

Brady, Ivan. "Foreword." In *Poetic Inquiry II: Seeing, caring, understanding: Using poetry as and for inquiry*, xi-xvi. Edited by K. Galvin and M. Prendergast. Rotterdam, The Netherlands: Sense, 2016.

Burford, James. "Sketching Possibilities: Poetry and Politically-Engaged Academic Practice." *Art/Research International: A Transdisciplinary Journal*, 3.1 (2018): 229-246.

Denzin, Norman. K. *Interpretive Autoethnography*, 2nd ed. Thousand Oaks, CA: Sage, 2014.

Faulkner, Sandra L. *Poetic Inquiry: Craft, Method, and Practice*, 2nd ed. New York: Routledge, 2019.

Faulkner, Sandra L. "Poetic Inquiry: Poetry as/in/for Social Research." In *The Handbook of Arts-Based Research*, 208-230. Edited by Patricia Leavy. New York: Guilford Press, 2017.

Faulkner, Sandra L. "Poetry Is Politics: A Poetry Manifesto." *International Review of Qualitative Research* 10 (2017): 89–96.

Faulkner, Sandra L., Bernadette M. Calafell, and Diane S. Grimes. "Hello Kitty Goes to College: Poems about Harassment in the Academy." In *Poetic Inquiry: Vibrant Voices in the Social* Sciences, 187-208. Edited by M. Prendergast, C. Leggo, and P. Sameshima. Rotterdam: Sense Publishers, 2009.

Fisher, Thomas. "Outside the Republic: A Visionary Political Poetics." *Textual Practice* 23 (2009): 975–986. doi:10.1080/09502360903361600

Galvin, Kathleen, and Monica Prendergast, editors. *Poetic Inquiry II: Seeing, Caring, Understanding: Using Poetry as and for Inquiry*. Rotterdam, The Netherlands: Sense, 2016.

Masciotra, David. "Rita Dove: 'The First Thing That Goes When a Government Becomes a Tyranny Are Words.'" *Salon*. February 5, 2017. https://www.salon.com/2017/02/05/rita-dove-the-first-thing-that-goes-when-a-government-becomes-a-tyranny-are-words/?utm_content=buffer00fe4&utm_medium=social&utm_source=facebook.com&utm_campaign=buffer

Orr, David. "The Politics of Poetry." *Poetry* 192 (2008): 409–418.

Parini, Jay. *Why Poetry Matters*. New Haven, CT: Yale University Press, 2008.

Prendergast, Monica. "Poetic Inquiry, 2007-2012: A Surrender and Catch Found Poem." *Qualitative Inquiry*, 21, no. 8 (2015), 678–685. doi:10.1177/1077800414563806

Rattle Poetry. Poetry is back in the news. https://www.rattle.com/respond/

Reale, Michelle. "Living One Day Is Easy, Living a Life Is Hard: A Sudanese Refugee in Sicily." *Cultural Studies <=> Critical Methodologies*, 15, no. 6 (2015): 490-491. doi:10.177//1532708615614023

Reale, Michelle. "We Never Thought It Would Be Like This": Refugees' Experiences in Sicily." *The Qualitative Report*, 20, no. 1, Article 6 (2015): 107-114. http://www.nova.edu/ssss/QRQR20/1/reale6.pdf

Rise Up Review! http://www.riseupreview.com/index.html

Writer's Resist. http://www.writersresist.com/

I: Poetic Inquiry as Pedagogical Practice and Community Building

Poetic inquiry creates a space for communication and interrogation.
—Laura Apol and Mark McCarthy

In this section, we offer chapters that demonstrate how poetry can be a pedagogical tool to address social injustices through community practice and a tool to practice reflexivity and show positionality. For example, Laura Apol and Mark McCarthy write about their use of literature in a class with future educators in "Pedagogy, Poetry, and Politics: Using Poetic Inquiry to Convey, Challenge and Co/Create a Response to Literature." They write "data poems" about their experiences training prospective teachers to uncover their positionality as educators and poetic inquirers and ask an important question:

> What are the boundaries among research, art, and teaching when it comes to highly charged issues in which our pedagogical, poetic, and political selves do not merely wish to *convey*, but also to *challenge* and *create*?

Poetic inquirers can use their pedagogical poetry practice to engage with this question. Using poems to document a researcher's and teacher's understanding of a social process promises to give new insights. Amanda N. Gulla and Molly H. Sherman, in "Difficult, Beautiful Things: Young Immigrant Writers Find Voice and Empowerment through Poetry," present a collaborative project with young immigrants in their work as an education professor and a high school English teacher. They integrated visual art and poetry into a workshop they designed for young immigrants to help them explore their identities and the immigrant experience together. The students learned to feel pride in their origins and stories, similar to the growth felt by Alexandra Fidyk's students. In "Poetics of the Body: Contemplative, Somatic, and Arts-Integrated Methods for Girls' Well-Being," Fidyk discusses her work with girls around body image and the importance of poetry as a performative practice. The girls found confidence in the lyric, "[a]s such poetic inquiry became poetry as process; poetry as performance; poetry as voice (symbol and word); poetry as remapping life." Poetic inquiry has much to offer our pedagogical practices in and outside of the classroom, for both students and researcher-teachers alike.

1.

Pedagogy, Poetry, and Politics: Using Poetic Inquiry to Convey, Challenge, and Co/Create a Response to Literature

Laura Apol,
Michigan State University

Mark McCarthy,
Michigan State University

This chapter began as a pedagogical study of our students' written responses to literature focused on Muslims in the Middle East. We wondered whether ongoing engagement with books by and about "Others" over the duration of a semester would sharpen students' awareness of their own identities and unexamined stereotypes they might carry. We chose poetic inquiry—specifically, the creation of "data poems"—as a research methodology to explore one student's thinking. The resulting poems did little to help us engage with the student or her responses, leading us to expand our inquiry into a range of poetic strategies and, in the process, to raise methodological questions that initially overshadowed but ultimately spoke to our pedagogical concerns. In rewriting student stances into poems, we created a space for conversation with one another, with our overarching pedagogical and political commitments, and with the methodology itself.

Keywords: teacher education, teacher inquiry, literature response, poetic inquiry methodology

Political and social rhetoric casts many groups of people as dangerous "others," especially those non-white, non-Christian, and non-U.S.-born.

This climate of xenophobia has risen recently in regard to Muslims, and given the pervasiveness of this rhetoric in contemporary news and social media, we feared that these stereotypes would show up in our teacher education classrooms, and in our students' future classrooms as well. One means to counter potential negative assumptions teachers may carry into the field is to provide experiences reading literature by and about diverse groups, enlarging students' perspectives and challenging ethnocentric views.

This paper began as a pedagogical study of the written responses of prospective teachers as they engaged with literature focused on Muslims in the Middle East. We wanted to know whether ongoing engagement with books by and about "others" over the duration of a semester would shape our students' thinking and sharpen their awareness of their own identities and the unexamined stereotypes they might carry. We chose poetic inquiry—specifically, the creation of "data poems" based on one student's journal entries—as a research methodology because we believed it would allow us to see more deeply into our students' thinking. The resulting poems, however, did little to help us engage with the student or her responses, leading us to expand our inquiry into a range of poetic strategies and, in the process, to raise methodological questions that initially overshadowed but ultimately spoke to our pedagogical concerns. We re-viewed and re-wrote student stances into poems, creating a space for conversation with one another, with our overarching pedagogical and political commitments, and with the methodology itself. Ultimately, this creative process foregrounded our stances as educators and raised questions about our own processes as poetic inquirers.

Goals and Background

Prospective teachers, who are often white and Christian, must be prepared to teach students unlike them; however, they often hold deficit beliefs about minority students.[1] Although "holding deficit beliefs" differs from viewing Muslims as a threat, each emerges from practices of othering. Reading, responding to, and writing about literature as a part of coursework have been effective in developing more positive views of other cultures among prospective teachers.[2]

In our classes, we use global literature as one means to support prospective teachers in understanding and validating cultures outside their own. At the start of this study, we intended to determine the effectiveness of this approach using poetic inquiry as a means to understand and convey student responses. However, our poetic renderings of student writing seemed to us decidedly unpoetic, leading us further into drafting poems that adhered less directly to the student work and functioned more freely as poems in their own right. As a result, our questions shifted from determining the efficacy of the pedagogy to exploring the methodology itself—eventually asking:

> What are the boundaries between research, art, and teaching when it comes to highly charged issues in which our pedagogical, poetic, and political selves do not merely wish to *convey*, but also to *challenge* and *create*?

Poet-scholars maintain that using elements of poetry in data collection, analysis, and write-up has the potential to make our thinking clearer, fresher, and more accessible,[3] and to make visible what might otherwise be overlooked.[4] Focusing on repetition of words and phrases foregrounds themes that emerge in analysis—themes that are made more visible through a developing relationship between the researcher and the data[5]— and consequently brings different insights than a straightforward prose presentation would allow.[6] Thus, documenting student responses in the form of poems not only can help us make better sense of those students' evolving understanding, but also allows us to communicate that understanding more powerfully to the readers of the research. The "poetic" in inquiry can be characterized by the use of a range of poetic elements found in effective literary poetry[7]; poetry "expresses something that feels inexpressible in prose."[8] Yet within the field of poetic inquiry, there are tensions regarding how research data are represented: what are the responsibilities of the poet-researcher vis-à-vis the data and the aesthetic of the poem? We were committed to an aesthetic "poetic" understanding of poetry in inquiry, and found ourselves questioning the methodological boundaries of poetic inquiry as we moved more deliberately toward increasingly poetic and political expression.[9]

Method

Mark was the instructor of a section of a required children's literature course specifically created for global educators-in-training—a cohort of elementary education majors. Laura directs the children's literature offerings in the Teacher Education program. Classes met weekly for three hours; five of the meetings were reserved for book discussion. There were roughly twenty students, most in their second year of university; most identified as female and white, and most were nineteen or twenty years old.

Central to the course was a commitment to social justice teacher education in response to growing xenophobia in the U.S. in 2016. Mark took an explicitly anti-Islamophobic position in teaching, selecting five texts with central Muslim characters.[10] After student-led book discussions, participants responded to the following open-ended prompt: *Has this book added to or transformed how you think of Muslims? If so, in what ways?* The students' written journal responses across all five novels comprised the data.

We examined this data by creating "data poems."[11] We focused on student journals and the themes expressed there because they represent the most direct engagement students had with texts. In our initial stages of data analysis, we read through all the journal entries in order to better hear each student's evolving "voice"—to hear what was said but also to listen to the silences, the "white space" in the response. We looked for direct and first-person statements about evolving views of Muslims.

Then, we turned these responses into poems: poetic transcriptions[12] which re-presented the data, in the process noting emerging themes across time[13]; determining and distilling the "essence"[14] of various sections; and identifying repetition, resistance, or connection-making. In the final step, we shifted to using our own sense of the "poetic"—and ultimately our own poems—to challenge students' engagements with the literature and themes of the course, eventually creating poetry that aligned with our pedagogical, poetic, and political commitments. As our purposes changed, our interactions with the raw material of the student journals changed, and the role we played in the creation of the poems changed as well.

Results

We focus here on Olivia (a pseudonym). Throughout her journal entries, she maintained that she simultaneously was and was not changing as she proceeded through the course. In several entries, she insisted that she did not see Muslims as "different," yet she repeatedly called attention to difference without awareness of these contradictions. We believed that by distilling what we experienced as Olivia's circuitous journal entries, we would see more of her thinking, and would be better able to understand and convey her stance toward the content of the course.

Poem 1: to convey

In the first poem, Mark conveyed Olivia's thinking by drawing a poem directly from her reflections. It was important to maintain the integrity of Olivia's discourse by using her exact words. Mark wanted to pull forward the strong phrases from her journals that best represented how he had come to know her in class. To make visible a sense of progression through the course, he followed the course structure, using her responses in the order in which she wrote them, only reusing words or phrases when Olivia did so herself. The strategy he used was to delete words and sentences until he had a series of phrases representing the skeleton of her thoughts.

Just Like Everyone Else

I still view them the same,
just like everyone else.

A different perspective,
learning more about them,
rid of the "single story"—
I was able to get rid of
stereotypes I created.

Father seeming more dominant
strengthened my understanding of
how I see couples in that culture.
Her friend was Muslim
and had to wear a headscarf,
but it seemed normal.

It gave me a better understanding of
the struggles Muslims have gone through.
I do not think that it has changed
what I felt before.
It didn't really change my view of
Muslims.

I didn't think about race,
especially being Muslim.
I hope certain nationalities become more accepted,
and hopefully one day all of them.

There were no differences,
which is how I view Muslims.

In this attempt to convey information from Olivia's journal in the form of a poem, Mark expected that a distillation of her ideas would provide intimacy and insight. However, the results were unsatisfying to us on two fronts: it did not help to convey Olivia's learning, nor did it result in what we considered to be a poem.

Poem 2: to convey

Because we were dissatisfied with the initial rendering, we tried a different strategy to create a poem. Like Mark, Laura relied almost exclusively on Olivia's own words, though Laura played more freely with the order. She began by highlighting those phrases that seemed to have some spark, then cut and moved them around to hear more clearly Olivia's overlaps, conflations, and confusion. Formatting the poem in couplets and repeating phrases across the stanzas intensified the repetitive qualities of Olivia's reflections, while opening and ending the poem with the same phrase foregrounded the circuitous nature of Olivia's responses. All the words belong to Olivia, though there are a few changes of form (singular to plural, verb tenses) to smooth the transitions between lines.

It Didn't Really Change My View of Muslims

I think reading didn't really change
my view of Muslims.

Muslims, surrounded by the war,
witnessed such terrible things at such a young age.

They witnessed terrible things,
but they are just like everyone else—

like everyone else but with the additional struggles
that they faced being a refugee.

Being refugees,
many do not have a happy ending.

Instead of happy endings, they move
with the hope that they are changing their future.

In the future, I hope that certain nationalities
will become more accepted.

The Muslims were accepted;
It was the refugees that were still a problem—

reminding me of the problems
we are facing today on the "refugee crisis."

The "refugee crisis" gives me a better understanding
of the things that Muslims have gone through.

I know that what they've gone through
affects them and who they are now,

but I still view them the same.
I think I didn't really change my view of Muslims.

Once again, the poem felt to us decidedly unpoetic and did not provide much additional insight into Olivia's thoughts. It was not just that the *poem* was lacking; it was also that Olivia's entries were disappointing in their content, leading us to speculate that the prompt seemed to have invited repetition and revisiting, thus adding to—rather than alleviating—Olivia's uncertainty in understanding and/or articulating the differences between Muslims, immigrants, race, nationality, and the like. We felt, then, that poetic transcription as a methodology had not proven to be an effective way to meet our goals for the study nor to engage with Olivia's responses pedagogically. Consequently, we had a desire to do more with Olivia's writing.

Poem 3: to challenge

In this third poem, we shifted from a focus on conveying to challenging Olivia's words. Olivia's journal entries serve as the springboard into a poem that addresses her writings, foregrounding moments where Olivia seems unaware of her own assumptions or fails to examine her own biases, even late in the course. At the center of the poem is Olivia's discomfort that the novels she read in class did not have happy endings—something she had come to expect in literature. Olivia's insistence that she views "them" (whoever "they" may be") as "the same" leads Laura, the writer of this poem, to conclude that Olivia is correct—there can be few happy endings if she (if we all) continue with overlapping uncritical categories of Muslims, immigrants, and refugees, with vague empathy for an othered "them," with a superficial understanding of history ("then" and "now"), and with little awareness of the identities of the characters that are encountered in literature.

So Few Happy Endings

Olivia has read about Muslims, about refugees and migration
and war,

and how each affects the others. She has sympathy
for *their* personal struggles, what *they* have gone through,
how *then* affects *now*.

She is making
connections, *Sky* to *Ground* and back again—[15]
and now she has learned
that not all Arabic fathers are dictators
and sometimes Muslim immigrants leave a place
expecting to return.

When Olivia reads that the character
has to wear a headscarf, it seems normal. That's what she says.

She says her views on Muslims are unaffected by her reading—
she doesn't even notice the characters
are Muslim. Except for the headscarf. And moving
to another country. And that dominant father.

She still views them "the same"—Muslims, refugees—
but for Olivia, what is *the same*?

Interchangeable categories:
Muslim/immigrant/refugee/immigrant/Muslim?
Or *the same* as those around them—those who are non-Muslim,
non-immigrant, non-refugee?

Perhaps only *the same*
as how she viewed them before: before this book, this class,
this university degree. This time in history.

Olivia says she understands the personal struggles
—of being a Muslim surrounded by war,
—of human migration,

but she does not like the outcomes
of the books she is assigned.
They do not have the happy endings
she expects. And while the Muslims
are accepted (she views them, after all, as *the same*)
the refugees are still a problem. They remind her
of problems we are facing today—a refugee crisis.
At a young age, children see terrible things.

Olivia has indeed arrived at some measure of truth:
war has its human effects. Children *do* see terrible things.
There *is* a crisis. And she is right:
as long as we live
in a world where Muslim, immigrant, and refugee
are interchangeable terms,
where views of *them* never change,
it will always be *the same*.

There will be so few happy endings.

Drawing on yet freed from a strict adherence to Olivia's own words, this
poem allowed us to speak back to some of the expressions she had used in

representing her responses to the literature. We were aware that we might seem unfair or unkind to Olivia in this poem, taking her words and arguing with her "after the fact." Still, it felt better to us, politically and pedagogically, to engage in this more active/reflective dialogue with Olivia and her understandings (even though the course had concluded) than to merely offer her journal entries in poetic form.

We felt, by this point, that we had met our pedagogical goal for our inquiry: we had learned something about our own teaching from the process of working with Olivia's journal entries in multiple formats. In future iterations of the course, we planned to create prompts that allowed for difference and nuance between readings rather than open-ended prompts that resulted in vague (and disappointingly repetitive) responses, and to engage our students in ongoing dialogue around those responses rather than allowing the journals to function solely as a personal/private repository for ideas.

That said, once more we felt that as a *poem* this rendering had little to offer; it seemed preachy and direct rather than nuanced and allusive; the language was not particularly rich, powerful, or evocative.

Poem 4: to co/create

In our inquiry to this point, we had challenged (in the abstract) Olivia's responses; though she would never see that challenge, we had been truer to our own political convictions by pointing out and pushing against (rather than merely carrying forward) some of her unexamined assumptions. Though this addressed some of our pedagogical and political goals, we still had not met our poetic goals; we had not yet created anything that we considered to be "poetic."

Part of the purpose of poetry is that it harnesses, through language, emotion that can lead to action. That sense of the power of language seemed to be missing when we were tied too directly to Olivia's own words and phrases.[16] As a result, we decided to experiment with co/creating with Olivia (in the abstract, through her journal entries) a new poem. Guided by poetic sensibilities and political convictions, Laura worked loosely with Olivia's journal entries, creating (with Olivia's own words in mind but not directly on the page) a poetic engagement not only with Olivia's ideas, but also with the ways Olivia's uncertainties represented larger cultural narratives and perspectives. The poem has at its center a highly publicized image (a photograph, taken August 17, 2016) of Omran, a Syrian child from Aleppo who—with the signing of the incoming president's Executive Order banning Muslim immigrants—would no longer be allowed to enter the United States. Anger toward that U.S. stance toward refugees becomes central to the poem.

Crisis: Immigrants, Muslims[17]

This, the long night—sirens
in the distance:

an airstrike in Aleppo,
an incoming president's promise
of protection from a so-called "national threat."

Now kindness
(that woman in a hijab,
that man bowing in prayer)
has no place here.

How do we move from one stance
to another? Look:

there is a boy in the back seat,
at a young age
bearing witness to terrible things—
blood on his face, dust on his shirt,
ferried by flashing lights.

What have we learned?
There are so few happy endings.

The latest wave:
Muslims, immigrants, refugees
(dust and blood, blood and dust)—
it makes no difference;
we view them the same—
as each other, as us,
as we always have.

The headscarf, the truck search,
the father with empty arms:
for Omran, Aleppo is no longer
home.

But here, far from his world
of nights loud with the drone of fighter jets,
here, we *do* make a difference—

here, we are closing the door.

Occasioned by Olivia's journal entries, this poem allowed us to use poetry to address issues of social justice that we had hoped would be evident for our students in the course. Like so many Americans, Olivia recognized there was a crisis, but couldn't really identify the problem or its source, much less imagine a solution. In this, our final poem, vague alignments (Olivia's "there are no differences," "I view them the same") give way to a huge difference—a government policy that both engenders and exploits difference, viewing all Muslims as a potential threat. Our goal was to speak not only to Olivia, but to engage broadly and poetically with current events—to use concrete images, repetition, line breaks, and the distillation of language to speak with more power about the context in which Olivia was reading and responding to literature, hoping that an understanding might, eventually, lead to action.

Conclusions

By drafting multiple poems from the same data set, we wished to call attention to the multiple ways poetic inquiry creates a space for communication and interrogation, making transparent the relationship between a particular student's informal journal responses and our desire to move our students beyond a simple and simplistic response to literature and into a sense of social responsibility.

It became quite clear to us in our early writings about this project that Olivia was responding to a problematic writing prompt—a prompt that (at least for her) failed to invite rich responses. Still, our continued engagement with Olivia's journals led us to different questions around the relationship between research, art, and activism. Using poetry not only to convey, but also to challenge and co/create allowed us to interact with Olivia's journal entries and our own pedagogical, poetic, and political commitments in transparent and unexpected ways. Ultimately, revisiting the data and rewriting our poems increased the complexity of our sense of the "poetic" in the inquiry.

Future research might lead us to ask: What do these differing engagements with student responses allow us to understand not only about the students' perspectives on the other in literature, but also about our own poetic registers and stances as researchers and writers? Does an explicit focus on the "poetic" enrich or undermine the integrity of the research?

This preliminary work allowed us to foreground questions about some of the methodological tensions inherent in poetic inquiry. We began with teacher-questions, but found ourselves, poem by poem, uncovering and exploring researcher-questions and our own activist concerns. We deliberately foregrounded the tensions inherent in these efforts toward poetic inquiry: the relationships between the researcher and the data, the goal for the research, the obligation and complication of "speaking with/to" the writings of a student who has already finished the course, the complexities of creating art when it means departing from a strict adherence to the data, the forever-complicated political stances we take as both teachers and researchers. As we make more visible and explicit our own engagements and convictions in inquiry, new questions emerge about the responsibility of the poet-researcher that are always and ever both pedagogical and political.

Notes

1. See, for example, Anderson and Stillman, "Student Teaching's Contribution"; Cochran-Smith, et al., "Critiquing Teacher Education Research"; Sleeter, "Preparing Teachers."

2. Mueller and O'Connor, "Telling and Retelling"; Haddix, "Beyond Sociolinguistics"; Brindley & Laframboise, "The Need."

3. Cahnmann, "The Craft, Practice, and Possibility."

4. Leggo, "Pedagogy of the Heart."

5. Butler-Kisber, "Artful Portrayals."

6. Faulkner, "Poetic Inquiry."

7. Sullivan, "On Poetic Occasion."

8. Prendergast and Belliveau, "Poetics and Performance," 202.

9. This study was Mark's first foray into poetic inquiry; Laura is an experienced poet-scholar. Rather than viewing our differing levels of experience as markers of "novice" and/or "expert," we saw our collaboration (and in particular our differing experiences and stances) as a means to ask different sets of questions from our distinct experiential perspectives as we moved more deeply into the work.

10. Barakat, *Tasting the Sky*; Healy, *When We Wake*; Laird and Nimr, *A Little Piece of Ground*; Nye, *The Turtle of Oman*; Sattouf, *The Arab of the Future*.

11. Cahnmann, "The Craft, Practice, and Possibility"; Eisner, "The Promise and Perils"; Richardson, "The Poetic Representation."

12. Richardson, "Writing: A Method of Inquiry."

13. Corbin and Strauss, "Grounded Theory Research."

14. Glesne, "That Rare Feeling."

15. A reference to two novels Olivia read in the course: Barakat, *Tasting the Sky*, and Laird and Nimr, *A Little Piece of Ground*.

16. In retrospect, it seems our attempts to create poems directly from the data faltered given that the journal entries lacked what Sullivan calls "poetic moments," thus leading to poems that evidenced little "poetry." As Prendergast and Belliveau put it, "Mundane data can only lead to mundane poems crafted from the data," "Poetics and Performance," 202.

17. The underlined words in this poem are taken from Olivia's journal entries.

Bibliography

Anderson, Lauren M., and Jamy A. Stillman. "Student Teaching's Contribution to Preservice Teacher Development: A Review of Research Focused on the Preparation of Teachers for Urban and High-Needs Contexts." *Review of Educational Research* 83, no. 1 (2013): 3-69.

Barakat, Ibtisam. *Tasting the Sky*. New York, NY: Farrar, Straus & Giroux, 2007.

Brindley, Roger, and Kathryn L. Laframboise. "The Need to Do More: Promoting Multiple Perspectives in Preservice Teacher Education through Children's Literature." *Teaching and Teacher Education* 18, no. 4 (2002): 405-420.

Butler-Kisber, Lynn. "Artful Portrayals in Qualitative Inquiry: The Road to Found Poetry and Beyond." *Alberta Journal of Educational Research* 48, no. 3 (2002): 229-239.

Cahnmann, Melisa. "The Craft, Practice, and Possibility of Poetry in Educational Research." *Educational Researcher* 32, no. 3 (2003): 29-36.

Cochran-Smith, Marilyn, Ana Maria Villegas, Linda Abrams, Laura Chavez-Moreno, Tammy Mills, and Rebecca Stern. "Critiquing Teacher Preparation Research: An Overview of the Field, Part II." *Journal of Teacher Education* 66, no. 2 (2015): 109-121.

Corbin, Juliet M., and Anselm Strauss. "Grounded Theory Research: Procedures, Canons, and Evaluative Criteria." *Qualitative Sociology* 13, no. 1 (1990): 3-21.

Eisner, Elliot W. "The Promise and Perils of Alternative Forms of Data Representation." *Educational Researcher* 26, no. 6 (1997): 4-10.

Faulkner, Sandra L. "Poetic Inquiry: Poetry as/in/for Social Research." In *The Handbook of Arts-Based Research*, 208-230. Edited by Patricia Leavy. New York, NY: Guilford Press, 2017.

Glesne, Corrine. "That Rare Feeling: Re-Presenting Research through Poetic Transcription." *Qualitative Inquiry* 3, no. 2 (1997): 202-221.

Haddix, Marcelle. "Beyond Sociolinguistics: Towards a Critical Approach to Cultural and Linguistic Diversity in Teacher Education." *Language and Education* 22, no. 5 (2008): 254-270. doi:10.1080/09500780802152648

Healy, Karen. *When We Wake*. New York, NY: Hachette, 2013.

Laird, Elizabeth and Sonia Nimr. *A Little Piece of Ground*. London, UK: Macmillan Children's Books, 2003.

Leggo, Carl. "Pedagogy of the Heart: Ruminations on Living Poetically."
    The Journal of Educational Thought (JET)/Revue de la Pensée Educative
    (2005): 175-195.

Mueller, Jennifer, and Carla O'Connor. "Telling and Retelling about Self
    and "Others": How Pre-Service Teachers (Re) Interpret Privilege and
    Disadvantage in One College Classroom." *Teaching and Teacher
    Education* 23, no. 6 (2007): 840-856. doi: 10.1016/j.tate.2006.01.011

Nye, Naomi Shihab. *The Turtle of Oman*. New York, NY: Harper Collins,
    2014.

Prendergast, Monica, and George Belliveau. "Poetics and Performance." In
    Reviewing Qualitative Research in the Social Sciences, 197-210. Edited by
    Audrey A. Trainor and Elizabeth Graue. London, UK: Routledge, 2013.

Richardson, Laurel. "Writing: A Method of Inquiry." In *Handbook of
    Qualitative Research*, 923-948. Edited by Norman Denzin and Yvonnis
    Lincoln. Thousand Oaks, CA: Sage, 2000.

Richardson, Laurel. "The Poetic Representation of Lives: Writing a
    Postmodernist Sociology." *Studies in Symbolic Interaction* 13, no. 1
    (1992): 19-29.

Sattouf, Riad. *The Arab of the Future*. New York, NY: Metropolitan Books,
    2015.

Sleeter, Christine E. "Preparing Teachers for Culturally Diverse Schools:
    Research and the Overwhelming Presence of Whiteness." *Journal of
    Teacher Education* 52, no. 2 (2001): 94-106.

Sullivan, Anne McCrary. "On Poetic Occasion in Inquiry: Concreteness,
    Voice, Ambiguity, Tension and Associative Logic." In *Poetic Inquiry:
    Vibrant Voices in the Social Sciences*, 111-126. Edited by Monica
    Pendergast, Carl Leggo, and Pauline Sameshima. Rotterdam,
    Netherlands: Sense Publishers, 2009.

2.

Contemplative, Somatic, and Arts-Integrated Methods for Girls' Well-being[1]

Alexandra Fidyk,
University of Alberta

As social media and media culture target the life of youth, dangerous and unrealistic cultural ideals of slimness (particularly among females) and beauty have distorted a healthy sense of well-being. Attentive to such concerns, a research project—*Poetics of the Body*—was developed to support girls'/students' self-image and sense of well-being through a unique combination of contemplative, somatic, and creative methods, where trauma-based techniques were carefully and invisibly interwoven. Leading out from embodied subjective experience, the girls were guided through processes of amplification, imagination, attunement, and witnessing, so to poetically story their lives via a life-size body map. Through ancient collective practices, a community of trust, safety, and care was built among participants. In addition, there were after-school conversations held with their teachers in order to support them to integrate new awareness of and attention to the body and feminine principles, thereby undertaking a poetic approach to learning.

Keywords: body image, body map, community response, emotions, girls, poetic storying, sensations, voice

Poetry is an utterance of the body.[2]

Public Health Agency Canada reports that ten to twenty percent of children and youth in Canada experience mental illness and that only one in five children and youth who need mental health services receives them.[3] As a result, Canadian public schools have become ideal and necessary places to address child and adolescent mental health.[4] Because educators and staff members in schools today are expected to undergo professional learning to acquire skills that support child and youth mental health,[5] the response requires the development of mental health resources, supports, and training for them.[6]

At the same time, the design and implementation of mental health models must cut through the cultural forces biasing Western conceptions of healthy functioning.[7] As remnant of the Enlightenment, the thinking function (as compared to the feeling function[8]) remains privileged in teaching and learning and encourages separation between the body and brain/mind. It demonizes right-brain sensibilities, which include the poetic, symbolic, relational, and imaginal realms. Abstraction, left-brain dominance, and dissociation by smart-tech cannot continue to dominate learning. The increasing emphasis on testing, rationalization, and technology within schools correspondingly "takes us further and further away from 'imaginative life,' alienating us from our embodiment and our lived world."[9] Within trauma studies, *imagination* has been deemed "absolutely critical to the quality of our lives."[10] Imagination as an egoic method is not the aim, although helpful. What is desired, rather, is imagination that arises autonomously through relationship with the creative pulse of existence— images that appear to us via intuition, instinct, the body, and the not-yet-conscious. Connecting the emotional, symbolic, and imaginal domains with learning develops the right hemisphere. The right hemisphere knows through contact with direct phenomena of lived experience and is interested in sensations, movements, emotions, feelings, and images that spontaneously emerge when we process internal and external events. For trauma experts Bessel van der Kolk, Peter Levine, and Sharon Stanley, we are moved, changed, and transformed as we surrender our abstract, logical, and sequential ways of knowing to the body-centered, relational, and poetic dynamics of our lived experience.[11] In order for this surrender to occur, the body's wisdom must be rediscovered: its finitude not resented, its limitations not abhorred, its thought not disembodied.

For mental health to be addressed by teachers, counselors, and administrators, a shift in understanding human physiology is needed — that is, *what the body knows* and *what the body remembers*.[12] As with "embodied interpretation," we must reunite the body-brain/mind conceptually and in research.[13] They are one and function as a unity. To heal trauma, we must bridge the dissociation between body and psyche, pay careful attention to what our bodies hold, and re-inhabit them. To achieve that, we must work

directly with bodies, rather than seeing them as second to our minds/brains. Teachers engaged in campaigns that seek to support child and youth mental health must then expect to be changed in their practice.

In response to the need for resources and teacher preparedness, a participatory poetic inquiry was conducted with eight grade-six "girls," aged ten to eleven. We were guided by the following question: *In what ways might girls' experiences with art-integrated activities and body-centered techniques inform educators about pedagogical practice and mental health interventions?* Our study unfolded through an *animated paradigm*—the ancestral home of *ispoesis*, a realm that supports a return to the imaginal and poetic basis of consciousness.[14] Its ontology reflects a worldview that includes and values images, intuition, imagination, feeling, the unconscious, transpersonal, transgenerational, transgender, imaginal, and emergent dimensions.[15] It calls forth practices, knowing, and values inherent to pre-modernity, traditional, and Indigenous peoples: ritual, ceremony, expressive movement—such as drumming, dancing, and chanting—community healing, dreams, visions, and ancestors, to name a few. And it is alive, animated, as are the poems, imaginative creations, and dreams that arise from it—here, a poem, to remain a poem, can have "no one interpretation, one meaning, one value."[16] Such dwelling radically reconsiders the ways that we come to know and thereby what we know. Thus, "withness of the body" makes body the starting point for our experience of the "circumambient world."[17]

As we worked within an animated paradigm, poetic inquiry—akin to arts-integrated inquiry—further guided us. Poetic inquiry brought forth visual images, art, and photography; it was philosophically aligned with those committed to communicating experiences of memory, identity, place, relationality, hope, fear, and/or desire. This quality was witnessed, for example, in the participants' tagline poetry: "#Brave," "Girls Can Do ANYTHING!" and "#Positive." It was also visible in their legends, which gave meaning to the colors and symbols of their body maps, such as the one entitled "Sorrows of life." It had a full vertical body split indicated by a thick, solid zigzag, which symbolized their "feeling ripped in half." The three-dimensional black buttoned side symbolized their[18] core self: "not perfect but who I am," and the other side, coated in glitter, was tagged: "what my mom expects." In this way, poetic inquiry aided to more authentically express their experiences. Sometimes phenomenological and existential, poetic inquiry was a way to know through rhythm, imagery, emotion, metaphor, and attention. As such, this poetry made "connections among intellect, emotion, spirit, and the body."[19] Similar to Helene Cixous's work that explored the relationship of the female body with language, this inquiry explored what the body knows and invited expression that "subverts the given structures and available forms."[20] Like performance poetry, their participant bodies released spoken word, writ black, writ loud:

> You Weirdo!
> You Suck
> Get Out!
>
> No. Be Brave.
> #Girl Power

As Cixous argued, "Write your self. Your body must be heard."[21] In this way, the poetic—raw feeling, aesthetic sound both oral and written, and form—can be a transgressive and powerful tool especially for those denied access to power, which is the experience of many women and girls, as demonstrated in the body map "Behind my 'perfect' life."

Methods were carefully chosen and layered wherein a *transdisciplinary praxis* emerged. Arts-integrated practices of imagination, coloring, tracing, painting, and play, and body-centered techniques of breathing, grounding, visualizing, mindfulness, and movement were integrated[22] alongside practices inherent to integrated body psychodynamics: attunement, containment, boundaries, breath, and agency; trauma studies: pedulation, resonance, relationality, somatic awareness, and somatic empathy;[23] and analytical psychology, particularly active imagination and symbol amplification, in order to support cultural inclusivity, bypass Western conceptions of health, and honor difference— that is, voice, body, gender, and story.[24]

The rhythmic interplay of these methods encouraged the participants' images of self depicted through their relationships to their bodies performed as poetry written on the body.[25] That is, their personal narratives became poetic symbols and slams inked upon life-size body maps. Like many women and girls before them, they found that lyric forms of language—the expressive and personal—helped to find themselves, their truths. Most of the girls included taglines, often integrating code such as ⊘, which meant, "Not allowed to be me." Similar to "Breath in Poetry—Breathe in experience, exhale poetry," a spoken-word poetry slam series in Edmonton, AB, our meetings became weekly gatherings in support of sharing voice and experience with poetry at the center.[26] As such poetic inquiry became poetry as process; poetry as performance; poetry as voice (symbol and word); poetry as remapping life. As with Instagram poets, who are seen as "inspiring a new generation of raw, emotional storytellers" and who are making a difference in their communities via social media, the girls' concise musings, while not written for that platform, would fit there perfectly[27]:

> My happy
> place is in more
> than just my
> Heart

Perhaps most important to this endeavor, poetic inquiry was committed to communicating sociopolitical and cultural concerns as an act of witness.[28] Just as the poet needs the listener/reader to bring a poem into its fullness, every "I" needs a "you" to hear and see her as she is. *Bearing witness*—which attends to the mover with an attitude of nonjudgmental compassion—says that your suffering matters. "Witnessing is different from 'observing' and 'looking at'; looking can be quite objectifying but witnessing means being actively present to the mover."[29] When we attune to others in an empathetic and nonjudgmental way, it "enables them to develop an awareness of their inner states and to experience, contain, and express the full range of emotions."[30] Witnessing also offers the recovery of aspects that were previously held unconsciously in their bodies. Witnessing the girl-participants permitted them/zir the felt experience needed to *feel felt*—that is, to somatically know they/ze were seen, heard, and accepted as ze/they were. It also enabled zir/them to express that which was most needed to be spoken. A moment poignantly articulated in the sharing circle by one participant:

> I Am—
> Not a girl
> Not a boy
> some ONE in-
> between

And another agreed:

> Why?
> Why do I
> have to get
> changed, do
> my hair?
>
> My brother, in
> sweats slouches
> on the sofa, and
> gets to go to the movies
> —like that!

Witnessing, like poetic inquiry, requires an openness to the other. As Jan Zwicky elaborates, "imagination allows us to enter the experience of another without appropriation, ownership, or reductiveness."[31] Taken further, witnessing can help us distinguish between our own feelings and those that belong to another; it teaches us not to impose our reality onto others, while preparing us to "create increasingly conscious and respectful relationships."[32]

Traditional means of witnessing occur in many cultures through *ceremony*. All cultures celebrate essential elements of life in different forms of ceremony. Stanley, in her extensive experience and research with First Nations Peoples, describes a ceremony as involving encounters that "contain and hold the disturbed energy of trauma along with the natural healing forces of life."[33] "In many ways," she continues, "the encounters of the new paradigm in Western healing practices, right-brain-to-right-brain affective embodied experiences that Schore (2012) advocates, are ceremonies that bring essential elements together for healing trauma."[34] Ceremony can take the form of a "contained intersubjective dialogue between two people of a group"; "a meditation, or the experience of sharing and embodying imagination and dreams, dancing, music, or other expressive forms."[35] Further, the elements that constitute a ceremony "include embodied intersubjective relationships, the rituals of sacred, uninterrupted time, the development of bodily based rhythm and movement, and somatic relational exploration of internal and environmental influences on human experience"[36]

As conducted, the design and enactment of the methods used with the participants embodied the four described elements of ceremony. Because ceremonies serve as a living, pulsating container they can "bring the fragmented elements of dissociative experiences together ... for acknowledgement, conversion, metabolism, and transformation of lived experience"[37] —as the girls did with old memories, disappointments, fears, and personal hurts and hopes. Our sharing circles, used at the beginning and end of our gatherings, invited the rhythmic ebb and flow of exploring new phenomenological material; encouraged its integration when witnessed; and enabled the new to be embodied into a *felt sense*, during which the "sense of interconnectivity" grew.[38] "Felt sense" from Eugene Gendlin is not a mental experience but an embodied physical one, "the lived body's sense of *felt* context in any moment"—itself a form of mirroring.[39]

In developing this ceremonial encounter to support well-being, a clear and caring intention for the participants and myself was required. To do so honored the unique transsubjective relationship at the moment and gave careful body-based attention to space, pace, time, pause, and connection between our environment and us. And further, an "ecology of relationship" grew among us as we engaged in the embodied, energetic field of care.[40] Following the intention was the greeting, a "moment of meeting" that fertilized the "right conditions" of the encounter and the potential conversion from sympathetic arousal to social engagement—a relaxed, parasympathetic response—the best healing condition because it provides immediate protection in traumatic moments.[41] The mindful-greeting involved a respectful presence and welcome, a moment of soft eyes and naming the other as ze/they/she ran into the library, our designated research space—Ms. J, Ms. M, Ms. S. Like a ceremonial dance, it set the theme and ethos of relational caring and respect for the girls as persons.

From intention and invitation, we engaged in breath work. We charged our bodies; we calmed our bodies. We grounded through eye contact and touch, and we expanded our capacity to hold. Conjoined by rhythm, the girls discovered new language—a poetics of breath, a poetics of touch, a poetics of presence—grounded through the sensual and sensorial. As such, a poetics of the body enabled them to discover new ways of knowing—co-being and-co-becoming.

As they woke up to increased charge, they used grounding techniques to draw their awareness into their bodies, such as feeling the pressure of their bums against the mat and floor. I guided them through body scans and visualizations, the first being the touchstone, an invitation to recall a memory or to imagine a place that made/would make them feel safe and content. They amplified this image—fleshed in color, shape, size, and texture. They then *felt into* their bodies: where did this symbol want to reside? For one, a Newfoundland beach scene from family vacations was painted on her feet, complete with seagulls and glittering sand. Her embodied sense of place is what poet John Haines called a "place of sense"[42]—that is, an aesthetic and spiritual presence that is attentive to where we dwell. Here, I am reminded of Heidegger's coupling: "poetry and dwelling belong together, each calling for the other."[43] Fittingly, these home dwellings began their body poems.

Vital for each girl-participant was to "safely experience [their/her] sensations and emotions."[44] This awareness was encouraged by presence, slowness, and a tactful invitation to scan internally, to notice sensations, then images, itches, niggles and affect, and/or their absence. Schooling commits violence against children and youth when they ignore their bodies. Prolonged periods of time when children are required to sit still, be quiet, and follow instructions without engagement deaden their minds and bodies quite literally. As a result, many have learned to dissociate, split out, or cut off from their bodies. The integration of contemplative practices supported the girls' sense of selves, taught skills needed to communicate inner affective states, and encouraged an attitude that honored their interiority. "Engaging the self-observing, body-based self-system, which speaks through sensations, tone of voice, and body tensions" aids to establish an awareness of or relationship with an inner presence, which in turn provides a secure place to return when needed.[45]

While the unique combination of methods aided to develop a community of trust, the sharing circles in particular aided to establish a new ethos because "each person had the opportunity to take an uninterrupted turn," in speaking to the topic, an equal chance to speak and be heard.[46] Our circle was formed with personal yoga mats—each deemed sacred space. The mats provided a concrete visual for the girls to come into relationship with their own energetic space, body, and that of the other. They also helped to demonstrate the importance of boundaries—physical, emotional, and intimate. We can only feel safe if we know that others will respect our boundaries—not moving in too close or too far away; hence, the development of character style (not personhood) based on our early experiences of inundation and abandonment. Boundaries also reflect the capacity to build, sustain, and discharge energy. If we don't have boundaries,

> we need defenses such as withdrawal, control, sidetracking, creating rules, scapegoating, humor, sex, rationalizing, intellectualizing, name-calling, perfectionism, black-white thinking, threats, gaslighting, coldness, sweetness, excessive concern for the other—all are handy ways to avoid feeling and to avoid communication. The healthy alternative is to state valid feelings.[47]

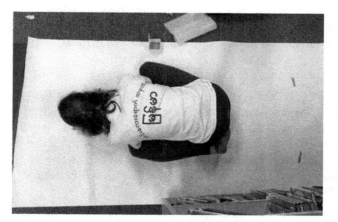

Moving from our circle, the girls worked comfortably and silently on the floor. The body-centered poetic process lasted sixty to ninety minutes. Directed by felt sensations, symbols were added each week, wherein "every carnal act and organ inscribes its own *imaginaire*"; "sensation is expression and expression sensation."[48] Some worked sitting to the side of their body maps, leaning in, while others sat upon their bodies working intimately through constant touch. They learned to attune with their bodies and experiences so to metaphorically voice the ways they perceived themselves, their lives—their stories. With increased detail, they amplified what they noticed, developing consciousness about and care for their inner worlds.

When we pay focused attention to our bodily sensations, we can recognize the ebb and flow of our emotions and, with that, increase our control over them. As van der Kolk discovered: "At the core of recovery is self-awareness ... Body awareness puts us in touch with our inner world ... [without such awareness and the ability] to observe the interplay between our thoughts and our physical sensations," there can be no healing.[49] Taken further, our inner worlds in meaningful relation to our outer worlds is that which moves us toward reflective self-conscious awareness of our dynamic, interconnected web of life and thus to empathy, mutuality, and reciprocity. In order to better understand the interrelatedness of these worlds, children and youth need to hear, feel, enact, speak, perform, write, and read poetry. As Judy Pinn describes, poetry facilitates an "enfolding of self with place, of the outer with the inner."[50] Poetry has always stitched passion to other, be it the beloved, place, or politics. Poetry keeps us in relation—the very thing trauma needs to release from the hijacking of current time by the past event. To encourage self-awareness, teachers must invite sensations, emotions, and bodies into the classroom and so into learning. When they do, they would be well advised to proceed poetically, that is, to practice and encourage "the arts of attentive observation and storytelling, writing and performing, [which] means experiencing the world as the living, breathing, dying, transforming, dynamic poem it is."[51]

Through a process of *ispoesis*, which integrated contemplative, somatic, and arts-integrated methods, girl-participants dwelt creatively in a new form of knowing that wished "to honor the places where commonality (community) and uniqueness (individual) meet."[52] Through poetics of the body, they were empowered to voice their lived experiences in relation to the ways they felt and saw themselves, and in doing became "political agents"[53] speaking truth for mental health.

Trauma research shows that attunement via human contact is central to physiological self-regulation. "Trauma [after all] is about loss of connection—to ourselves, to our bodies, to our families, to others, and to the world around us."[54] Thus, those who become displaced or exiled, an ever-increasing number of people in Canada, Canadian schools, and the world—people who have lost their connection to land, language, culture, and family—often experience complex trauma. One consistent finding across trauma studies highlights relations: "Traumatized human beings [mammals] recover in the context of relationships: with families and loved ones."[55] By extension, this paradigm reforms the guiding ethics in both conducting research and opening up relations within the school community and beyond. Here the values of *relationality* and *relational accountability* governed, reflecting interconnectedness, empathy, humility, and care— qualities inherent to a sense of belonging to a much larger cosmos imbued with spirit.[56] This shift welcomes diversity in culture and language— including the arts, tradition, and science—thereby allowing greater complexity and potentiality in understanding and practice.

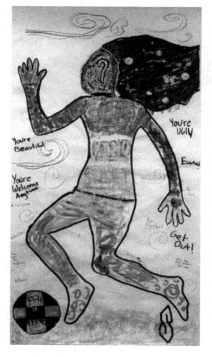

The changes required to meet whole school approaches[57] must occur not in teachers' cogitations, "but in the affective embodied experiences of … their brain/mind/body."[58] Educators must have access to new knowledge, skills, and learning opportunities whereby they too can experience relational and somatic approaches necessary to integrate the body and arts, especially the poetic, into their classroom practice. In addition, they must be willing to become vulnerable in their own bodies and learning: less certain, more curious. Without empathy for their own and others' lives, compassion and care become abstractions and an enduring response to mental health will not be possible.

Notes

1. This chapter is based upon "'What the Body Remembers': Integrating Fields and Methods to Support Girls' Well-Being," a keynote presentation given at the Jungian Society for Scholarly Studies: "Emerging …" Conference at Portland State University, Portland, OR (June 27-30, 2018). This research was funded by a grant from the Alberta Advisory Committee for Educational Studies (2016).

2. Maxwell, quoted in O'Driscoll, *The Bloodaxe Book*, 224.

3. Public Health Agency Canada (PHAC), 9; CMHA; PMA; WHO.

4. Wei et al., "Comprehensive School"; Leblanc et al., "Psychosocial Health."

5. Kutcher, et al., "Educator Mental Health Literacy."

6. Wei et al., "Comprehensive School."

7. Unger, "Introduction"; Leblanc et al., "Psychosocial Health."

8. Feeling is the psychological function that evaluates or judges what something or someone is worth. In Jung's view it is a rational function, like thinking, in that it is decisively influenced not by perception (as are the functions of sensation and intuition) but by reflection. In his words, "a feeling is as indisputable a reality as the existence of an idea" (CW 16, par. 531).

9. Galvin and Prendergast, "Introduction," xiii.

10. van der Kolk, *The Body Keeps*, 17.

11. van der Kolk, *The Body Keeps*; Levine, *Trauma & Memory*; Stanley, *Relational and Body-Centered*; Sieff, *Understanding and Healing*.

12. Singh Baldwin, *What the Body Remembers*.

13. Galvin and Todres, "Poetic Inquiry," 307.

14. Hillman, *The Dream*.

15. Fidyk, "Conducting Research"; Fidyk, "The Influence of Cultural."

16. Hillman, *The Dream*, 126.

17. Whitehead cited in Keller, *From a Broken Web*, 236.

18. The intentional inclusion of multiple personal pronouns seeks to respect diverse identifications, especially those who stand on the continuum, between and beyond, the hegemonic markers of "male" and "female"— typically referred to with the personal pronouns he/him/his and she/her/hers. Among some genderqueer, non-binary, gender creative, questioning, trans, and Two-Spirit people, "they/them" (or most accurately they/them/their/theirs) is/has become a choice of personal pronoun (along with *ze/zir* and others). In solidarity with, respect for, and inclusivity of friends, colleagues, and diverse readership, "they" will be used alone as well as alongside "she" and or "he." When herein used, note the Standard English language rule of pronoun-noun agreement will not be followed. In support of the campaign to raise awareness of gender-neutral pronouns and diversity in gender identities, see: https://www.su.ualberta.ca/services/thelanding/learn/pronouns/. I would like to thank Alison Brooks-Starks who shared this site with me and offered comment on this footnote.

19. Neilsen, "Lyric Inquiry," 99.

20. Cixous, "The Laugh," 99.

21. Cixous, "The Laugh," 335.

22. Rosenberg et al., *Body, Self, & Soul*; Rosenberg and Kitaen-Morse, *The Intimate Couple.*

23. Levine, *Trauma & Memory*; Stanley, *Relational and Body-Centered*; Rosenberg et al., *Body, Self, & Soul.*

24. van der Kolk, *The Body Keeps*; Levine, *Healing Trauma*; Levine, *Trauma & Memory.*

25. Gastaldo et al., *Body-Map*; Devine, "The Moon, the Stars"; MacGregor, "Mapping the Body"; Weinand, "An Evaluation"; Karlsson, "Visual Methodologies."

26. Breath in Poetry.

27. Epstein, "Don't Call Them."

28. Prendergast, "Introduction," xxxvi-xxxvii.

29. Stromsted and Sieff, "Dances of Psyche," 57.

30. Ibid.

31. Zwicky, *Wisdom and Metaphor*; Neilsen, "Lyric Inquiry," 95.

32. Stromsted and Sieff, "Dances of Psyche," 58.

33. Stanley, *Relational and Body-Centered*, 77.

34. Ibid.

35. Ibid.

36. Ibid.

37. Ibid.

38. Stanley, *Relational and Body-Centered*, 78.

39. Stanley, *Relational and Body-Centered*, 79.

40. Gendlin, *Focusing*; Galvin and Todres, "Poetic Inquiry," 310.

41. Hockley, *Being in Relationship.*

42. Stanley, *Relational and Body-Centered*, 78.

43. Haines, *Living off the Country.*

44. Heidegger, "Poetically Man Dwells," 93.

45. van der Kolk, *The Body Keeps*, 215.

46. van der Kolk, *The Body Keeps*, 238.

47. Wilson, *Research Is Ceremony*, 41.

48. Katherine, *Boundaries*, 115.

49. Kearney, "What Is Diacritical Hermeneutics?" 8.

50. van der Kolk, *The Body Keeps*, 208-209.

51. Pinn, "Restor(y)ing," 45-46.

52. Borhani, "Living with Words," 103-104.

53. Wiebe and Sameshima, "Sympathizing with Social Justice," 27.

54. Galvin and Todres, "Poetic Inquiry," 314.

55. Levine, *Healing Trauma*, 9.

55. van der Kolk, *The Body Keeps*, 210.

56. Wilson, *Research Is Ceremony*.

57. Education Alberta; McHale et al., "Promoting and Improving"; JCSH.

58. Schore, *The Science of the Art*, 12.

Bibliography

Borhani, M. T. "Living with Words: This 'Vale of Soul-Making.'" In *Poetic Inquiry: Enchantment of Place*. Edited by P. Sameshima, A. Fidyk, K. James, & C. Leggo. Wilmington, DE: Vernon Press, 2017.

Breath in Poetry. (n.d.) https://www.breathinpoetry.com

Canadian Mental Health Association (CMHA). Edmonton Region. https://edmonton.cmha.ca/document-category/mental-health/

Cixous, H. "The Laugh of the Medusa." In *Feminisms: An Anthology of Literary Theory and Criticism*. Edited by R. R. Warhol & D. Rice Herndel. New Brushwick, NJ: Rutgers, 1991.

Devine, C. "The Moon, the Stars, and a Scar: Body Mapping Stories of Women Living with HIV/AIDS." In *Border Crossings* 2008: 58-65. http://www.digitalsinternational.org/cms/content/Carol%20Devine%20-%20Body%20Mapping%20%20Border%20Crossings.pdf

Education Alberta. 2016. https://education.alberta.ca/media/3576206/working_together_to_support_mental_health.pdf

Epstein, R. "Don't Call Them Instagram Poets: How the Social Media Outlet Is Providing a Platform for a New Generation of Authors—and They Want You to Know." *Marie Clarie*. May 3, 2018. https://www.marieclaire.com/culture/a20071698/instagram-poets-trend/

Fidyk, A. " 'What the Body Remembers': Integrating Fields and Methods to Support Girls' Wellbeing." Jungian Society for Scholarly Studies Conference, Portland State University, Portland, Oregon, 2018.

Fidyk, A. "The Influence of Cultural and Familial Complexes in the Classroom: A Post-Jungian View [invited]." In *The Precarious Future of Education: Risk and Uncertainty in Ecology, Curriculum, Learning, & Technology*, 71-108. Edited by j. jagodzinski. New York: Palgrave Macmillan, 2017.

Fidyk, A. "Conducting Research in an Animated World: A Case *for* Suffering. [invited]" *International Journal of Multiple Research Approaches, Special Issue: Depth Psychological Research Approaches* 7, no. 3 (2013): 378-391. http://mra.e-contentmanagement.com/archives/vol/7/issue/3/article/5290/conducting-research-in-an-animated-world--a-case

Galvin, K., and M. Prendergast. "Introduction." In *Poetic Inquiry II— Seeing, Caring, Understanding. Using Poetry as and for Inquiry*, xi-xvii. Edited by K. T. Galvin & M. Prendergast. Rotterdam, The Netherlands: Sense Publications, 2016.

Galvin, K., and L. Todres. "Poetic Inquiry & Phenomenological Research." In *Poetic Inquiry. Vibrant Voices in the Social Sciences*, 307-316. Edited by M. Prendergast, C. Leggo & P. Sameshima. 2009.

Gastaldo, D., L. Magalhaes, C. Carrasco, and C. Davy. *Body-Map Storytelling as Research: Methodological Considerations for Telling the Stories of Undocumented Workers through Body Mapping*. 2012. http://www.migrationhealth.ca/undocumented-workers-ontario/body-mapping

Gendlin, E. *Focusing*. New York: Bantam Books, 1980.

Griffiths, J. *Wild: An Elemental Journey*. New York, NY: Tarcher, 2006.

Haines, J. *Living off the Country: Essays on Poetry and Place*. Ann Arbor, MI: University of Michigan Press, 1981.

Heidegger, M. "Poetically Man Dwells." In *The Green Studies Reader: From Romanticism to Ecocriticism*, 88-95. Edited by L. Coupe. London, UK: Routledge, 2000.

Hillman, J. *The Dream and the Underworld*. New York: William Morrow, 1979.

Hockley, L. *Being in Relationship: The Ecology of Individuation*. Jungian Society for Scholarly Studies Conference, Portland State University, Portland, Oregon, 2018.

Joint Consortium for School Health (JCSH). "What Is Comprehensive School Health?" 2008. http://www.jcshcces.ca/upload/JCSH%20CSH%20Framework%20FINAL%20Nov%2008.pdf

Jung, C. G. "The Psychology of the Transference." In *The Practice of Psychotherapy, The Collected Works of C. G. Jung*. Translated by R. F. C. Hull. 16 Bollingen Series. Princeton, NJ: Princeton University Press, 1966. 163-167.

Karlsson, J. "Visual Methodologies." In *Research Methods and Methodologies in Education*, 94-101. Edited by J. Arthur, M. Waring, R. Coe, & L. Hedges. Los Angeles, CA: Sage, 2012.

Katherine, A. *Boundaries*. Center City, MN: Hazelden, 1991.

Kearney, R. "What Is Diacritical Hermeneutics?" *Journal of Applied Hermeneutics* 1 (2011): 1-14.

Keller, C. *From a Broken Web: Separation, Sexism, and Self*. Boston, MA: Beacon Press, 1986.

Kutcher, S., Y. Wei, A. McLuckie, and L. Bullock. "Educator Mental Health Literacy: A Programme Evaluation of the Teacher Training Education on the Mental Health & High School Curriculum Guide." *Advances in School Mental Health Promotion* 6, no. 2 (2013): 83-93.

Leblanc, M., P. J. Talbot, and W. M. Craig. "Psychosocial Health in Youth: An International Perspective. In *Handbook for Working with Children and Youth: Pathways to Resilience across Cultures and Contexts*, 165-188. Edited by M. Ungar. Thousand Oaks, CA: Sage Publications, 2005.

Levine, P. *Trauma & Memory. Brain and Body in a Search for the Living Past.* North Atlantic Books: Berkeley, CA, 2015.

Levine, P. *Healing Trauma: A Pioneering Program for Restoring the Wisdom of Your Body.* Boulder, CO: Sounds True, 2008.

MacGregor, N. H. "Mapping the Body: Tracing the Personal and the Political Dimensions of HIV/AIDS in Khayelitsha, South Africa." *Anthropology & Medicine* 16, no. 1(2009): 85-95.

McHale, K., N. C. Council, and M. Maidrag. "Promoting and Improving Emotional Health through Building Resilience in Children and Young People Using Whole School Approaches." 2015. http://www.westsuffolkccg.nhs.uk/wp-content/uploads/2013/01/APPENDIX-5B-Improving-Emotional-Health-Building-Resilience.pdf

Neilsen, L. "Lyric Inquiry." In *Handbook of the Arts in Qualitative Research*, 93-102. Edited by J. Gary Knowles & Ardra L. Cole. Los Angeles: Sage Publications, 2008.

O' Driscoll, D, Ed. *The Bloodaxe Book of Poetry Quotations.* Northumberland, England: Bloodaxe Books, 2006.

Partners for Mental Health (PMH), Canada. http://www.partnersformh.ca

Pinn, J. "Restor(y)ing a Sense of Place, Self and Community. In *Changing Places: Re-Imaging Australia*, 38-47. Edited by J. Cameron. Double Bay, New South Wales: Longueville Books, 2003.

Prendergast, M. "Introduction: The Phenomena of Poetry in Research." In *Poetic Inquiry: Vibrant Voices in the Social Sciences*, xii-xlii. Edited by M. Predergast, C. Leggo, and P. Sameshima. Rotterdam, The Netherlands: Sense Publishers, 2009.

Public Health Agency of Canada (PHAC). "The Health of Canada's Young People: A Mental Health Focus." http://www.phac-aspc.gc.ca/hp-ps/dca-dea/publications/hbsc-mental-mentale/weight-poids-eng.php

Rosenberg, J. L., and B. Kitaen-Morse. *The Intimate Couple.* Atlanta, GA: Turner Publishing, 1996.

Rosenberg, J. L., M. L. Rand, and D. Asay. *Body, Self, & Soul: Sustaining Integration.* Atlanta, GA: Humanics Trade Group, 1985.

Schore, A. N. *The Science of the Art of Psychotherapy: The Latest Work from a Pioneer in the Study of the Development.* New York. W. W. Norton, 2012.

Sieff, D. *Understanding and Healing Emotional Trauma: Conversations with Pioneering Clinicians and Researchers.* London, UK: Routledge, 2015.

Singh Baldwin, S. *What the Body Remembers.* Toronto, ON: Alfred A. Knopf, 1999.

Stanley, S. *Relational and Body-Centered Practices for Healing Trauma: Lifting the Burdens of the Past.* New York: Routledge, 2016.

Stromsted, T., and D. F. Sieff. "Dances of Psyche and Soma: Re-Inhabiting the Body in the Wake of Emotional Trauma." *Understanding and Healing Emotional Trauma: Conversations with Pioneering Clinicians and Researchers*, 46-63. New York: Routledge, 2015.

Unger, M. "Introduction: Resilience across Cultures and Contexts." In *Handbook for Working with Children and Youth: Pathways to Resilience across Cultures and Contexts*, xv-xxxix. Thousand Oakes, CA: Sage Publications, 2005.

Van der Kolk, B. *The Body Keeps the Score: Brain, Mind, and Body in the Healing of Trauma.* New York, NY: Penguin Books, 2014.

Wei, Y., S. Kutcher, and M. Szumilas. "Comprehensive School Mental Health: An Integrated 'School-Based Pathway to Care' Model for Canadian Secondary Schools. *McGill Journal of Education/Revue des sciences de l'education de McGill* 46, no. 2 (2011): 213-219.

Wiebe, S., and P. Sameshima. "Sympathizing with Social Justice: Poetry of Invitation and Generation. *Art | Research International: A Transdisciplinary Journal* 3, no. 1(2018): 7-29.

Wienand, A. "An Evaluation of Body Mapping as a Potential HIV/AIDS Educational Tool." *Centre for Social Science Research*, working paper 169 (2006): 1-32.

Wilson, S. *Research Is Ceremony: Indigenous Research Methods.* Halifax & Winnipeg, Fernwood Publishing, 2008.

World Health Organization (WHO). http://www.who.int/features/factfiles/mental_health/en/.

Zwicky, J. *Wisdom and Metaphor.* Kentville, NS: Gaspereau Press, 2003.

3.

Difficult, Beautiful Things: Young Immigrant Writers Find Voice and Empowerment through Art and Poetry

Amanda N. Gulla

Molly H. Sherman,
Harvest Collegiate High School in New York City;
Lehman College, University of New York

This chapter describes a collaboration in aesthetic education between an education professor and a high school English teacher of refugee and immigrant students in the Bronx, New York. In a co-taught workshop, we integrated visual art and poetry into the English curriculum; these students explored paintings through the lens of what it means to be a "hyphenated American" and wrote powerful poetry in response. We explored ideas about identity, heritage, displacement and its concomitant traumas, as well as some of the more optimistic aspects of the immigration experience. The experience of writing poems in response to art had a positive impact on the students' engagement and confidence in themselves as writers.

Keywords: aesthetic education, English language learner, adolescent, immigrant, poetry, ekphrastic, voice, refugee, community

This chapter describes a collaboration in aesthetic education between an education professor and a high school English teacher of refugee and immigrant students in a newcomers' high school in the Bronx, New York. According to Maxine Greene, "Aesthetic education is an approach to teaching and learning that teaches what it means to pay heed to the appearances of things, the sounds of things, to be responsive to new vistas and new forms. It is—deliberately and delicately—to move students to fresh insight and awareness."[1]

In a co-taught workshop, we integrated visual art and poetry into the English curriculum; these students explored paintings through the lens of what it means to be a "hyphenated American" and wrote powerful poetry in response. We chose art and poetry that explored ideas about identity, heritage, displacement and its concomitant traumas, as well as some of the more optimistic aspects of the immigration experience and multicultural identity. Then students wrote poems responding to the art. We began with Frida Kahlo's *Self Portrait on the Borderline between Mexico and the United States*, then continued our study of the complexities of American identity through George Ella Lyon's poem "Where I'm From," Jacob Lawrence's *Migration Series*, and Romare Bearden's *Black Odyssey*, as well as a selection of poetry from sonnets through modern works.

In response to each of these works, students were encouraged to "notice deeply," a practice that Lincoln Center Institute defines as, "to identify and articulate layers of detail in a work of art through continuous interaction with it over time."[2] The students began to move from observation and description to interpretation as they generated questions in relation to their observations. They considered not just what they were seeing, but the choices the artist made in creating the work and the meaning and significance of those choices.

We developed this way of teaching in the midst of a presidential campaign whose rhetoric was increasingly hostile toward immigrants. Our purpose was to create a space for students to develop and communicate their stories and insert their voices into a threatening national conversation as a "who" rather than as a "what,"[3] by writing poems in response to works of art that evoked aspects of their lived experiences. For most, it was their first experience of expressive writing in English. Through the poetry workshop, students had conversations in which they discovered their common feelings of alienation and struggled to communicate effectively. The process of reading and discussing each other's poems helped to build a strong supportive community across the various cultures in the classroom. For many, these were the first poems they had ever written in any language.

This notion that works of art could be doorways to lead us into expressing our own experiences is rooted in Greene's belief that "cultural, participatory engagement with the arts" could provoke "an initiation into new ways of seeing, hearing, feeling, moving."[4] These provocations have the power to engage what Greene called the "social imagination," which she defined as, "the capacity to invent visions of what should be and what might be in our deficit society, in the streets where we live and our schools. Social imagination not only suggests but also requires that one take action to repair or renew."[5]

For students who are new to the United States, their previous education is too often haphazard and based upon their family's ability to pay. The twelfth-grade students at the international school in which we worked are mostly identified as Students with Interrupted Formal Education (SIFE). Most of these students arrived in the Bronx traumatized by extended family separations, poverty, crime, war, and oppression based on gender, political, religious, or socioeconomic designations. These students had spent or were still spending so much energy on survival that reflective, introspective thought was often too painful and repressed in the face of the need to survive and succeed and, most simply, learn English.

Given the range of reading and comprehension levels in each classroom, we agreed that teaching students to develop meaningful literacy would be best served by first learning to "read" visual art. Starting with art enabled students to engage in intellectually stimulating discussions about symbolism and creative choices that carried over into subsequent discussions of literature, as well as into their writing. Furthermore, the symbolic imagery in the works of art we studied reflected the students' own experiences back to them in ways that they understood and wanted to express. Telling their stories necessitated finding their voices. Seeing how Kahlo, Lawrence, and other artists had found and expressed their voices showed the students that this was possible.

Our initial foray into the creative writing process was through an activity created by the New York City Writing Project's Melicca McCormick, inspired by Sherman Alexie's character Junior in *The Absolutely True Diary of a Part-Time Indian*. Trying to figure out where he fits in as an "apple" (red on the outside and white on the inside), Junior looked at the small and large of who he was. This brainstorming work was important front-loading for the work to follow as much of the thinking and discussion would allow students to start their "Where I'm From" poems at a higher level. The conversations often returned to the public discourse around immigrants and how alienating that could be. Students wanted to show the complexity of their identities to those who dehumanized them through caricatures. The power to connect to another's heart through language was a conversation from the day poetry was introduced. Here is an example from Marisol,[6] a student who was one of the more advanced speakers in the class but had not previously written any poetry.

Marisol's Tribes

I know that to them I'm just an immigrant. Someone who is here to "have babies, take their jobs and money." This is a misconception because I am more than that. Sure, I am an immigrant, but I am also a person who works hard and has hopes and dreams. I belong to that tribe.

I belong to the tribe of those who vehemently dislike to ask others for favors. I belong to the tribe of readers because Quentin Jacobsen's misfortunes make them forget, but still remember their own. And the tribe of those who cease to exist as the rain pours down.

And the tribe of people who drink hot chocolate with the purpose of burning their tongue, just to spend the rest of the day feeling it with their upper lip.

And to the tribe of El Ensanche Duarte in San Francisco de Macorís who are coming in and out of Dona Juana's house because she had a stroke last night.

And the tribe of people whose organs all sink down to their feet when they see that someone, because they wish they could sit in their underwear at 3 am at a kitchen counter with them and talk about the universe.

And the tribe of people who wish to be doctors but sit in their room alone whispering to themselves over and over, "I can do it, I can do it, I can do it."

And to the tribe of people who are happiest with the feel of the wind on their face and hair as they're swinging back and forth in the playground at the park.

And from the tribe of people whose favorite color is that of red roses when their petals turn a red wine at their base.

And to the tribe of people who look out into the night sky and wish she was still sleeping next to me, but then, I remember that in the morning the flowers that grew over her will bloom.

In the process of writing their "Tribes" poems, the students described their lives both literally and metaphorically, which laid the groundwork for subsequent writing and also deepened their understanding of the literature they were reading.

English Language Learners Building a Vocabulary of Creative Expression

Students who are struggling with language are, by necessity, literal, and often seek the language learners' holy grail: formal vocabulary instruction. It is well documented that out of context vocabulary learning yields little growth and deflects from the higher thinking that the learner could employ while engaging with the new language. The opportunity to ask open-ended questions that seek no singular right answer is hugely freeing for anxious speakers who must not only consider the concepts they wish to inquire about, but the language to express them. The open questioning encouraged our students to think more deeply. They were being asked not to be certain but to wonder. Instead of the usual school experience of being questioned by teachers, they were now the questioners, and their curiosity determined the direction of the discussion. When we studied Kahlo's *Self Portrait on the Borderline between Mexico and the United States,* one student asked what it meant that Kahlo held a cigarette, then another hypothesized that the cigarette might be suggesting that Kahlo felt that life in the United States was unhealthy, because the hand that held the cigarette was on the United States side of the portrait. Once a significance had been assigned to that cigarette, students began to notice other images of smoke and fire in the painting and to see connections between various symbolic elements. The more they saw, the more they went back for a deeper look and asked further questions about the details and composition of the painting. A very important pedagogical goal for English language learners (Ells) is for them to be able to engage in authentic discussions. We became acutely aware of how their ideas and questions were building on one another and worked to develop a vocabulary of metaphors and examples of how to use them in creative writing.

After the students had engaged in this process of unpacking symbols and metaphors through paintings and literature, we felt that even those who had never heard of poetry before that year were comfortable enough with both reading and writing poems that they could take on some more traditionally canonical works and writers. This comfort with poetry is not to be taken for granted, as even many of the graduate students in our university's English Education program had expressed discomfort with poetry and asked for help in how they might teach it in their own classrooms. Interestingly, the Ell students did not exhibit fear or frustration. Because they were able to understand the logic of language and structural choices made by poets, the students were able to recognize similarities to the kinds of choices they had made in their own work. In the process of poetic analysis, they easily made connections between the artistic choices made in the poetry and fiction they read and those that were made by the visual artists whose work they analyzed.

One example of how this played out in class involved Bashita, a Bangladeshi student who, like many language learners, had been initially resistant to creative writing. This young woman found herself captured by her independent reading book, *I Am Malala*. When Bashita was inspired by Malala's story to write a poem about her own life, she incorporated insights related to the painting *Face Reality* by Laurie Cooper, which we had studied alongside Paul Laurence Dunbar's poem "We Wear the Mask." Having already studied sonnets and iambic pentameter, Bashita wanted to express her truth in the manner of Dunbar and Cooper, but she said that she wanted to "do something hard" and create a poem entirely in iambic pentameter. She worked in the classroom during lunch seeking the symbols and language to express her feelings, not only of being an immigrant, but of gender bias in her culture. She worked every day for several weeks in order to produce a truth she had buried deeply.

> How can educating girls be Haram?
> Is her mind more dangerous than a gun?
> Is God pleased by those who praise by killing?
> Quran, Bible, and Torah proffer love.
> Neighbors spot my hijab … a double-take.
> Eyes glancing like doves, woodpeckers, and hawks.
> Judge others not, lest ye be not judged.

> Malala combated the faceless ghosts.
> Slithering into her home through airwaves.
> Her voice is a missile to millions of others;
> a shield protecting girls' education
> against darkness petrified by knowledge.
> Her insistent eye turned evil to stone.

The image of this young woman furiously focused on her screen or tapping out syllables as she researched ideas and words to both honor Malala and express her truth is unforgettable. She was confident, determined to be heard. She had found and valued her voice.

"Miss … this is me!"

The work throughout the year led to a visual art and poetry project based on Jacob Lawrence's *Migration Series* and Romare Bearden's *Black Odyssey*. The students studied *Black Odyssey* with the art teacher and then in English class they analyzed the paintings and the accompanying text of the *Migration Series.* They were comfortable with poetry and had developed a strong community in which they learned from and supported each other's creative work. The teacher built lessons around the students' own writing. Kids would get shout-outs in the hall from students in the other classes. Through a grant from The Professional Staff Congress of the City University of New York (PSC-CUNY), we were able to produce an anthology of the students' writing with color prints of their artwork. The anthology was titled *Nobody Knows the Stories of Others,* after a line from one of the students' poems. The opportunity to publish and be heard was motivating, but so were moments like the following.

After viewing each of the sixty panels of *The Migration Series* and the accompanying text, students were given books containing all of the panels and asked to select one or more that connected to their experience as an immigrant. They were looking for a "feeling" connection to the image. Kelvin, a sweet boy with limited English, who was often absent as he worked off the books on a construction job to pay the rent, was in class that day. A few minutes into the activity he raced across the room with the book splayed open in his hand, excitedly pointing to a page and repeating, "Miss … this is me! That's what I did. I looked like that!" I was unsure of what he meant at first. The image was from panel #24,[7] whose accompanying text said, "The children were forced to work in the fields. They could not go to school." The panel had an image of children bent over picking cotton in a field.[8] Here is Kelvin's poem, written almost in one draft.

> Working since I was a child in my uncle's fields.
> Getting up when the sun rose and coming back when the sun was going down.
> My heart throbbed with sadness because I could not get an education like my friends
> I could not have
> the same opportunity as them.
>
> Tired of
> planting the field
> weeding the field
> carrying bananas in a bag bigger than me.
> Bending hundreds of times every day to get potatoes
> feeling that my back is going to break
> walking in shoes covered in mud.
>
> I went to school without books, both the school and I didn't have any
> and only one pencil

and a piece of paper,
walking into my class
with everybody looking at my broken shoes.

Bashita's take on the same panel indicated how art can elicit a sense of empathy as the image of children working in the fields elicited this memory:

As I go to school my friends watch me
with my books in my hand.
They never have had the opportunity to step on the school porch.

While I carry my books, my friends carry tiffin to rice paddies
to the person who is working there,
instead of bringing books to school.

Monday morning, I watch my neighbor
carrying a massive fishing net
holding it over his shoulder
and his ten-year-old daughter following him
wherever he goes with a small basket.

While I carry my books
and go to school
waving my hand to say bye to them.

Conclusion: Writing Difficult, Beautiful Things

By placing the study of works of art at the center of the curriculum for shared, guided inquiry through observation and questioning, aesthetic education encourages students to imagine other possible ways of being in the world. Central to these experiences, which Maxine Greene saw as "integral to the development of persons—to their cognitive, perceptual, emotional, and imaginative development," is the students' own artmaking because it fosters a "distinctive mode of literacy" that Greene believed "must be grounded in actual experiences with the materials of at least one of the arts."[9] The supportive, discursive writing community that developed brought together diverse cultures and personalities. The opportunity to produce an anthology of their writing and artwork provided concrete validation of the students' hard work and growth. The pride they had in the book continues on as students return to ask for copies for their college professors who had seen the work and wanted copies of their own to use as examples of what is possible when young writers are guided to find and use their voices.

Notes

1. Greene "Aesthetics and the Experience," 317.

2. Holzer and Noppe-Brandon *Community in the Making,* 6.

3. Arendt. *The Human Condition.*

4. Greene. *Variations on a Blue* Guitar, 6.

5. Greene. *Releasing the* Imagination, 5.

6. All students' names are changed to protect their privacy.

7. Lawrence, *The Migration Series.*

8. *Museum of Modern Art*
https://www.moma.org/interactives/exhibitions/2015/onewayticket/pan
el/24

9. Greene "Aesthetics and the Experience," 319.

Bibliography

Alexie, Sherman. *The Absolutely True Diary of a Part-Time Indian.* New York, Little, Brown, 2007.

Arendt, Hannah. *The Human Condition.* Chicago. The University of Chicago Press, 1958.

Dunbar, Paul Lawrence. "We Wear the Mask." In *The Complete Poems of Paul Lawrence Dunbar.* Pantianos Classics, 1922.

Greene, Maxine "Aesthetics and the Experience of the Arts: Towards Transformations." *The High School Journal* 63, No. 8 (May 1980): 316-322.

Greene, Maxine. *Releasing the Imagination: Essays on Education, the Arts, and Social Change.* San Francisco. Jossey Bass, 1995.

Greene, Maxine. *Variations on a Blue Guitar: The Lincoln Center Institute Lectures on Aesthetic Education.* New York, Teachers College Press, 2001.

Gulla, Amanda, and Molly Sherman. eds. *Nobody Knows the Stories of Others: An Anthology of Poetry and Art Work by the Students of Kingsbridge International High School.* New York, PSC CUNY, 2015.

Holzer, Madeleine, and Scott Noppe-Brandon. eds. *Community in the Making: Lincoln Center Institute, the Arts, and Teacher Education.* New York. Lincoln Center Institute Series on School Reform, 2005.

Lawrence, Jacob. *One Way Ticket: Jacob Lawrence's Migration Series.* New York. Museum of Modern Art. https://www.moma.org/interactives/exhibitions/2015/onewayticket/panel/24

Lyon, George Ella. "Where I'm From." In *Where I'm From: Where Poems Come From.* Spring, Texas: Absey, 1999.

II: Poetic Inquiry into Place and Local Identities

Our embodied relationships with the places where we live can be a way to begin to care for human and non-human.
—Sheila Stewart

In the second section, we showcase work that speaks to the use of poetic inquiry rooted in places far and near, and deepening our relationships with our own identities. The chapters in this section question the binary between nature and culture, between art and science, between body and language. Lee Beavington writes ecopoetry to bridge the modern divides among nature, human, and machine, and to show how poetic inquiry can, "(re)connect us to the land, give rights to nature, and honor Indigenous peoples." Poetry can be a way to refuse the human/non-human dialectic and work as social justice by giving voice to the animal and material world. The poet scholars use their reflective practice of poetry writing as a way to honor Indigenous peoples and their lands. Sheila Stewart juxtaposes settler colonialism and poetry "grounded in body and place" to explore questions such as, "In a world where some people are deemed at home and others disposable, how might I write from a grounded place of attunement to water, land, and body? As a poet, how might I contribute to developing a more equitable world?" Poetry can be a response to inequities.

Poets can use their identities and locations as a means of connecting to larger issues of place, space, race, and belonging. Poetry can be used to witness and as an ordering principle in moments of personal or social chaos. Anne Sullivan wrestles with her place in Nigeria as a visiting Fulbright (White) scholar in "Learning Calabar: Notes from a Year in Nigeria," using poetry as a way to anchor and explore her white body in another place, to show how poetry helps us bear witness to violence and social unrest. Margaret McKeon considers experiences as a social justice advocate working with the Canadian Truth and Reconciliation Commission on the legacy of Indian Residential Schools in "Opening into

Relational Responsibility with Poetry." McKeon uses lyric verse to show how relationality around land is an ethical practice and invites us to create new worlds through poetry: "Poetry can be world-creating because it creates experience. It lingers in intimacy to know the broader world deeply. Through poetry, as artful inquiry, I dwell in complexity rather than easy conclusions. Welcome here. Dip your toe in the river."

Poetic inquiry can help us interrogate assumptions and understandings of gender, race, and class. In the chapter "Race and Identity in Post-Apartheid South Africa: Making Coloredness Visible through Poetic Inquiry," Heidi van Rooyen's poems about race provide "insights into the contextual, emotional, and psychological experience of coloredness." Van Rooyen argues that "reclaiming coloredness" through poetry and narrative can help "project a positive self-image in the face of pervasive negative racial stereotyping, and perhaps as a way to finally negate shame," affirming poetic inquiry's role in healing and reclamation. John J. Guiney Yallop also speaks to Indigenous identity through the use of poetry as a personal journey to discovery, reclamation, and integration of marginalized identities. He writes of needing to return to "the place of my birth, the place where my body had begun, a place where I have often gone to heal," when he was diagnosed with prostate cancer. While there he discovered his grandmother was Aboriginal. Guiney Yallop wrote poetry to make sense of this newfound identity, to release prior understandings of who he was and to embrace who he is becoming: "Releasing is what happens when I am moved by the voice and words of a poet. Releasing is what happens when I write or perform my own poetry." Poetic inquiry both uncovers buried and forgotten identities within us and exposes the inequities created when we refuse to place identity in communion with place.

4.

Ecopoetics of the Amazon

Lee Beavington,
SSHRC; Simon Fraser University

The Amazon basin boasts the world's largest river and tropical rainforest, with a surprisingly thin soil that supports our greatest terrestrial biodiversity. During the Interdisciplinary Amazon Field School, a partnership between Kwantlen Polytechnic University and the Calanoa Project in Colombia, students are immersed in this jungle landscape, from boating through flooded forests to trekking through primary tropical rainforest. As an instructor for this field school, and a poet-scientist-philosopher, I include ecopoetry throughout this experience to help students engage with this unfamiliar climate and geography and provide a political voice to rekindle a relationship with the land. This chapter addresses the following questions through a poetic ecological lens: How does poetry offer a voice to the more-than-human? What poetry embodies the Amazon? How can poetic inquiry (re)connect us to the land, give rights to nature, and honor indigenous peoples?

Keywords: ecopoetics, Amazon rainforest, environmental ethics, ecology, field school

I typed the word "Amazon" into Google. The first eight *pages* of results all related to Amazon.com, the behemoth internet retailer that once upon a time wanted to become the world's biggest bookstore. When I told colleagues that I had a ticket to the Amazon, they assumed I was visiting Amazon.com headquarters in Seattle rather than flying to South America. When I told a student, "There's no internet in the remote Amazon," she thought I was somehow referring to Amazon.com's mobile app.

The Amazon, gone from wild haven to civilized corporation, has lost her native voice. The Earth's greatest terrestrial biodiversity and largest river have been branded into an online market-based metropolis with little to no regard for its namesake. Amazon.com is clearly an *it*, while many industrial exploitative entities are all too eager to treat the genuine Amazon as an *it*, harvested historically for rubber trees and today for hardwoods, slashed and burned for pastured cattle, mined for gold, and drilled for oil.

This chapter addresses the following questions through geo-ecological and poetic inquiry lenses[1]: How does poetry offer a voice to the more-than-human? What poetry embodies the Amazon? How can poetic inquiry (re)connect us to the land, give rights to nature, and honor indigenous peoples? I answer these questions through the use of ecopoetry about my experiences in the actual Amazon as part of a school experience. The poems here serve as webs of reciprocity. Even the detritus of the world can be brought alive by poetry, revealing an evocative relationality that whispers countless threads of interconnection. Cloud, rain, river, wing, human, root, and soil are all interwoven in an unbroken tapestry, disturbing the illusion of a human/nature divide.

We are defined by our actions and words. How we speak about the world defines, in turn, how we see and interact with the more-than-human. Botanist and indigenous scholar Robin Wall Kimmerer knows the importance of language use and right speech.[2] When a forest is a noun, it is referred to and treated like an object. Burn it, cut it, dissect *it*. When a verb is used instead, the forest becomes active, a living creature that suffers and thrives. Poetry plays with language this way. Ecopoetry is the use of poetic language—including rhythm, imagery, and sensory evocations—to elicit a relational connection with the natural world, and question privileged positions and human-entrenched hierarchies. Poetic inquiry both rallies poetry for the purpose of elucidating nascent insights and builds connective tissue that blurs the barriers separating humans from each other; ecopoetry focuses on breaking down human-nonhuman barriers, and thus opens an avenue toward environmental ethics. If we can appreciate that the surrounding environment is every bit a part of us as we are a part of it, then perhaps we can foster a shift toward ecocentric politics valuing all animate (and even inanimate) life as holding inherent value.

Poetry and nature experiences both possess the power to attune the senses, animate the seemingly inanimate, and foster a reciprocal relationship with the more-than-human. Such sensorial engagement can sew new threads of interconnection among subjects, human and otherwise. As Robert Bringhurst contends, "Forests are highly developed [nonhuman] civilizations"[3] and "the tamer they are, the less they can teach us."[4] The wild is a process, an ongoing dance between our corporeal bodies and the immersive biosphere. Our DNA is interwoven with nature the same way roots are woven into and with the earth. Bringhurst continues, "[Poetry] is the language of the world: something humans overhear if they are willing to pay attention."[5] The poems included in this chapter are in search of a wild interconnectivity, a way of questioning the anthropocentric worldview by channeling the voice of the Amazon. Poetry can awaken our wild senses and focus perception to cultivate a felt relationality among animals, plants, and the immersive biosphere.

The Interdisciplinary Amazon Field School[6] is a partnership between Kwantlen Polytechnic University (KPU) near Vancouver, British Columbia, and the Calanoa Project in Colombia. Calanoa was founded by Marlene and Diego Samper as an arts, ecology, design, and sustainability learning center, located on the banks of the Amazon River. Students in this field school come with diverse backgrounds and interests, yet they all engage in an immersive cultural and ecological experience, from hearing a shaman speak in his maloka to trekking through primary tropical rainforest. As an instructor for this field school, and a poet-scientist-philosopher, I include ecopoetry throughout this experience to help students engage with this unfamiliar climate and geography[7] and provide a political voice to rekindle a relationship with the land.

Rise and Fall

look down
everything goes down
the world falling

fruit

petal

pollen

leaf

spore

seed

look up
no—
this is not rain
these ten thousand specks

insects
six-legged mist
of the Amazon canopy
tricked into the mouth
bat and bird
spellbound
this cloudburst of bugs
partners in rainforest exfoliation

watch
this rain of excretion
become soil

wisps of wildwood
crumbling bark
twigs shed like tears
no consequence

spinneret spider molt
toppled ant
fledgling feather
howler monkey fur
iguana skin flake
poison dart frog fleck
single morpho butterfly wing
flutters to rest

nothing sleeps long here

rise
and fall

every wing and grave

rise
and fall

roots fueled by rain

rise
and fall

trillions of leaves
sweat ascendant tears
every tree felled
cuts a piece of cloud
out of the sky

Traveling to the Amazon from Canada is an enormous privilege for both instructors and students, a reality that is not forgotten. Significant effort is made to engage in reciprocity, through such acts as gift-sharing (e.g., bringing salmon from BC), making dinner for our Colombian hosts, circles of gratitude, and bringing eyeglasses and other items difficult to acquire in the remote Amazon (even Amazon Prime cannot deliver here). I fully acknowledge the irony of privileged travel resulting in a better understanding of privilege and entitlement. In many ways, this is a challenging journey for students. Heat, sweat, mosquitoes, tarantulas, and a pronounced culture shock leave many of them feeling permeable and vulnerable. The hope is to cultivate cultural, ecological, emotional, and social literacy through this immersive experience, leading to the acknowledgment, understanding and perhaps even integration of other worldviews.

Our journey begins in the Andes, specifically Bogotá, the capital of Colombia. We travel up to Monserrate, a mountain overlooking the city and housing a church. Mist creeps over this sacred place, which could be called the birthplace of the Amazon River. Looking down at Bogotá, a city of more than eight million people, could not feel more distant from tropical jungle. Yet some of the rain that descends here from the heavens will end up in the Amazon River, a reminder of the web of relationality that integrates all life.

Monserrate

I stand on the Andes
where stone bridge spirits
shiver next to angels

Bogotá stretches below
a city tide that never ebbs
where sin and salvation bicker
over each drop of rain

privileged cloudwalker
I have traveled long
to be a tourist in this church

blessed by this black Mary—
continental divide
apostles cling to her mist
afraid to depart solid rock

How far down the mountain

does Mary's blessing carry?

does it reach

the pink river dolphins in the Amazon River
  swimming beneath cruise ships

the indigenous carving bloodwood
  into wooden elephants

the gold diggers from Canada
  come to claim their legal prize

their open pit mine
  cuts a community out of the earth

the priest who stood up and said
  you have to shoot me to stop me

a week later, murdered.

In the Amazon Rainforest, there is constant sound and movement. Sit still long enough, and you can hear the forest raining down bits and pieces of leaf, bark, insect, feather, and fur. This so-called detritus falls to the forest floor and gets eaten by the soil. The roots suck up the resultant minerals, as well as the deluge of rainfall. So much water moves through roots, trunks, branches, and leaves that these trees help form their own climate.[8] A large tree in the Amazon can transpire three hundred liters a day. Cutting this tree down sucks rain out of the rainforest.

A shaman spoke to us in the Amazon, saying, "The richness is in the forest."[9] These poems are my offering to this richness, and a call to remember the true name and worth of all things wild. The shaman added, "If you are against nature, you are against yourself," and if this is true, then we need to make every effort to understand nature in order to better understand ourselves.

Amazon Orchestra

The path is a river of sound
I shiver between symphonies
shrill cicadas and mosquito quiver
hind leg of grasshopper bows
forewing's euphonic string
jaguar stalks the podium
every player in this animal orchestra
tunes to her stride
limbed into rhapsody

The path roars at midnight
perfect pitch of equator black
lyrics unlit into a polyfaunic
my ear turns eye
the silent octave of tarantula
viper's hiss
a slither on my eardrum
melodies that amplify

The path is choral confession
hunger and lust
moon rises into choir's first encore
frogs collate their cries
into medleys moist with hormone
until the wave of croaks recedes
and I am alone
with sirens unseen
flinch at each footstep
fear venom that sizzles
on tongues timbred with savage song
a harmony that devours light

The path is sonic oscillation
rising with the breathing earth
below the rhythm of the rainforest
a realm of howls and hymns
gravid air vibrates with prey
territory lyricked by fang
with leaf cutter's cadence
a valley of percussive cacophonies
drives the blind thump of my heart

Notes

1. Charlton, *Fundamentals of Fluvial Geomorphology;* Ricklefs, *The Economy of Nature;* Galvin and Prendergast, "Introduction"; Leggo, "Yearning for Words"; and Thomas, Cole, and Stewart, *The Art of Poetic Inquiry.*

2. Robin Wall Kimmerer, *Braiding Sweetgrass.*

3. Robert Bringhurst, *Tree of Meaning,* 275-276.

4. Bringhurst, 272.

5. Bringhurst, 145.

6. http://www.kpu.ca/amazon-interdisciplinary-field-school and http://www.calanoaamazonas.com

7. Beavington, "Poetic Pedagogy"; Gorrell and Colfax, *Writing Poetry*; and Thomas, "Geopoetics."

8. Wright, et al., "Rainforest-Initiated Wet Season."

9. Shaman in discussion with author, 14 May 2017.

Bibliography

Beavington, Lee. "Poetic Pedagogy in Science Education." In *Poetic Inquiry: Enchantments of Place*, 355-363. Edited by Pauline Sameshima, Alexandra Fidyk, Kedrick James, and Carl Leggo. Wilmington, DE: Vernon Press, 2017.

Bringhurst, Robert. *Tree of Meaning: Thirteen Talks*. Kentville, NS: Gaspereau Press, 2006.

Calanoa Amazonas. (n.d.) Retrieved from http://www.calanoaamazonas.com

Charlton, Ro. *Fundamentals of Fluvial Geomorphology*. London: Routledge, 2008.

Galvin, Kathleen T. and Monica Prendergast. "Introduction." In *Poetic Inquiry II – Seeing, Caring, Understanding: Using Poetry as and for Inquiry*, xi–xvii. Edited by Kathleen T. Galvin and Monica Prendergast. Rotterdam, The Netherlands: Sense Publishers, 2016.

Gorrell, Nancy S., and Erin Colfax. *Writing Poetry through the Eyes of Science: A Teacher's Guide to Scientific Literacy and Poetic Response*. Sheffield: Equinox, 2012.

Kimmerer, Robin W. *Braiding Sweetgrass: Indigenous Wisdom, Scientific Knowledge and the Teachings of Plants*. Minneapolis, MN: Milkweed Editions, 2013.

Leggo, Carl. "Yearning for Words, Learning with Words: Poetic Ruminations." *LEARNing Landscapes* 5, no. 1 (2011): 149–155.

Ricklefs, Robert E. *The Economy of Nature: A Textbook in Basic Ecology*. New York: W.H. Freeman, 1993.

The Amazon Interdisciplinary Field School. (n. d.). Retrieved from http://www.kpu.ca/exchange/field-schools/amazon

Thomas, Suzanne M. "Geopoetics: An Opening of the World. In *Poetic Inquiry II—Seeing, Caring, Understanding: Using Poetry as and for Inquiry*, 191-201. Edited by Kathleen T. Galvin and Monica Prendergast. Rotterdam, The Netherlands: Sense Publishers, 2016.

Thomas, Suzanne, Ardra L. Cole, and Sheila Stewart, eds. *The Art of Poetic Inquiry*. Halifax, NS: Backalong Books, 2012.

Wright, Jonathon S., Rong Fu, John R. Worden, Sudip Chakraborty, Nicholas E. Clinton, Camille Risi, Ying Sun, and Lei Yin. "Rainforest-Initiated Wet Season Onset over the Southern Amazon." *Proceedings of the National Academy of Sciences* 114, no. 32 (2017): 8481–8486. https://doi.org/10.1073/pnas.1621516114

5.

Opening into Relational Responsibility with Poetry

Margaret McKeon,
University of British Columbia

My ancestral bloodlines lead me here, to a sloshing birth on land that was promised to be a Papaschase Cree Reserve but is instead the prosperous University of Alberta. Before my first heartbeat or screaming breath, I'm a colonizer here. I am raised in a Western worldview, which has a foundation of seeing itself as universal to humanity, named by Santos (2014) as cognitive imperialism. For me, decolonization is not just about human rights or social justice. Nor is it outside of these. Wilson (2008), describes an Indigenous way of understanding responsibility as emerging from and being accountable within relationships, these being relationships to places, people, and ideas. In this chapter, I share my journey toward understanding ethical relationality, particularly as it centers around land. As a poet, I draw on lyrical writing, rich with the poetic gifts of metaphor, and poetry to weave vivid space of exploration.

Keywords: decolonization, relational responsibility, land, story, metaphor, ancestral knowledge

Gypsy Stolen

I leave without saying or where I'm headed

unsure if by foot or car
or horseback

forget how to ride but I trust this animal

lean into her warm muscled smoothness

her wiry mane

pack dreams that jar me awake with restless sweat
in rough bags that grip her powerful hunches

the days I'm crazy in tight rolls on top

she will know what's next

I'm awake. Well, not quite awake. And my eyes squint open against eyelids weighted by ancient fears and plenty of violence. Four heart valves strain with accumulated plaque to keep me alive. Pump, squish, pump, squish.

My ancestral bloodlines lead me here, to a sloshing birth on land that was promised to be a Papaschase Cree[1] Reserve but is instead the prosperous University of Alberta. The Papaschase required to disperse. A top-notch hospital built. I am born on a June evening.

Before my first heartbeat or screaming breath, I'm a colonizer here. Maybe the clay-heavy river could clear out my bloodlines a bit. Carry away some of my excess ancestral and white-skinned privilege and colonizer's education.

"You're all wonderful people—thoughtful and kind— but you're entirely missing the mark." (I'd thought I was getting somewhere with my learning.) "This is about reconciliation and everything here is from your Western ways."

I'm working on reconciliation and decolonizing and my nose is bleeding onto another glass wall, a sneaky wall composed of my ideas and ways: "the way we do and know things around here" … in our Western normative circles.

In Canada, the Truth and Reconciliation Commission on the legacy of Indian Residential Schools calls for our institutional and personal engagement with reconciliation. Generations of Indigenous children were forcibly removed from their families and communities to attend government-mandated schools, run by churches delivering a curriculum of civilizing and Christianizing (and often abuse). Well-meaning and "doing God's work," they delivered cultural genocide.

I grew up among social justice activists but I do not easily use this language for my work. Poetry and bloodied glass walls have grown me leery of taking language for granted. I am nourished by the fruits of Canada's strong social justice movements: publicly funded health care, old age pension, employment insurance. Social justice now closely knits with human rights ideals and legislation.

I recently visited the Canadian Museum for Human Rights at the sacred meeting of the Assiniboine and Red Rivers. In the first hall is a timeline that shows the evolution of human rights. The second hall features Indigenous Perspectives: "First Nations, Métis, and Inuit peoples have concepts of rights and responsibilities based on worldviews in which everyone and everything is interrelated."[2] It is a beautiful space, whose walls and tapestries extend up through the exhibits on the higher floors, though its concepts and language do not. The words here taste different. No progress narrative. Humans aren't the sole focus.

Western thought has a foundation of seeing itself as universal to humanity, named by Boaventura de Sousa Santos as cognitive imperialism.[3] For me, decolonization is not just about human rights or social justice. Nor is it outside of these.

In this chapter, I share my journey toward understanding ethical relationality, particularly as it centers around land. My position is a map of how my responsibilities grow from my relationships. As a poet, I draw on lyrical writing, rich with the poetic gift of metaphor, and poetry to fully and expressively weave this space of exploration. Poetry can be world-creating because it creates experience. It lingers in intimacy to know the broader world deeply. Through poetry, as artful inquiry, I dwell in complexity rather than easy conclusions. Welcome here. Dip your toe in the river.

I sit on a grassy bank alongside *kisiskâciwani-sîpiy*, the North Saskatchewan River, which sings to the few June mosquitoes that brave a stirring breeze. It doesn't matter how old I am or if it will rain later. A matted spider web of relationships surrounds me and composes me: strands of food and clothing, prosperity and loss, past, present, and future encircle me and reach in all directions.

Among the stems of sacred *misâskwatômin*, Saskatoon berry shrubs, I spill tears of the Irish famine and pee Chilean water from Chilean grapes I ate with breakfast. These waters flow downriver to Fort Carlton and Fort Pitt where Treaty 6 was signed in 1896 between the Canadian crown and the nêhiyawak, Anihšināpēk, Nakota and Dene, and other nations. I sit by the singing river.

Cree scholar Shawn Wilson describes an Indigenous way of understanding responsibility as emerging from and being accountable within relationships, these being relationships to places, people, and ideas.[4]

I call on my loving Irish and German ancestors to help guide my relationships: With the Indigenous lands on which I live my life. With the Indigenous and other non-Indigenous peoples who inhabit them. Within weaving between the Euro-Western knowledges in which I was raised and the Indigenous and ancestral Celtic knowledges of which I'm a learner.

My bloodlines flow from colonists and the brutally colonized. We are settlers to North America where we have sometimes survived and sometimes thrived, been poor and well off, powerless and powerful, loving and abusive.

In my dreams, I climb through mosquitoes to reach Mt Featherstonhaugh. Striding across its rounded rock top, I strain to peek under the English nameplate, engraved for my Anglo-Irish great-grandfather who engineered part of the northern British Columbia leg of the Canadian National Railroad. In my dreams, I fly over the vast territories of the Dakelh-speaking people, bolting down steel lines and English names, waving to Great-Grandfather still stuck on his small mountain. But then I'm awake. Well, not quite awake.

I need to think more about these, relationships and relational stories, that contain my curricula of responsibility, my gifts of life purpose.

Inquiring into and healing power imbalances of past and ongoing colonization (and destruction) of peoples, land, and ways of knowing form a central work of our time, a decolonizing work that is at core about relationship. Shawn Wilson tells me that understandings of relationship define both my sense of self and of responsibility.[5]

In the decisions around whether to build a new dam or not, we should consider not just whose knowledge, but what kinds of knowledge and what kinds of relationship "count" in this decision. Maybe it's not a dam. Maybe it's pipeline. Potawatomi ecologist Robin Wall Kimmerer and Kathleen Dean Moore write about pipeline confrontations at Standing Rock in 2016, describing, "Two lines, facing each other on a North Dakota highway. On one side, concrete barriers protect a row of armored vehicles and helmeted police with assault rifles."[6] Meanwhile, on the other side, "a young man rides a white horse whose legs are stained with blood. A woman, wearing a scarf to protect her lungs from tear gas, wafts sage smoke over a boy to give him strength, wash away hate, and remind him of his sacred purpose."[7] *Two lines, facing each other on a North Dakota highway, strike me through the heart.*

"Here, on a highway stretching across trampled prairie grass, the fundamental contest of our time is playing out. It's a confrontation not only between two groups of people, but between two worldviews."[8] *Two lines tear open my sense of self.*

"...between the lines vibrates with tensions of race, historical trauma, broken treaties, money and politics, love and fear. But the underlying issue that charges the air, mixing with the smells of tear gas and sage, is the global contest between two deeply different ideas about the true meaning of land."[9] *Two lines through the long grasses, and I come from the Humvees, yearn for a white horse.*

I yearn for reconciliation with the land, the earth, the deep beating heart on which I tread my feet. *Are you there, Earth? It's me, Margaret.*

We exist in webs of relationships: with ourselves, with other people, and the-more-than-human; with ideas and places; with the past, present, and future. What I believe counts as knowledge defines how I identify and know my relationships and therefore name as my responsibilities. Understanding knowledge as the domain supremely of cognitive thought produces much different personal and communal networks of relationships and responsibilities than when I am able to value also bodily, emotional, and intuitive-spiritual knowing.

I want to learn how to walk with worldviews differently. To open myself to experience land, people, and ideas in more generous ways, ways that do not just belong to my head.

Doctoral studies brought me to Coast Salish territories and an ocean coast lined with fertile soils and tree giants. I seek out the few remaining ancient trees to rest my head on spongy rippled bark, gently inquiring into the ancient knowledge of Douglas fir or cedar. Among the tall trees of my doctoral studies, I've been learning about coming to know as gradual opening of my being. I work on healing my bark-thick resistances to what I don't understand or perceive. I'm healing myself into knowledge. Through poetry, I learn to inhale and exhale other knowing. More and more the world sounds and feels different than I could have imagined.

> Short months ago I heard nothing.
> Now, even in the city, I perceive the surround
> of trees and plants that line the sidewalk.
>
> My breastbone echoes with quieter than quiet presence:
> stillness so still it is movement, while rumbles
> of cars and trucks fade
> behind the pregnant sliver of new moon.
>
> Stars appear dimmer in the city
> but don't be tricked by this light trick of perception.
> Our peril sees as if all fires are dim,
> as if there are no other watchers.
>
> Every child knows the ignored teacher signals
> louder and louder and angrier,
> knows to turn her head and be still.

Dolores Whelan in her work with the Celtic calendar teaches of the rhythms of seasons serving as guidance for the creative transformation of personal and communal worlds.[10] The Celtic Calendar organizes four seasons into *giamos,* a more feminine period dominated by darkness, deep being, transformation, and receptivity, and *samos,* a more masculine period dominated by brightness, active doing, and productivity. The death and stillness of winter allow for the land's rebirth in spring. Similarly, for people, transformation lives in the times of stilled hands and the discomforts of interiority.

Stillness? What about productivity! Efficiency! Action! In my worldview, shame boils through me when I stop producing. From the privilege of stillness, I open my eyes, peer around at the ocean, mountain, animal worlds that all exist in balanced cycles of growth and dying back. Dying back is trust that another spring comes anew. In surrendering to loss, I'm awake with ancient seeds in my hands to greet the sunrise. Intuition rises up through my dreams.

Dawn Still Sings Its Creation
For the crows who leave their work each winter night to gather

From the bottom of a small pool, I wonder
about welcoming learning like a foliaged
stillness welcomes bathing chickadees

In our seasons of doing and being,
a balanced circle of rivers and calm,
I too walk frozen, mesmerized,
under the waterfalls of doing

Do we mistake ourselves for our machines
and their continual summers of doing,
only occasionally, catastrophically,
apocalyptically, breaking down

We might seek machine fixes
that will re-imagine themselves

Or we might strip naked, hang safely on trees
the ideas and identities of our needy belongings,
and return to the ancient places
where our kind have always gathered

where earth belches a warm heat,
water we've almost forgotten

where past, present and future
cacophonate our linearity-weary senses

where teachers may be winged or hoofed,
and oceans lullaby our timeless cells

Until spring's mornings when we return anew
disheveled and eager, to our living productivities

Knowing that without rituals of nakedness,
we've no ask of others for change
and our created world has ceased its creation

We paint change with our words on repeat, until
rewriting our own idea worlds of perception,
how your pain and my pain vibrate in my belly

We needn't notice but we are all thresholds
and day is still born at night

Metaphor, one of the sacred gifts of poetry, allows us to hold diverse elements together and can help bridge and heal tensioned opposites. I believe that all stories of ideas, places, and people have some kind of truth—it may be physical truth, emotional truth, historical truth, spiritual truth, trauma truth. Mostly we attend and hotly debate a certain kind of truth—"facts." A world described only in facts can be dizzying and doesn't make sense, because it isn't the whole world.

On a long spring road trip, we trace the curve of the waking earth. Northern Montana's grassy prairie, surprise valleys, and sprinkled mountain ranges flow past outside. "But it's a fact—there's a birth certificate from Hawaii." Jonas is sputtering because a Republican politician on the radio is very certain that President Obama was not born in the USA.

I suggest that maybe rather than just fake-truths, there are deeper kinds of truth that weave together to make every person a whole person and every perspective a whole perspective, even if the core of that perspective is fear. Maybe it's a matter of perceiving more richly.

As we close in on a remote border crossing back into Canada, Jonas responds, "so you mean actually listen to them?" (the Republicans).

Dream of Grandmothers

A great battlefield was drawn, armies marched
from both directions. Grandmothers ringed the field
from so far back, their numbers, wholeness wove a womb.

With every swing of sword or axe, raging enemies
dissolved into each other and were lost. Those
gawking and those running away, none survived.

At fear's bottom of fighting, a long river runs clear.
Your heart and the land beat softly. Children dream
as a night bird sings silver to the rising new moon.

Manulani Aluli Meyer describes, from her Hawaiian worldview, three types of knowledge. The first two are knowledge that floats in the head and knowledge gained through experience. The third and highest form of knowledge is Aloha because there is service to Others. Here, knowledge is drawn into the self and the self is transformed: "Aloha is intelligence with which we meet life."[11]

Seeking deeper intelligence, I take up a pedagogy of drawing ideas inside myself and attending to the felt experience of resistance—how is it layered with fear, anger, or shame? From this transformative dwelling, I return into the worlds of ideas, places, and people from a different soil and with new openness and clarity. I return with new ability to witness what before consumed me.

This is a pedagogy of coming to know myself deeply, so that I can be of better service to my relationships of ideas, places, and people. It is challenging myself to become more than open-minded, to grow into being open in spirit, in emotion, and in bodily presence. It is mapping my interior landscapes as a key to understanding external ones.

Before doctoral studies, I inhabited a rockier salt coast of Western Newfoundland. Teaching alongside Mi'kmaw cultural educators, we asked students to learn about their own ancestry. We celebrated particularly Mi'kmaw ancestry, but I learned about bringing these Mi'kmaw teachings inside myself and to seek and honor my own ancestors and their stories. To remember my great-grandfather on his mountain.

I honor the Mi'kmaw teachers who have so affected the course of my life. Their teachings called me awake and call me into dreams. I hope I will always be waking up.

On Settler Identity and Colonialism[12]: A Reader Response
For those who carried the ceremonies while they were illegal

I escape for a walk. Mind brimming with listless chatter,
birdsong on the wind feels distant, impenetrable. In rain
I rest my numb body against a cedar, pray for healing.

Just a book, but they've gripped in sticky hands the heart
of my immigrant's insecurity and shame. I say,
Thank you for showing me this,
while my hands grope about my ribs for the hollow.

Colonialism made bare dis-entitles the exile's arrival,
de-territorializes her property. Text that is insistent,
illegal. illegitimate on the Land

Examining clenched fingers, I find it true: generations in
and I'm clung still to a steep face between the origins
I've forgotten and a landed breath of true responsibility.

I'm of the race of white blight. The rot in potato famine.
The apocalypse in climate. The extra in extraterrestrial.

I can't let go. I can't let go with such violence I chew
incessantly, my fingernails down to fear-worn knuckles.

But fall! It's painful for it's rebirth, but soil rises to cradle
a flailing heartbeat. Moss swells with tears' water and salt.

Nova Scotia: after Cornwallis and a Mi'kmaw Scalp bounty,
residential school, clear-cutting, still Eagle knows Mi'kmaw
lullabies and the Mi'kmaq know *kipu*/Eagle as I never will.

Know *n'sit nogama*, storied responsibility for each being
that walks, flies and swims Mi'kmaw territory,
even I am invited to heal in Sweat Lodge

I am responsible—we are responsible. For breathing. For
naming our own responsibilities. But do that, name them.
what are your responsibilities here?

Notes

1. Donald, "Edmonton Pentimento." Donald recounts the history of the Papaschase Cree in Edmonton.

2. https://humanrights.ca/exhibit/indigenous-perspectives

3. Santos, *Epistemologies of the South*.

4. Wilson, *Research Is Ceremony.*

5. Ibid.

6. Kimmerer and Moore, "The White Horse," par 1.

7. Ibid

8. Kimmerer and Moore, "The White Horse," par 2-3

9. Kimmerer and Moore, "The White Horse," par 3

10. Whelen, *Ever Ancient Ever New.*

11. Meyer, "Manu Aluli Meyer."

12. Lowman & Barker, *Settler: Identity and Colonialism.*

Bibliography

Donald, Dwayne. "Edmonton Pentimento: Re-Reading History in the Case of the Papaschase Cree." *Journal of the Canadian Association for Curriculum Studies* 1, no. 3 (2004): 21-53.

"Indigenous Perspectives," Canadian Museum of Human Rights. Accessed September 2, 2018, https://humanrights.ca/exhibit/indigenous-perspectives

Kimmerer, Robin. W. and Kathleen D. Moore. "The White Horse and the Humvees—Standing Rock Is Offering Us a Choice." *Yes! Magazine.* November 5, 2016. http://www.yesmagazine.org/people-power/the-humvees-and-the-white-horse2014two-futures-20161105.

Lowman, Emma. B., and Adam J. Barker. *Settler: Identity and Colonialism in 21st Century Canada.* Winnipeg, MB: Fernwood, 2015.

Meyer, Manu. A. "Manu Aluli Meyer on Epistemology." YouTube Video, 9:57. October 2010. https://youtu.be/lmJJi1iBdzc.

Santos, Boaventura de Sousa. *Epistemologies of the South: Justice against Epistemicide.* Boulder, CO: Paradigm Press, 2014.

Whelan, Dolores. *Ever Ancient Ever New: Celtic Spirituality in the 21st Century.* Dublin, Ireland: Original Writing, 2010.

Wilson, Shawn. *Research Is Ceremony: Indigenous Research Methods.* Halifax, NS: Fernwood, 2008.

6.

The Ground Beneath Our Feet: Poetry and Settler Colonialism

Sheila Stewart,
New College Writing Centre, University of Toronto

In this chapter, I ask how I might write from a grounded place of attunement to water, land, and body. Living beside Lake Ontario, in Toronto, home of many Indigenous peoples, I begin to explore connections between settler colonialism and poetry, particularly my family's relationship to settler colonialism. I examine a literary anthology, *A Pocketful of Canada* (The Canadian Council of Education for Citizenship, Robins 1946), which my parents acquired shortly after immigrating to Canada. This literary digest of Canada "others" Indigenous peoples through its imagery and racist choice of work. The work of current Indigenous poets provides a welcome probing analysis, particularly that of Billy-Ray Belcourt and Gwen Benaway. My own poetry and imagination are deeply shaped by my parents' lives in Ireland; more recent work inquires into my connection with this land. Three of my poems anchor this chapter, probing my relationship with spirituality, religion, and colonialism.

Keywords: body, land, Indigenous, settler colonialism

only the land gets me

> Gwen Benaway
> from *Passage*
> 2016

there is a dirt road in me.

it hurts to be a story.

i am the boundary between reality and fiction.
it is a ghost town.
you dreamt me out of existence.

Billy-Ray Belcourt
    from *This Wound Is a World*
    2018

Altar

I set up altars everywhere I go—
polished pocket stone,
daisy, or dandelion in a pinch, shell
shaped like your ear,
a bowl of water,
           comfort

I'm not religious
    no no no
    I say no no no

       leave that question
             or alter—

I inquire into what it is to be grounded in both body and place. I live beside Lake Ontario, in Toronto, home of many Indigenous peoples. This was the territory of the Wendat and Petun First Nations, the Seneca, and the treaty holders, the Mississaugas of the Credit River. The territory was the subject of the Dish with One Spoon treaty between the Anishinaabe and Haudenosaunee and allied nations to peaceably share and care for the resources around the Great Lakes. Nine watersheds flow into Lake Ontario around Toronto. I live between the Humber to the west and the Don to the east. In a world where some people are deemed at home and others disposable, how might I write from a grounded place of attunement to water, land, and body? As a poet, how might I contribute to developing a more equitable world? This chapter begins to explore connections between settler colonialism and poetry, trying to understand the ground on which we stand.

I begin with stone and shell to speak of land or place. Our relationship with land can be an anchor in the desire to write and teach in ways that contribute to a more just world. I am often overwhelmed by the increase in racism, drone bombing, waves of people fleeing their homelands in dangerous conditions, the traumas of displacement and oppression so many people are experiencing, climate degradation, the pressure of the university, students' anxiety and my own. Our embodied relationships with the places where we live can be a way to begin to care for human and non-human; I inquire into my connection with this land.

While born in Canada, my first poetry collection,[1] about my relationship with my mother, is rooted in Northern Ireland, my parents' homeland. Their landscapes were familiar to me: the River Lagan in County Down near Glen Farm where my mother grew up; the Cusher River in my father's village of Tandragee which flooded the millworkers' homes each spring. I wrote about my mother's sense of displacement. This inherited kinship with and desire for other lands is often shared by children of immigrants. I grew up near the Avon River in Stratford, Ontario, going to the Stratford Theatre to see Shakespearean plays. Our Stratford was modeled after and longed to be as important as the "real" Stratford in England.

In my second collection,[2] I wrote about High Park, Toronto, streets and cafés, family, and body. To write *from*, *to*, and *with* the present moment and the body is also to engage with memory and loss. My doctoral work used poetic inquiry as methodology to explore the dynamics of shame, grief, and silence as they relate to writing, authority, family, and church; I inquired into my uneasy relationship with my father, a United Church minister. Poetry is the plumb line I use to uncover and reclaim embodied knowing; such writing is an embodied, feminist practice, a spiritual quest(ioning). How is this quest or practice shaped by being a settler living on colonized land? Certainly, I am the beneficiary of having grown up in Canada. Plenty of Stewarts and other Scots-Irish assumed ownership of this land. In light of the Truth and Reconciliation Commission and the calls of Indigenous activists, artists, and scholars, I ask: How might I understand land, reconsider my relationship with it, and my place here?

When my daughter first learned about residential schools and the role of the church, she said, "Did Grandpa know about that? What did he do?" My father had been a Presbyterian minister in Ireland and joined the United Church on immigrating to Canada in 1955. Our family was part of the postwar wave of immigration from the preferred countries of the United Kingdom and Western Europe. The history I grew up learning was that of colonization, but it was not called that and was, as such, invisible to me.

Poetry can both aspire to contribute to a more equitable society and reinforce the status quo, in some cases directly contributing to the project of colonization. I turn to a shelf full of books I grew up with. *A Pocketful of Canada* was on my parents' bookshelf.[3] Below Robins's name as editor on the title page is "The Canadian Council of Education for Citizenship"; this book was a kind of manual on how to be a Canadian citizen. The book jacket illustration includes rivers, trees, the parliament buildings, tepees, totem poles, a man fishing, and another hunting. Wood engravings by English-born artist Laurence Hyde include the front cover and end pages' images of the natural world, figures on horseback waving guns who appear to be "cowboy and Indian" in chase, and a campfire by a lake. A man tends the fire, a woman sits beside it, canoe on the shore. Opposite the title page, a larger engraving depicts a young Indigenous woman embracing a deer, trees and grass surrounding them. We see her naked upper body, her braid with a feather. These illustrations, which could be called typical Canadiana images, are the precursors to the current reality of the Missing and Murdered Indigenous Women and Girls.[4]

Edward Said's concept of orientalism situates these images in the context of how culture contributes to the imperialist, colonial project.[5] The word "pocketful" connotes a kind of innocence or sweetness. What is the pocket full of? Candy? Cash? Racist stereotypes? How much can a pocket contain? Used as a school textbook, this book is but one of many used through twentieth century Canada to develop and reinforce enticing mythologies of the two founding civilizations, English and French, developing a barren land. The three poems by Duncan Campbell Scott are among the most egregious with their images of savages and a "weird and waning race."[6] Scott was a much-revered poet and bureaucrat at the time, and understood to be instrumental in the establishment of residential schools. In a sense, books have been my altar, so I need to reckon with how some major elements of Canadian literature have been based on racism and entwined with the settler colonial project of negatively portraying and erasing Indigenous peoples.

The past few decades have seen a burgeoning of Indigenous literatures, with Indigenous poetry emerging as a powerful, at once deeply personal and political art form. Gwen Benaway and Billy-Ray Belcourt are two young, queer poets who engage profoundly with the body as a site of colonization. Both grapple with issues of violence, land, love, gender, and language. Of Anishinaabe and Métis descent, Benaway begins her book, *Passages*, with the poem "Lake Michigan":

> when the question
> has no easy answer,
> I weave a second life
> to please the curious.
>
> where are you from
> is do you belong,
> who claims you
> in softer words.
>
> I answer here,

this land between countries and water,
the Great Lakes
where my ancestors
grew and died
along the shoreline
of every waterway.[7]

Benaway's book is in homage to the Great Lakes, arranged in five sections, each named after one of the lakes.

In *This Wound Is a World*, Billy-Ray Belcourt celebrates love and the body, in all their woundedness. From the Driftpile Cree Nation, Belcourt, like Benaway, is a theorist and academic, as well as a poet. Like Benaway, he wears his scholarship lightly in that his poems are direct and visceral. In "Boyfriend Poems" he writes, "my body, like the land, was up for grabs." He writes, "everyone is lonely / but no one knows / what to do about it."[8] His book won the 2018 Griffin Poetry Prize, following Indigenous poets who won the two previous years: Jordan Abel for *Injun* (2016) and Liz Howard for *Infinite Citizen of the Shaking Tent* (2015).

I turn now to a recent poem, rooted in Ireland, but attending to a recent social/political moment.

Whatever is in Your Mind

I.

Your thick whitewashed walls,
big fireplace, Donegal
stone cottage.

Aunt Ena and you, Uncle Bonar—
your trifle went round my heart like
velvet. Courgettes from your garden
quickly fried
in butter,
fresh wheaten bread.
Melting. I didn't

want to say the wrong thing.

Uncle Bonar, with your shock of silver hair,
you watched me labor over
my diary and letter home.

It can be easier, you said. *Just write quickly
whatever is in your mind.*

II.

Emanuel African Methodist Episcopal Church
—massacre in Charleston
already faded from our screens.
How can I hold it?
Just write quickly,
or any way at all.

Her mother said, *The girl loved to talk.*
A thirty-two-year-old paralegal
Heather Heyer. Charlottesville.
Her mother addresses the man who
drove his car into the demonstrators:
This isn't a video game.

Bonar, you didn't fly
the bloody Union Jack.
Humor and caution got you through.
After the war, your Belfast linen
business in decline.
Troubles—such an understated word.
Careful what you said,
kept the peace,
prepared the potatoes, beans and carrots.

III.

Bonar, you said, *You're doing great,*
but avoid that political stuff.
My Amnesty International
Christmas card a clue.

Bonar, I'm speaking to you from King Street,
Yonge Street, York, Simcoe, Baldwin,
bowing to the Queen's English.
Statues, war memorials,
shells of residential schools.
My mind a trap I want
to flee.

How might I write a world where some bodies are prized and others
deemed disposable? Unarmed Black and Indigenous men and women are
shot by the police in Canada, as well as in the States. I can neither flee my

mind nor write whatever is in it. I need instead to try to understand what shapes it.

Language and the Queen's English are tied up in the hierarchical way people are viewed and the material and discursive differences of their lives. In teaching a Women and Gender Studies course called Writing the Body, I ask students to consider the relationship between their bodies and their writing. I ask: *How might writing help us inhabit our bodies/selves more fully? How can our bodies help us inhabit our writing more fully?* As an instructor I need to ask these questions of myself. And further questions: *How might we reconsider our relationship to bodies of land and water? What might these relationships mean for our writing?*

The work of Toronto poet and essayist Maureen Scott Harris engages powerfully with the natural world, including the Don River. Harris writes in "Opening the Griefcase," "my writing still struggles with the same seemingly insurmountable difficulty; again and again it refused to be in my experience. How often I live beside myself."[9] I struggle, too, to be in my experience and to write from it. "Opening the Griefcase" is a lyric essay about giving up a baby as a young woman of twenty-one and the effect this had on Harris's life and writing. Harris, like myself, grew up as a minister's daughter, where silence, particularly about difficult emotions, was the norm. She writes, "We weren't a family practiced in sharing feelings, especially not bad feelings like anger or sadness. All extravagant feeling was unseemly, but bad feelings were a kind of dirty secret. Maybe we felt that bad feelings made us bad people, or that we were—or ought to be—above the failings of ordinary people."[10] Like Harris, I needed to be careful not to feel or say the wrong thing.

Concern about saying the wrong thing is a problem for a writer and educator interested in social change. I have followed the advice given to many writers to write what I know. In part, this has meant writing from a kind of woundedness, which has a fair bit to do with how gender was shaped in my family and time. As a white person, I need to also speak and write about racism and other forms of oppression, rather than leave this work to people of color who are directly affected by it and bear a greater cost in confronting it. I am the only person in my family of origin born in Canada but I am never asked, "Where are you from?"—the invasive question many racialized people—Indigenous, Canadian-born and immigrant—are frequently asked.

Striving to contribute to a more equitable society can seem like a lot of less-than-fruitful striving and lead to burnout. The long meetings, busyness. Sometimes the rush from event to demo is largely *rush*; there is little time for contemplation. The college where I work is a hub for activist students and professors. The combination of activism and academia can be lethal in terms of pace and overwork. Poetry requires slowness and attention.

At age thirteen in our trip across Canada pulling our trailer, or caravan as my parents called it, I wrote each evening in a red scrapbook, like a school project. At the time, this cross-Canada camping trip was something many middle-class families did once. I used a ruler to draw pencil lines half an inch apart down the page and printed the date at the top left and miles traveled top right. Drew maps of states and provinces, recorded where we ate and when we stayed at the Happy Valley Trailer Park and Dogwood Campgrounds of British Columbia. Pasted in postcards after I copied out the captions in red. Drew a sun with a smiling face for sunny days, a cloud with a grim mouth and rain coming down like tears. Just the permitted facts.

The insides of our sleeping bags were patterned with Wild West scenes. Rodeos, roundups. I'd copied out the postcard caption: *Indians riding wild buffalo provide a unique event at the Calgary Stampede.*

Postcards of the totem poles in Stanley Park.

What else could I write? Choked by the habit of restraint. Certainly nothing about my body.

I will end with a poem called "Billy Stewart's Geography," based on my father's grade school geography notebook.[11] Words from his notebook are italicized and indented in the poem. While shocked by the explicit racism in my father's school notes, I had only to turn to books from my childhood to find colonialism has bled into settler colonialism in Canada. I wrestle with the layers of words which shape my relationship to bodies of land and water.

Billy Stewart's Geography

There was a dark tunnel which we all knew about.

See him at a school desk with an inkwell, carefully dipping his
       pen, copying from the board, circa 1930. An index inside the
       front cover of his hardcover notebook.

Although Abyssinia is very mountainous
it is making wonderful progress under Italian
control.

My schoolboy father tours me through Ceylon, Rhodesia, Belgian
Congo, Italian East Africa rivers and trade.

> *Liberia, a very backward state, founded*
> *for liberated American slaves.*

> <u>*The Sahara*</u>
> *Wherever water reaches the surface an oasis*
> *is found. These oases differ in size from a few*
> *square yards to areas as big as Ulster.*

Once a year on the Fourteenth of July, my father goes to
Warrenpoint on the Irish Sea.

The trio of festival days begins with the Twelfth. The Orangemen
come to Tandragee with their brigade. The painted banners
display their lodge number and King William on a white
horse emerging from the Boyne River. Mothers and children
line the streets, cheer on their menfolk as they march and
drum. The crowd compare the men on parade from
Ballymore, Cordrain, Tullymacann, and beyond. My father's
sisters and mother start making ice cream at 5 a.m., sell out
mid-afternoon.

The Thirteenth is the Sham Fight in the neighboring village of
Scarva where people enact the battle. "Who won?" some
Protestants would ask with a wink and a smile.

From Christmas on, the children dream of the Sunday School
train excursion. They arrive at the station early clutching
their train tickets and food chits.

My father told me, *There was a dark tunnel which we all knew*
about, and as the slow train went through it, boys kissed girls,
and everyone ended up in different seats. Newry station, ten
kilometers to Warrenpoint and the great day began.

On the last page:

100 years ago Canada was roamed by hunters. The Hudson Bay
Company was king. Today there are 10 and a half million
inhabitants. The natives have dwindled. Today they are given
settlements. There are only 100,000 Indians.

Each page of the notebook filled. The schoolmaster's text from
book to board to notebook.

There was a dark tunnel which we all knew.

As a United Church minister, did he know about the Mohawk
Institute Residential School, Brantford, 1828 to 1970? Closed
when I was ten, I visited it later as a museum.

Dad, did you really think
the Twelfth was fun for Catholics? *William, of Glorious, of*
Pious, and Immortal Memory shouting from the closet.

Did you know about the Gordon Indian Residential School in
Punnichy, Saskatchewan, begun in 1889, closed in 1996? I
didn't know. I was thirty-five when it closed.

There was a dark tunnel.

Maps and pages failing.

Notes

1. Stewart, *A Hat to Stop a Train.*

2. Stewart, *The Shape of a Throat.*

3. Robins, *A Pocketful of Canada.*

4. "National Inquiry into Missing and Murdered Indigenous Women and
Girls."

5. Said, *Orientalism;* Said, *Culture and Imperialism.*

6. Robins, 181.

7. Benaway, *Passage*, 3.

8. Belcourt, *This Wound*, 35.

9. Harris, "Opening the Griefcase," 75.

10. Harris, 71.

11. "Billy Stewart's Geography" first appeared in "Christ Would Break Your Tongue," *Art/Research International: A Transdisciplinary Journal*, 3(1), 258–265.

Thank you to Abby Bushby for generously discussing the Indigenous lands on which Toronto is located.

Bibliography

Belcourt, Billy-Ray. *This Wound Is a World: Poems*. Calgary, Alberta: Frontenac House Poetry, 2017.

Benaway, Gwen. *Passage*. Neyaashiinigmiing, Ontario: Kegedonce Press, 2016.

Harris, Maureen. "Opening the Griefcase." In *How to Expect What You're Not Expecting: Stories of Pregnancy, Parenthood, and Loss*, 135-148. Edited by J. Hiemstra & L. Martin-Demoor. Touchwood Editions, 2013.

"National Inquiry into Missing and Murdered Indigenous Women and Girls." n.d. http://www.mmiwg-ffada.ca/.

Robins, John D., ed. *A Pocketful of Canada*. Toronto: WM. Collins Sons & Co., 1946.

Said, Edward. *Orientalism*, 1st ed. New York: Pantheon Books, 1978.

Said, Edward. *Culture and Imperialism*, 1st ed. New York: Knopf, 1993.

Stewart, Sheila. *A Hat to Stop a Train*. Toronto: Wolsak and Wynn, 2003.

Stewart, Sheila. *The Shape of a Throat*. Winnipeg, Man: Signature Editions, 2012.

Stewart, Sheila. "Christ Would Break Your Tongue." *Art/Research International: A Transdisciplinary Journal* 3, no. 1 (2018): 258–65.

7.

Learning Calabar:
Notes from a Year in Nigeria

Anne McCrary Sullivan,
National Louis University

When I set out for a year of teaching in Calabar, I didn't know my destination was the fifth largest slave-trading port of West Africa or that this corner of Nigeria was once Biafra, where a bitter civil war filled the U.S. news with images of starving children. I had no idea that in learning the history of Nigeria, I would learn to recognize the voice and the repercussions of dictatorship, and my learning would come to resonate with disturbing political directions in my own country. Living in close proximity with aftermaths of cultural ravaging and civil war, and with ongoing corruption, my learning became personal as well as political. The poems of this chapter constitute an ongoing effort to witness, explore, understand, and communicate. They present documentation in support of Dionne Brand's observation: "The ruin of history visited upon a people does not wipe out the steadfastness of beauty."

Keywords: Africa, Nigeria, Calabar, Biafra, slavery, acrostic poems, arts-based research, poetry of witness

My Finger Inquires of the Map—Where?

Here! Right here is Ekorinim. Here I sat,
looked down the hill to the Calabar River.
There, across the river, Oron, where I went
in an overcrowded boat with a small
refrigerator and a goat, to visit
Ekpe masks, traditional costumes.

And there, downstream, Creek Town,
where Etim led me on dirt streets, pointing,
"This is where ...." "This is where ...."
He put a helmet on my head, loaded me
onto the back of a motorbike. We rode
to the once home of Mary Slessor
who stopped the killing of twins.

Parrot Island. Where is that? Farther toward
the Atlantic somewhere. I never went there.
There had been kidnappings. At Parrot Island,
entering the river, slave ships paused to fire
a cannon announcing their arrival.

This river has no slave castles, no witnesses
to its history. At Old Calabar, foreign traders
were not allowed to build on shore—no homes,
offices, castles. They lived, conducted business
on their ships. In canoes, Calabar traders came
and went, dressed in European suits.

Invisible thousands passed out of this river's mouth.
Nothing now to point to, the barracoons rotted,
replaced by docks and jetties. An ordinary traffic
moves on the river through mangrove forests
once lush, made sparse by invasive palms.

There are no colors on this map, only lines, black
and white. I get my colored pencils, color the river blue,
add labels, make notes, "This is where ...." "This is where ...."

Calabar, Nigeria was not a place I ever learned about in school. I could
not have located it on a map.

I did not know about the richness of a culture that predated the slave
trade along the banks of the Calabar River.

I did not know that Calabar was the fifth largest slave-trading port of
West Africa.

I did not know that Nigeria was a colony of Great Britain until as late as
1960 when it became an independent nation.

I did not know that this southeastern corner of Nigeria was once called
Biafra, site of a bitter civil war that filled the U.S. news of the late 1960s
with images of starving children.

I knew nothing of attempts at democracy that were time and again thwarted into brutal dictatorships.

My ignorance was immense when I set out to spend a year living and working in Calabar, though I had, at least, learned to locate it on a map and had given myself a crash course on current politics.

En route to Calabar, I made a required stop in Lagos.

Before Calabar—at the Consulate in Lagos,
Review of procedures, conferrals with medics.
I will be mostly on my own, it seems.
Emergencies ... *Well, at such a distance, we'll do the best we can.*
Fruits and vegetables must be disinfected.
If I have trouble with mefloquine, split the pill, take twice a week.
Now I sit in the final briefing, look at gruesome, bloody images, advised:
Give false information. Shred everything. The purpose of this is to Scare the crap out of you.

Consistent with images of Nigeria in the Western press, this advice, grounded in fear, was intended to keep me safe. If I had not done a little homework, if I had not had experience with other African nations, that briefing might indeed have "scared the crap out of me." Even so, it was sobering, and there were specific things I hadn't thought of, most notably the high danger of fire because of faulty wiring. "If an appliance begins to smoke, get it outside before it begins to burn. When leaving the house, unplug things." This bit of information foreshadowed what I would learn of failed and failing infrastructure.

I first heard of Calabar when I was in Accra, Ghana, at the Pan-African Literacy for All Conference. There I met Bernedette Cornelius-Ukpepi. She approached me with a paper she had written, asking for advice. When I had read the paper, my primary observation was that her research question called for qualitative research, but she had used quantitative methods, and the results seemed skewed. She told me that at the University of Calabar where she worked, they did only statistical research. She had never heard of qualitative and wanted to know more. We continued our communications via email, but after a year, it seemed clear that if we were going to do substantial, meaningful work, I would need to go to Calabar. I applied for a Fulbright, it was granted, and somewhat to my astonishment I found myself heading for Nigeria, ignorant as a microbe, with no idea even of how much there would be to learn.

It would be a while before I would know the history of Calabar, but I immediately began learning the aftermath and human consequences of that history. I was plunged into the context of Nigeria's deep poverty, lack of infrastructure, absence of safety nets, and, operating everywhere, a legacy of corruption, the roots of which, I have come to see, extend back to colonialism.

I was, of course, privileged, protected, cared for by my neighbors in the compound to which the university assigned me. I was welcomed and accommodated by colleagues at the university. I would move unscathed through the poverty that characterized the vast majority of people whom I saw on the streets and encountered in markets daily. Although I shared the inconveniences and discomforts related to lack of electricity and sometimes lack of running water, these were small things in comparison, and I was afforded the privilege of observing, witnessing the profound dignity with which people lived in circumstances of ongoing extreme duress. My deepest learning would come from observing and interacting with my neighbors, my assigned driver, my assigned cook. My learning would be facilitated by the discipline and focus of making poems.

> Dennis explains I must sit in the back,
> Right side. *It is customary.*
> I let him open the door, not wanting to
> Violate custom, slip inside.
> Every day I will take my assigned place,
> Ride uncomfortably comfortable to school.

> *

> This takes me by surprise. I'm told
> Her name is Mary. Hauling my history,
> Embarrassed by servitude, I must accept this

> Cook who comes with the house,
> Overcome my resistance as she
> Organizes spices and pots in my
> Kitchen. *Prof, what would you like for dinner?*

> *

> The awareness of disorder generates in the human mind
> a spontaneous ordering response.
> —Gregory Orr[1]

Gregory Orr has written extensively about poetry as an ordering principle in moments of personal or social chaos. "Faced with disorder," he writes, "the human mind needs to respond with an ordering principle that will sustain it and console it."[2] Suddenly dropped into a context of social disorder, poverty, and dysfunctional government, experiencing that disorder in marginal but tangible ways (power outages sometimes days long, leaking roofs, lack of resources, lack of medical support), I found poetry helpful, its compression, its control, and its small aesthetic satisfactions. Poetry served as a lens through which I could bear to gaze at the dignity of Nigerians around me as they struggled to construct order within the economic and social disorder of a largely non-functioning state.

My personal chaos included the discovery that the classes I thought I would be teaching I would not, in fact, be teaching. I was assigned to teach a plethora of courses, graduate and undergraduate, including Bilingual Education, Environmental Education Research, and Ecotourism, none of which I had expected or planned for. The work I had proposed to do with faculty would occur in addition to the heavy teaching load, serving on graduate student committees, and participating in departmental meetings and Faculty Senate. Among other adjustments, my Western expectations in relation to time were severely challenged.

I began writing acrostic poems like "Briefings," "Driver," and "The Cook" (above), small poems with strict demands of form constructed from the left margin, where the title is written vertically and governs the entire structure. My conscious reason for choosing the acrostic form related to its smallness. I could draft these poems when I was waiting for something to happen—for my driver to come, for the meeting to start, for my students or my colleagues to arrive.

> Cars don't start sometimes. Including
> Ours—old Toyota assigned and (not)
> Maintained by the university.
> I call Dennis. *I'm coming, Prof.*
> Nevertheless, he does not come. I'm
> Going to make another cup of tea.

I also came to understand that the strict control demanded by the acrostic form helped to anchor me in circumstances that were beyond my control and out of control. They steadied me and helped me to cope as I was learning to live my Nigerian life and learning to comprehend the lives around me. Some of those lives were bitterly hard.

Death is never ordinary,
Even here where it comes so early so often, here in this
Neglected nation where a rat comes in the
Night, takes a piece of your wife's leg.
Infection follows. And then one morning you
Say quietly, when I am seated in the back, *Prof, my wife dey die.*

*

Determined that his children will be
Educated in Calabar, not sent to relatives in
Nsukka to work on the farm, he tells me that a
Neighbor helps.
I know why he is often late. But he
Says only *Sorry, Prof.* No excuses, no complaint.

*

Dennis's son and daughter meet me at the
Entry to their mud-walled house.
Neighbors smile, say *Good day, Mma,*
Nod respectfully. I follow Dennis
Inside. Two overstuffed chairs fill the room. We
Sit—the children, Miracle and Happiness, on his lap.

*

During the night I heard the heavy rains' enormous
Energy beating, banging on roofs, thrashing the trees.
Nine o'clock this morning, Dennis came. Late. He had
Not answered the phone. *Prof, the roof let water
In. A wall split open. The children were
Shivering.* The landlord? *He said there is no budget for repairs.*

*

Christian as this country claims to be, God
On every set of lips, prayer
Resonating in all its chambers high and low, a
Rancid, rat-infested corruption
Usurps justice everywhere, through bribery,
Patronage, and outright theft. Empty prayers
Thrill the ear, and all around us: suffering.

I was invited to participate in a field trip guided by one of my colleagues, an all-day venture with about thirty-five students, which would end with a visit to the Slave Museum at the banks of the Calabar River.

I came out of that museum profoundly disturbed. As we had moved room to room, I felt my distress growing, and my whiteness felt like accusation. Nobody glanced at me accusingly. Nobody seemed to notice my whiteness at all, nobody but me. In fact, it seemed that the students were rather detached from what we were seeing and the story it told. They would occasionally make a joke of some sort, not an uncomfortable joke, just a joke. When we were back outside, I said something to my colleague about the horror of it. She said rather dismissively, "Yes, it was a terrible time, but it was a long time ago."

In that moment I learned that she and I were emblematic of our two countries. Her country was distanced from that awful history, not forgetting and certainly still affected by it, but not holding it in ordinary consciousness. My country, on the other hand, was still mired in guilt and repercussion. We are still in the trauma of slavery, still dealing with it, or perhaps more accurately still *not* dealing with it. Nigerians, after all, have had other deep traumas to live through, and those consequences are closer to their moment—colonialism, dictatorship, civil war, and ongoing traumas of poverty resulting from corruption and theft of what should have been national treasure but became instead the personal treasure of a few. Billions of dollars in oil have been extracted from the Niger Delta, and there is no national network of drivable roads, no electrical grid that can deliver power for more than a few hours per day, no drinkable water from the tap. Schools are bare shells, often with unwindowed openings, no chalkboards, no books. Hospitals are few and shabby, without equipment or medicines. Where did the money go? There are many ways to wage war against people. War does not always require guns and bombs. Not every war *calls itself* a war. Even a war that *does* call itself a war, like the Biafran War of 1967-70, can call upon weapons that are neither gun nor sword nor bomb. A conscious, deliberate policy of starvation secured the victory of the Nigerian government in that war.

When Orr writes about poetry as an ordering principle in the face of disorder, he is most often referencing deep and terrible personal or social chaos.

What do I know of chaos?

What do I know of poverty?

What do I know of the broken glass embedded in compound walls?

What do I know of corruption that keeps electricity from flowing and makes fuel for generators disappear?

I lived for a short time in the presence of profound disorder, surrounded by it, touched by it—a mere brush on the sleeve. Chaos, for me, had an end date, specific, ticketed, and assured. If chaos in these poems matters, it is the chaos observed, not the chaos undergone. And what does it mean that chaos is ordered and encoded in these poems? No change will be effected in the lives of my Calabar neighbors and colleagues.

Perhaps the value of these poems lies in the tribute they pay, the attention they direct to people who do know chaos, who live in it with dignity, day after day, year after year, no ticket out, mired in corruption and its resultant poverty-for-the-many, wealth-for-the-few.

> Bernedette comes
> Early like me, bounces into my office, almost
> Running, sometimes skipping, girl-like, smiling.
> Nearing the desk, she rounds the corner for a quick
> Embrace. *Good morning, my prof!*
> Do you know, Bernedette, how much you mean to me?
> Extremely unlikely. Only once have I seen you despondent.
> The morning after heavy rains rushed mud and muck under
> The door of your office. No filing cabinets, no bookshelves,
> Everything was on the floor. Piece by piece you set it in the sun
> to dry.

Elliot Eisner often called for utility in arts-based research.[3] Some have suggested that utility may lie in bearing witness, in calling to attention, making visible, opening understanding or empathy.[4] The question of utility is at the forefront in my thinking now. There is no question that the poems I wrote in Calabar, the process of making them, had utility for me, grounding me, training my focus, teaching me to see. But can they do something in the world? That remains for me an open question.

Living and writing in Nigeria, I have been led to think about my own country's challenges, past and present, including not only issues of race but also issues of corruption and violence. In Nigeria, corruption is endemic, raw, barely hidden. In the U.S., it seems to me increasingly that we have prettied up corruption, codified it, made it legal, declared that corporations are people, established "respectable" mechanisms for enriching the few and keeping the poor poor.

As for violence, I was often asked during my year in Nigeria and when I returned, "Weren't you afraid?" "What about Boko Haram?" I have said that as the year went by, from my perspective in Nigeria, the U.S. looked like the scary place. In Nigeria, we knew where violence was likely to occur, who would be doing it, and why. In the U.S., violence was random. It could occur anywhere, in a school, a church, a theater, in any part of the country. You never knew who might become violent or why. Much scarier.

I also know a whole lot more about what authoritarian leaders look like, self-glorifying, surrounded by affirming sycophants, feeding a glorifying press, suppressing opposition. Until recently, I would not have related such observations to the politics of my own country. Things change.

Things are changing in Nigeria, too. Incrementally and not in a straight line, things are getting better. Many good people are doing good work. The democracy is strengthening. There is still a long way to go, but the journey is progressing.

My year in Nigeria was one of the most challenging of my adult life. It was also one of the most wonderful. I miss my Calabar friends and neighbors terribly.

> Working at the desk by my window
> I never know which of my neighbors will appear
> Naming me again, *Prof? Are you there?*
> Delivering news of gates, generators, babies, weddings,
> Ordinary news for the most part, but some
> Wondrous afternoons the children come, all of them. To sing.

The colorful Nigerian dresses that I wore every day in Calabar hang now, unworn, in my closet. I am in a different context, a troubled context with unresolved business. For a white woman to wear those dresses in the U.S. would be to risk creating affront. I stand sometimes and look at them, symbols of a period of deep, sometimes painful, mostly joyful learning in a country rich with resourceful, resilient, people.

> Not what you think. Not what
> I thought before I bounced myself across the
> Globe, hung my silly clothes in a new closet.
> Every day I wake to a different sun,
> Reorient. I have found a dressmaker.
> I greet my colleagues and learn and learn
> Although they still believe I came to teach.

Notes

1. Orr, *Poetry as Survival.*

2. Orr, *Richer Entanglement,* 15.

3. Eisner, "On the Difference"; Eisner, "Persistent Tensions."

4. Forché, "Twentieth Century Poetry"; Forché, "The Poetry of Witness."

Bibliography

Eisner, Elliot. "On The Difference between Scientific and Artistic Approaches to Qualitative Research." *Educational Resesarcher* 10, no. 4 (1981): 5-9.

Eisner, Elliot. "Persistent Tensions in Arts Based Research," 2005. http://med646.weebly.com/uploads/1/7/1/8/17184224/eisner.pdf

Forché, Carolyn. "Twentieth Century Poetry of Witness." *American Poetry Review* 22, no. 2 (March-April 1993): 17.

Forché, Carolyn. "The Poetry of Witness." In *The Writer in Politics.* Edited by William H. Gass and Lorin Cuoco. Carbondale: Southern Illinois UP, 1996.

Orr, Gregory. *Poetry as Survival.* Athens, GA: University of Georgia Press, 2002.

Orr, Gregory. *Richer Entanglement: Essays and Notes on Poetry and Poems.* Ann Arbor: University of Michigan Press, 1993. 15-23.

8.

Race and Identity in Post-Apartheid South Africa: Making Coloredness Visible through Poetic Inquiry

Heidi van Rooyen,
Human Sciences Research Council in South Africa, ZA

South Africa takes great pride in its vibrant and diverse democracy. But, there is much-unfinished work in the new South Africa. During Apartheid, the label "Colored" was applied to all people with mixed-race ancestry and with it varying degrees of privilege and misfortune. While the perspectives of the majority Blacks and minority Whites have dominated the country's reconciliation project, the story of coloredness, of those neither this nor that, suspended somewhere between white and black, has been largely invisible. In contemporary South Africa, some reject the racialized label in an attempt to move forward from this discriminatory past. Others believe a necessary part of moving on lies in unearthing the stories of this past that have shaped who we are and color what we bring to this new democracy. Using both found and generated poems, this chapter explores issues of race, class, identity, and belonging for those classified as Colored. It argues that in order to achieve social cohesion, this complex and contested identity needs to be unpacked, these stories must be told as they are an important part of the country's history.

Keywords: race, identity, coloredness, poetic inquiry, South Africa

Introduction and Background

In South Africa, the term colored has a particular meaning. It does not refer to Black people in general as it does in many other contexts, as in Britain and the United States. Since 1927, Coloreds were one of four classified ethnic groups identified during the period of white rule in South Africa alongside Whites, Blacks, and Indians.[1] This system of classification remained post-democracy in 1994, even though much of the apartheid legislation was abolished. Apartheid constructed a hierarchical society in which race functioned as the most salient category of identity. It defined how resources were allocated, where people lived and went to school, and who they married and had sex with. Bound to the political system, race became inextricably tied to social life through its entrenchment in law and policy. Coloreds held an intermediate status in the South African racial hierarchy, distinct from the historically dominant white minority and the majority black population. This in-between status, of being close to whiteness, yet seeing blackness as other, of privilege and oppression is an enduring feature of colored identity.

Coloreds are descendants of the sexual liaisons between colonialists, slaves, the indigenous Khoisan, and other groups who settled in the country.[2] Coloreds are often stereotyped as being "mixed breed," of being without identity, land, or culture. This stereotype is contrasted with the image of Black people as proud, "pure breeds" with history, culture, and identity going back centuries.[3] These ideas were informed by social Darwinism, which implied that people born as a result of miscegenation lacked the positive characteristics of the "pure races" they combined, but embodied all the negative ones.[4] Coloredness has often been tainted with notions of negativity, deviance, and illegitimacy.[5]

While the perspectives of the majority blacks and minority whites have dominated the country's reconciliation project, the story of coloredness has been largely invisible.[6] A necessary part of the South African story lies in uncovering the social meanings and consequences of this bureaucratically constructed identity. Poetry and poetry inquiry offer a creative avenue for doing some of this work, for unpacking the story of colored identity in the new South Africa.[7] While I identify as colored, and had been writing poetry for a few years, I had not written on issues of race and identity for academic purposes. I had also not used poetry in my research work. Poetic inquiry provided a useful opportunity for bringing the personal and political together.

Methodology

I used found and generated poems[8] to capture insights into the contextual, emotional, and psychological experience of coloredness. Found poems were developed through my reading of South African literature addressing issues of identity and belonging among coloreds during the Apartheid period and post-democracy. Following Glesne; Richardson; Sullivan, Butler-Kisber, Commeryas, and Stewart, in reading I noted recurring themes.[9] The following four themes seemed to characterize coloredness: a negatively defined identity, a sense of marginalization, assimilation with whiteness, and an intermediate status. In each theme, I noted words, images, and phrases that seemed to capture the essence of the theme. In staying true to the texts, the writer's unique rhythm, pauses, emphasis, syntax, and diction were replicated in creating the poems. Although no words were altered, "poetic license"[10] was used to rearrange the words in a different order than in the original text, and in some cases, repetition was used for emphasis. In addition to the found poems, in engaging with the literature on coloredness, I also generated a poem capturing my experience of living this identity.

Coloredness Negatively Defined

Coloreds were defined in a negative fashion, as an artificial category imposed from above by the White elite for political purposes. Wicomb, in her analysis of colored identity, traces links of shame with lack of visibility and recognition from the ways the group was described in the Population Registration Act of 1950.[11]

> The definition of a colored
> is someone that is not black
> and is not white
> and is also not an Indian.
> In other words
> a non-person.
> They are the leftovers.
> They are the people that were left after the
> nations were sorted out.
> They are the rest.

In addition to being defined in a negative fashion, or as an artificial category imposed by the white government, coloreds were believed to carry a number of inbred characteristics resulting from miscegenation.[12] As a group, coloreds often struggled to represent themselves as a genuine people with their own peculiar history, customs, and identity.

> No matter how respectable you become
> or your level of personal achievement
> the taint of that original sin
> remains entrenched.

You will be reminded
how early colonists
plucked vagrant colored women off the beach
put them in their kitchens as slaves
and fucked them like beasts
to produce
you—
half-caste
bastard.

You will be reminded
you were
conceived in sin.
That you are defective
a special breed
physically stunted
lacking in endurance
prone to dishonesty
licentiousness and drink.

You will be reminded
you are
God's step-children.

Assimilation

To survive in this hierarchical society that pitted ethnic groups against
each other and made white privilege the ultimate goal, coloreds opted to
assimilate with white.[13] The hope was that assimilation of whiteness and
promotion of its interests would lead to acceptance. Acceptance was
viewed as the best possible chance for colored people to maintain a status
of relative privilege.[14]

Coloreds strove to demonstrate
their white-mindedness.
White man's culture represented achievement.
Conformity with its values and practices,
a measure of social development
and individual accomplishment.
Their advanced levels of culture and civilization,
the ultimate ticket for inclusion
into the body politic.

Assimilation was also more intimately expressed and felt, informing hierarchies in families and communities governed by degrees of lightness of skin color and straightness of hair.[15] For some, assimilation required disowning your colored identity, your roots, your family, your community. Those with light skin could cross the racial barrier and obtain better housing, education, and job opportunities, and were able to marry white people.

> The surest route for social advancement
> was by being white in mind, spirit, and achievement.
> This desire for assimilation
> evident amongst those
> willing to disown their identity,
> turn their backs on friends,
> family, and former lives.
> Prepared to take the risk of exposure
> in an attempt to pass for white.

Intermediate Status

Coloreds have an in-between status, of being close to whiteness, yet seeing blackness as other. This intermediate status of coloreds was experienced in several conflicting ways. One way to navigate this was to assimilate.[16] While coloreds tried to hold onto privilege, they also feared being demoted and subordinated in the hierarchy like Blacks. But, no matter how well you assimilated, you always knew that you were "not quite white" enough.

Erasmus has written of her personal experience of being steeped in this way of thinking: "knowing that I was not only not white, but less than white; not only not black, but better than black."[17] This sense of feeling less than white, but better than black continues to shape relations between coloreds and Blacks. Black people view coloreds with suspicion and resentment because overall they benefited more from the social system than Blacks located at the bottom of the hierarchy. Similarly, coloreds were wary of the Black group that could vent its frustrations and displaced aggression toward Whites onto them.[18] Magardie also shows how less than white, better than black emerges within coloredness, too, not just in relation to Blacks. She points to a prejudice—not just directed at "the Blacks" but at other coloreds who look and act "too black."[19] Light-skinned-person-of-color privilege existed under Apartheid, and it exists today. Instead of checking this privilege in terms of how they locate themselves in relation to the majority in this country, far too many coloreds either see themselves as victims of the national democratic project, or as superior to other Blacks. This intermediate status also expresses itself as a sense of marginalization in relation to both Blacks and Whites. The lament that "first we were not white enough and now we are not black enough" has become a common refrain amongst colored people who feel alienated from the post-apartheid order.[20] Many coloreds feel marginalized in the post-apartheid dispensation, and are especially resentful at what they perceive to be a preferential allocation of resources to Blacks, especially in the Western Cape, where their needs are just as great.[21]

Engaging with other writers on this topic was instructive in reflecting on aspects of my identity. In response, I generated the following poem.

> I looked different.
> In a family from charcoal black
> to breadcrust brown
> sallow yellow and
> off-white cream
> I could pass for white.
> I talked different.
> I didn't talk colored.
> I twanged.
> Words spilled out
> careful and clipped
> stripped of blackness
> and of home.
>
> That accent helped me
> navigate a path
> away from the stench
> of the oil refinery
> that made grannies sick
> and left children
> with permanent colds.
>
> That twang
> gave me safe passage
> past the gangsters
> shoring up their despair
> and sagging jeans
> with knives and needles.
>
> But a twang
> doesn't cover all your holes.
>
> You can talk like them

move in their circles
buy their homes
drive their cars
but you still leave your family
coughing against pollution
dodging gangsters
running out of hankies
to wipe the kids' snotty noses.[22]

Conclusion

While legalized racial discrimination no longer exists in South Africa, race continues to play a powerful role in social and political life insofar as people continue to use apartheid-manufactured racial categories to identify themselves and others.[23] The experience of coloredness in contemporary South Africa's race politics is complex and contradictory.[24] While there was a strong tendency for people to accept a separate identity for colored people under the apartheid system of government, many argue that this offensive creation of apartheid or of racist mindsets should simply be dismissed.[25]

Others hold the view that as offensive as the term colored was, people continue to resort to it lacking any other word that would demarcate this particular racial identity created and then reified by recent apartheid legislation.[26] There remains for many a need to assert and to acknowledge this ethnic, cultural, and/or racial identity as it evokes a sense of self, community, and belonging.[27] If shame defined colored identity from the start, reclaiming coloredness can be viewed as an attempt to project a positive self-image in the face of pervasive negative racial stereotyping, and perhaps as a way to finally negate shame.[28] The complexities of colored identity need to be unpacked further. This paper has shown that it is possible to use arts-based approaches such as poetry to provide new avenues for acknowledgement and articulation of Coloredness in post-apartheid South Africa. Creative methods such as poetic inquiry, narratives, spoken portraits, and art give voice to the speaker rather than the researcher, privilege narrative, and capture depth of experiences.[29] All of these are critical ingredients for a reimagining of the race and identity project in this country.

The underlying assumption is that there is something fundamentally wrong with this identity and that some ideological transformation of the bearers of the identity will resolve the problems.[30] But this work needs to be done within the larger context of identity constructions in South Africa.

Rather than being merely human or South African citizens, South Africans continue to identify themselves as racial subjects. The deep infiltration of apartheid's racial menu into the everyday race thinking of South Africans plays itself out in myriad daily social interactions, and reproduces in social life that which has been declared statutorily obsolete.[31] Membership of these races is based on physical characteristics and the attribution of distinct characteristics to each group. Associated with each of these are sets of social scripts that operate as a resource that continues to be drawn on in the performance of raced identities.[32] The fact that in contemporary South Africa, debate continues about whether coloreds are "real blacks" speaks to the continuity of these raced identities, as well as the deep-seated and uncomfortable issues that haven't been resolved by the rainbow nation project.[33] Unless these issues are addressed, they will continue to fester in a cauldron of bitterness that could boil over. Evidence of this appeared during sporadic service delivery protests in parts of Gauteng and the Western Cape where coloreds have gone on the rampage and things have taken an ugly, racial twist.[34]

A reimagining and re-representation of coloredness may locate the community as a subgroup of a larger African identity. Magardie argues that doing this will negate the sense of non-belonging that remains an undercurrent of the identity.[35] This re-representation need not mean that coloreds lose the specificities of their own identity as there are a multitude of ethnicities in the broader African identity. However, this reconstruction is not something that is entirely dependent on coloreds themselves, it requires all South Africans to change their perceptions and ways of interaction.

Notes

1. Christopher, "To Define the Indefinable."

2. Adhikari, "Contending Approaches"; Adhikari, "Hope, Fear, Shame, Frustration."

3. Ibid.

4. Ibid.

5. Hendricks, "Debating Coloured Identity"; Adhikari, "Contending Approaches."

6. Hendricks, "Debating Coloured Identity"; Bornman, "Emerging Patterns."

7. Butler-Kisber, "Poetic Inquiry."

8. Faulkner, "Concern with Craft."

9. Glesne, "That Rare Feeling"; Richardson, "Poetic Representation"; Sullivan, Butler-Kisber, Commeryas, and Stewart, "Constructing Data Poems."

10. Butler-Kisber, *Qualitative Inquiry*, 87.

11. Wicomb, "Miskien."

12 Adhikari, "Contending Approaches"; Adhikari, "Hope, Fear, Shame, Frustration."

13. Ibid.

14. Adhikari, "Contending Approaches."

15. Erasmus, "Oe!"; Erasmus, "Contact Theory."

16. Adhikari, "Contending Approaches"; Adhikari, "Hope, Fear, Shame, Frustration."

17. Erasmus, "Introduction," 13.

18. Bowler and Vincent, "Contested Constructions."

19. Magardie, "It's Time to Talk."

20. Adhikari, "Not Black Enough"; Hendricks, "Debating Coloured Identity"; Bowler and Vincent, "Contested Constructions."

21. Magardie, "It's Time to Talk."

22. Adhikari, "Hope, Fear, Shame, Frustration." Refers to Kole Omotoso's description of the phenotypical features of coloreds as ranging "from charcoal black to breadcrust brown, sallow yellow and finally off-white cream that wants to pass for white."

23. Dolby, "The Shifting Ground"; Zack, "The Fluid Symbol."

24. Bowler and Vincent, "Contested Constructions."

25. Bornman, "Emerging Patterns"; Bowler and Vincent, "Contested Constructions"; Magardie, "It's Time to Talk."

26. Wicomb, "Miskien"; Bornman, "Emerging Patterns."

27. Zegeye, "A Matter of Colour."

28. Wicomb, "Miskien."

29. Faulkner, "Concern with Craft."

30. Hendricks, "Debating Coloured Identity."

31. Bowler and Vincent, "Contested Constructions."

32. Ibid.

33. Magardie, "It's Time to Talk."

34. Hendricks, "Debating Coloured Identity"; Magardie, "It's Time to Talk."

35. Magardie, "It's Time to Talk."

Bibliography

Adhikari, Mohamed. "'Not Black Enough': Changing Expressions of Coloured Identity in Post-Apartheid South Africa." *South African Historical Journal* 51, no. 1 (2004): 167–78. https://doi.org/10.1080/02582470409464835.

Adhikari, Mohamed. "Contending Approaches to Coloured Identity and the History of the Coloured People of South Africa." *History Compass* 3 (2005): 1–16. https://doi.org/10.1111/j.1478-0542.2005.00177.x.

Adhikari, Mohamed. "Hope, Fear, Shame, Frustration: Continuity and Change in the Expression of Coloured Identity in White Supremacist South Africa, 1910-1994." *Journal of Southern African Studies* 32, no. 3 (2006): 467–87. https://doi.org/10.1080/03057070600829542.

Bornman, Elirea. "Emerging Patterns of Social Identification in Postapartheid South Africa" 66, no. 2 (2010): 237–54. file:///C:/Users/Tar/AppData/Local/Mendeley Ltd./Mendeley Desktop/Downloaded/Bornman - 2010 - Emerging Patterns of Social Identification in Postapartheid South Africa.pdf.

Bowler, D, and L Vincent. "Contested Constructions of Colouredness in the Kuli Roberts Saga." In *The 2011 Critical Studies Seminar Series Hosted by the Departments of Politics and International Studies & Sociology at Rhodes University.* 2011. https://www.ru.ac.za/media/rhodesuniversity/content/politics/documents/Contested Constructions of Colouredness.doc.

Butler-Kisber, L. "Poetic Inquiry." *Journal of Critical Inquiry into Curriculum and Instruction* 5, no. 1 (2004): 1–4.

Butler-Kisber, L. *Qualitative Inquiry: Thematic, Narrative, and Arts-Informed Perspectives.* London: Sage, 2010.

Christopher, A. "To Define the Indefinable: Population Classification and the Census in South Africa. *Area* 34, no. 4 (2002): 401-408.

Dolby, Nadine. "The Shifting Ground of Race: The Role of Taste in Youth's Production of Identities." *Race Ethnicity and Education* 3, no. 1 (2000): 7–23. https://doi.org/10.1080/713693014.

Erasmus, Zimitri. "Contact Theory: Too Timid for 'Race' and Racism." *Journal of Social Issues* 66, no. 2 (2010): 387–400. https://doi.org/10.1111/j.1540-4560.2010.01651.x.

Erasmus, Zimitri. Introduction: Re-Imagining Coloured Identities in Post-Apartheid South Africa. In *Coloured by History, Shaped by Place: Perspectives on Coloured Identities in Cape Town.* Cape Town: Kwela Books, 2001.

Erasmus, Zimitri. "'Oe! My Hare Gaan Huistoe': Hair-Styling as Black Cultural Practice." *Agenda* 13, no 32 (1997): 11–16. https://doi.org/10.1080/10130950.1997.9675579.

Faulkner, S. L. "Concern with Craft: Using Arts Poetica as Criteria for Reading Research Poetry." *Qualitative Inquiry* 13, no. 2 (2007): 218–34. https://doi.org/10.1177/1077800406295636.

Glesne, C. "That Rare Feeling: Re-Presenting Research through Poetic Transcription." *Qualitative Inquiry* 3, no. 2 (1997): 202–21. https://doi.org/10.1177/107780049700300204.

Hendricks, C. "Debating Coloured Identity in the Western Cape." *African Security Review* 14, no. 4 (2005): 117–19. https://doi.org/10.1080/10246029.2005.9627597.

Magardie, K. "It's Time to Talk about Coloureds—and They're Gatvol." *Daily Maverick.* 2018. https://www.dailymaverick.co.za/opinionista/2018-06-04-its-time-to-talk-about-coloureds-and-theyre-gatvol/#.WyOOW6czbIX.

Richardson, L. "Poetic Representation of Interviews." In *Handbook of Interview Research: Context and Method*, 887-91. Edited by J. F. Gubrium and J. A. Holstein. Thousand Oaks, 1993.

Sullivan, A., L. Butler-Kisber, M. Commeryas, and M. Stewart. "Constructing Data Poems: How and Why—A Hands-On Experience." In *Extended Pre-Conference Session at the Annual Meeting of the American Education Research Association.* New Orleans, LA. 2002.

Wicomb, Zoë. "'Miskien of Gold Gemake.'" In *Snow on the Cane Fields: Women's Writing and Creole Subjectivity*, 205-34. Edited by Judith L. Raiskin. Minneapolis: University of Minnesota Press, 1996.

Zack, Naomi. "The Fluid Symbol of Mixed Race." *Hypatia* 25, no. 4 (2010): 875–90. https://doi.org/10.1111/j.1527-2001.2010.01121.x.

Zegeye, Abebe. "A Matter of Colour." *South African Historical Journal* 44, no. 1 (2001): 207–28. https://doi.org/10.1080/02582470108671396.

9.

Claiming Identity in the Presence of Oppressive Silenc(e) (ing)

John J. Guiney Yallop,
School of Education at Acadia University

While spending a week on the island of my birth, recuperating from the emotional impact of surgery for prostate cancer, I became aware that my maternal grandmother was Aboriginal. This discovery changed my identity (by then a subject of my research for more than a decade), my body (which had already been changed by the surgery), and how I live in the world (a life defined by difference since childhood). Rather than turn to this discovery with anger, which I was told was expected because this information had not been given to me sooner in my life journey, I embraced my new identity. I soon discovered, however, that this newfound identity I embraced was not always welcomed, particularly by some who had come to accept/expect my difference as gay/queer. This suite of poems, with narrative reflections, explores what it means to, sometimes tentatively and repetitively, claim one's identity.

Keywords: identity; Aboriginal; Indigenous; queer; gay

In July of 2009, while spending a week in Newfoundland, the island of my birth, recuperating from the emotional impact of a radical prostatectomy following a diagnosis of prostate cancer, I became aware that my maternal grandmother was Aboriginal. This discovery that my ancestral heritage came, in part, from what we now call North America changed my identity (by then a subject of my research for more than a decade), my body (which had already been changed by the surgery), and how I live in the world (a life defined by difference since childhood). Rather than turn to this discovery with anger, which I was told was expected because this information had not been given to me sooner in my life journey, I embraced my new identity and began calling myself Aboriginal or Indigenous, and began presenting and publishing about what it means to discover this new identity. I soon discovered, however, that this newfound identity I embraced was not always welcomed, particularly by some who had come to accept/expect my difference as gay/queer. This suite of poems, with narrative reflections, explores what it means to, sometimes tentatively and repetitively, claim one's identity.

The cancer diagnosis came as a 50th birthday gift shock, an intrusion into the life that I had anticipated for my family and for myself after our move to Nova Scotia from Ontario. In accepting an appointment to Acadia University, and after moving my family and our lives to this place, I was now going to die and leave them alone to fend for themselves. Yes, I was being a bit dramatic! A diagnosis of prostate cancer is not the end of the world, particularly when one is in a province that has some of the best medical practitioners in the world for treating this type of cancer. I was not being handed a death sentence; I was being given a diagnosis, and a number of choices to make in regards to that diagnosis. Once I let the drama pass, however temporarily, I was able to turn to those choices.

Still, cancer is, well, cancer, and it was not something I was expecting to be dealing with in the first year of my appointment in this new career. I guess we never expect, even though we might fear, that such bad news will come our way. I had not expected it, even though, less than two months before, my sister had died of cancer, and her diagnosis came as early in her life as my diagnosis had come in my own life. It was, perhaps, because of that compounding and complicating reality that it felt more urgent that I get some support for my daughter who was just nine years old at the time. Her aunt had died; would one of her dads be next? We met with my urologist, later to be my surgeon, as a family. He was wonderful. He explained to my daughter that the cancer her dad had was not like the cancer her aunt had died from. Even though all surgeries had risks, he said that they had done hundreds of those types of surgeries at the hospital where I would have my surgery, and that he was very confident I would recover well. He told my daughter that she may have to bring me glasses of water for the first couple of weeks, but after another few weeks I would be back to being able to do with her whatever I had been doing with her prior to my surgery. This was going to be a challenge, not a defeat.

Poetry has, for much of my life, been a way for me to process my reality, to deal with it. I wrote poetry through the process of cancer diagnosis, of surgery, of recovery. I also wrote poetry through other crises or challenges in my life, particularly experiencing homophobia as a youth and on into my adult years. If poetry through those times did not bring me justice, it at least brought me an understanding of the injustice I was experiencing as I was facing bigotry, prejudice, or simple ignorance worn comfortably. Through difficult times, poetry has also allowed me to access my humor. I sometimes joke that I did not actually write poetry during the surgery, but I do recall, as I was being wheeled into the room, with its shiny table and bright lights, saying to myself, "This would make a good poem." I put together a chapbook of twenty-five poems that, in a sense, document my journey through prostate cancer. I called it *Notes to My Prostate*.

After the surgery, and my recovery, I returned to work, but the recovery, while amazing in terms of what the body can do to heal itself, felt like there was something missing. I felt a need to return to the place of my birth, the place where my body had begun, a place where I have often gone to heal. I went to Newfoundland. While there, in a conversation with the mother of a friend who spent much of her childhood in the small town where my parents had lived and where I grew up, I was told that my maternal grandmother was Native. This news, that I was, as Mary Jane (Crocker) Harvey's grandson, Aboriginal, came as a shock, though a much different kind of shock than the other one that had changed my body. I confirmed with older family members and other community members that this fact, though unknown to me, was widely known in the community. I called my daughter, who is also Aboriginal, and my partner, whose maternal great-grandmother was Aboriginal, to share this news. I returned to work with a different sense of who I am. I had gone to Newfoundland to allow my body to recover; I returned with a body calling me to rediscover it, even to discover it for the first time.

> Grandmother blesses me
> with a gift,
> a new identity
> to fold into who I am,
> to fold myself into—
> to become.

> My Aboriginal Ancestors walked this land
> before my European Ancestors arrived here.

> My body
> bends across the ocean
> like a bridge
> constructed with my bones
> tied with my own flesh.

In an earlier piece, I wrote about how I embraced this newfound identity, even attending a *Forum for Aboriginal Academic Staff*, organized by the Canadian Association of University Teachers. I put together a research project to (re)discover my maternal grandmother, and to come to a better understanding of what this new information, new for me at least, meant for me moving forward in my career and in my life. I presented some of that early poetry in the church, now a home, where my grandmother would have attended the Roman Catholic Mass. I printed and distributed a book of poetry (*Who is Mary Jane Harvey? A Grandson's Poetic Explorations of Memories, Stories, and Gifts*) to the participants in the project, many of them quite old. I wanted each participant to see and hold the work I created with the help of their generosity, the sharing of their stories, to give them yet another gift from the life of the woman, my grandmother, they so greatly admired. This is what poetry can do. I was grateful to have poetry, to have been able to do that. Three of the participants have since died. I used the poetry from that book to create other renderings of the research, presenting at conferences and submitting more writing for publication.

During a conversation following one of my presentations, an audience member who had also discovered her Aboriginal ancestry as an adult told me that I would eventually become angry, if I was not already angry, about not being told earlier about my Aboriginal heritage, about lost opportunities from not knowing. While I have had many emotions since discovering this new identity, I have not been able to call any of them anger, particularly anger over loss. I try to use anger in productive ways (except when I use it in less than productive ways) and I was not able to see how being angry about this new information would add anything to my life going forward. I certainly felt grief at not having known my grandmother; she died when I was a one-year-old. I also felt gratitude, however, for this opportunity to get to know her in ways I would never have been able to do so without the research experiences I have had through my graduate and doctoral studies, and from my first research project in my new appointment, a project that further explored identity using poetic inquiry. Anger would, nevertheless, find its place, and this chapter is likely written with some of that anger.

While I felt that this new knowledge was a gift, one that I enthusiastically shared with family, friends, and colleagues, I soon discovered that not all saw it as such. A white man, and out as gay for decades, I had been perceived and received in particular ways. Not everyone was ready to let those perceptions be changed, and some, who perhaps saw their reception of my queerness as a gift *they had given me*, a gift of tolerance or acceptance I should be grateful for, were less than impressed that I now appeared to be flaunting another identity. Did I not already have enough identities, and should I not be grateful that my marginal identity of queer is now so widely accepted that it is now, in the view of some perhaps, part of the mainstream?

> Displacing your judgment
> onto my body,
> your judgments harm
> like the diseases your ancestors
> (and mine)
> brought to this land
> unintentional
> or deliberate
> depending on the person arriving
> and the crown they stood under.
>
> Inclusion is a cause
> until you find me
> inside the circle you thought you had defined;
> you move it
> to find a new center
> from which you can control
> belonging.
>
> I am not interested
> in your fucking (dis)approval
> of who I am.
> I have traveled this path before,
> familiar territory of just enough
> but not too much,
> and acknowledgement is required.
>
> Cancer was taken out of me,
> but I see it again
> in your (un)spoken words,
> and uninvited actions to set me straight
> or white.

I seem to have arrived at a point in my life when reclaiming my humor, rather than re-igniting my anger, is a more spontaneous response to some of the heterosexism and homophobia, as well as racism, I encounter. Still, anger, as well as sadness, is always also there because I know I am privileged in terms of the positions and powers I have been able to hold. If I am to be grateful, however, for the freedoms I have that neither I nor many others had previously, I will be grateful to those who fought for those freedoms, those who even died for them, and to those who fought alongside my queer brothers and sisters; I will not be grateful to those we fought, those who finally capitulated, finally acknowledged that we were worth something, that we had to be tolerated, accepted, celebrated. But this new reality was different. Margins were suddenly popular, suddenly a place to get into, and anyone appearing to try to occupy them had to be approved. What is (perhaps not) surprising about this disapproval of my new identity (or, when disapproval seemed unwise, just ignoring aspects of identity) was that it came, certainly in the majority of, if not in all, cases, from non-Indigenous people. I was being told by the descendants of colonizers that my identity as an Aboriginal Person did not meet with their approval; I wasn't really Native because … Because what? Because it did not fit with their picture of me? Because it meant that my whiteness was now in question? Because it meant that my queerness might now also mean something else? Because my Indigeneity could not be packaged in the way they had packaged the Indigeneity of others whom they saw as victims they could help in order to assuage their guilt? Because I wasn't Native *enough* (in their eyes)?

> You're okay
> with gay,
> but not with the Native blood
> that flows in my veins.
>
> Queer is a label
> you can theorize,
> but Aboriginal
> is a landscape you cannot cross.
>
> My Two Spirits
> cannot be contained
> by your ambitions.
>
> A Sweat
> brings me home
> to a place
> where you cannot find me.

Unlike coming out as gay, and struggling to find my place in a world where I was seen as sinful, sick, and criminal, and unlike recovering from cancer, when I was seen as vulnerable and in need of help (which I was), sharing my newfound identity of Aboriginal was not a demand for justice or a cry for help. I had experienced the privilege of whiteness, and I was not asking for help with this newfound identity. I wonder if it was this matter-of-factness about it that appeared to cause some people considerable consternation.

I seek to know
the twoness of who I am.

If I listen long enough
even the wind will whisper its answers.

The ocean has been telling me
for years;
I am still learning to hear.

I breathe in
the tranquility of being
holding two voices
that speak through one,
two ways of being
in one life.

I recently said, not entirely joking, that I go to conferences to release. Reading, writing, and sharing poetry is a way for me to release. This releasing, a word that was offered to me by the person who conducts the Sweats I attend on Friday nights, pushes out what I no longer feel a need to carry, what is holding me back, and creates a space for new, healthier realities to enter. Releasing is what happens on Friday nights when the sweat flows out of my body and the tears roll down my cheeks. Releasing is what happens when I am moved by the voice and words of a poet. Releasing is what happens when I write or perform my own poetry. Releasing is what happened to me recently as I neared the end of my first marathon. The emotions bubble or burst to the surface and I am overcome with what I have been holding, with what has been holding me, that I was not even aware of. A new body is created. A new path opens, and I run into it.

It begins with an opening
of the pores,
a preparation for what is to come.

It pushes up from the inside,
from deep hollows
of memories
where the mind cannot go.

A grunt.
A panting.
And, sometimes, tears.

Releasing
is through every pore
of the body,
and through the constricted
stretched
throat,
and through the top
of the head.

The body is transformed
into a unifying
peace.

It is easy for me to slip into seeking approval; it is familiar territory for
me, but not territory I am willing to stay in once I discover I am there.

I will not test
the stories of my ancestors,
voices ringing through my body
calling me back
to who I am.

I will listen
and learn
with the memories that rise
from the rocks,
the grandmothers and grandfathers,
in the Sweat Lodge.

I will spread my mind
into the space
created by my body's openings,
my sweat flowing
carrying the pain,
the toxins,
I did not know I had.

And

I work to listen,
to pay attention
to the fire

and the wind.

The four directions
receive
my offerings
and I lean into
each one
as I turn.

Prayer Ties
of gratitude
and requests
offered with acceptance
of unfolding being/becoming.

A Sweat
opens me
to the moment.
Ancient ceremony
guiding me
to now.

And

Aging, broken body
becomes home
to a new understanding
of me,
a new (way of) being in the world.

I am healed by surgery and modern medicine,
but I am made new by a gift
from grandmother,
a new call
into being.

Tears fall from my eyes.
Joy rises from my gut.
My throat opens
to gift
and to be gifted.

I bow my head
toward the Ancient Ones
and receive the heat
over my back

pressing through me
with words from my ancestors.

Come.

Open.

Give.

III: Poetic Inquiry as Praxis and Connection

The body, the breath and the word put together have power.
—Kimberly Dark

The third section of this anthology concerns the role of poetic inquiry in public and private practice to produce stronger connections among people and ideas. The poets in this section present meditations on poetic inquiry, musings on the possibilities and potentialities for poetic inquiry as political practice that can connect the personal to political, the single story to collective dialogue. In "Love and Bones Continued: Finding Dialogue about Histories Shared and Diverse through Poetic Inquiry in a Time of Discord," Bonnie Nish presents work on a poetry project that engages community members to get them "writing and thinking in different ways about life and words." Poetic inquiry can help us start dialogue, as Nish discovered in the project that brought Jews and Palestinians together through poetry.

Kimberly Dark shares two poems and the argument that poetry is like incantation—we can bring things into being through recitation. "Poetry, which arranges the breath, offers more frequent line breaks and spaces for the body to enter the text through breath: "Language conjures, / maybe not the leaf itself / but urge to leave the building." Sarah K. MacKenzie-Dawson considers how a pause, a breath can be part of our social justice practice in "Stitching Inward: Pausing Poetically Toward Connection, Possibility, and Praxis." If we stay with a pause and reflect in this space, we may be able to see our connection: "We can no longer consider ourselves, our contexts, our actions to be exclusive. Rather, we become aware that we are threads within the larger social fabric of humanity—our breath, our beings, our becoming—our lives are shared." The specificity in poetry connects to the universal. And the breath in poetry is a space for meditation on our connections.

Poetic inquiry can slow time through reflective practice. Robin Reynolds Barre also considers the pause in the chapter "Chronos Eats His Children:

A Poetic Inquiry into Time as a Social Justice Issue." Barre suggests that when we are balanced with time and recognize that some do not move in linear motions with time, we can engage in embodied and just poetic practice. "Time is a social justice issue when the indigenous, ethnic minorities, differently abled, the elderly, those suffering from mental illness are pathologized when they will not or cannot kneel before the Clock King." Robert Christopher Nellis furthers the practice toward social justice in considering how a focus on human-animal relationships as interconnected in a both/and web can teach us, in "Toward a Poetics of Graceful Pedagogy: Interspecies Encounter and a Certain Silence." Our deepest conceptions of our selves situated in space and time are challenged to connect more meaningfully with other beings, past and present. The chapters here "move toward praxis and presence, breath and connection, embracing the pausibilities of poetry" and poetic inquiry. The poet authors reveal how they have learned to see things differently through poetic practice.

10.

Chronos Eats His Children: A Poetic Inquiry into Time as a Social Justice Issue

Robin Reynolds Barre

If we listen carefully to the words used when we talk about time, and when we pay close attention to our relationship with time in our culture, we see a form of social injustice and violence of which we are often unaware. This essay is a poetic inquiry into Western culture's concepts of time as soul violence and as a social justice issue. We become aware that these experiences of time can be understood as agendas imposed by a corporate capitalistic system. Only one view of time is deemed acceptable and effective—linear, hegemonic, non-relational, agenda-ed—and it must be in service to the system. It excludes and pathologizes other ancient, holistic, and poetic ways of experiencing time. Through a series of original poems, references to mythic deities related to time, musings, and arguments the author seeks to de-pathologize and reclaim other ways of being in and with time.

Keywords: chronos, cultural time, myth, pathology, social justice, time

In Greek mythology, Chronos, the god we know as Time,[1] is one of the original creators of the world. Out of his own being he brought forth "the calm Aether and likewise Chaos, the empty space which had no firm bottom and was filled with darkness."[2] Chronos, "the lord of clock time,"[3] assures our inexorable march through the years. Chronos did not really eat his children; I took poetic license. It was his great-grandson Kronus, a Titan, who did so.[4] Yet when we believe that only one god rules time, we get eaten by Time, our lives devoured. This chronological monotheism is a social justice issue.

Poetic language and poetic considerations not only encourage thoughts on the social implications of chronological monotheism but also articulate a bridge between time as a human construct and Time as the world itself. Through poetic inquiry we can explore Time as a mythic, deified presence—even a poetic presence—and its complexity, diversifying our experience of time and respecting those who move through time in less linear ways.

Chronological time is measured by the sun rising and setting, the moon waxing and waning, the earth turning. It is gauged by the minerals of the earth. The unit of time we call a "second" is based on the oscillation frequency of the Cesium-133 carbon atom.[5] When we are in a balanced relationship with Chronos, we observe the world around us, notice patterns, cycles, and rhythms, and have an *embodied* sense of time. These rhythms and patterns are integral to poetry. Poetry in its truest form— spoken, chanted, sung—is embodied language; poetry, then, is a bridge between chronology, the bodies we inhabit, and the essence of the material world. Here I point to Tempus as another incarnation of Time, whose name alludes to tempo. There are others as well.

The Greek god Kairos is also associated with time. He is not a gentler god but his presence gives us a strikingly different experience. He rules over what we might call sacred time. Kairos stories our lives and weaves the narrative thread of our chronological days. He is an invitation into mythic Time, "the Timeless center."[6]

Metanoia—Afterthought; Fortuna; Occasio—the Occasion worth marking; and Mnemosyne or Memory—close relative of the Titan Kronus—are other divinities of time. I submit that we exclusively worship Chronos, or we are led to believe that he is the only one we should bow down to. This temporal colonization[7] excludes Kairos and unbalances Chronos. Without the "temporal oscillations"[8] between Chronos and Kairos, time becomes ravenous, consuming, and Titanic—untethered from the heavens and ungrounded from the earth. Our disembodied management of time leaves the cosmos and our bodies forgotten.

The radical imposition of linear time becomes a social justice issue when those who know other ways of marking time are pathologized. Those who cannot or will not fall in line with hegemonic agenda-ed time are often pathologized and become victims of temporal colonization. I think of children who have the diagnosis of ADHD; their meander through the fields of time rather than following the arrow of mechanized time[9] is pathologized as "time blindness."[10] I think of those who are grieving a terrible loss, or the elderly who move slowly and for whom Mnemosyne is a dear companion. We cannot even let plants grow in their own sweet time. Genetic modification research is quickly closing in on the ability to make plants grow faster.[11] The monopoly of standardized time and its accompanying norms and expectations do violence to other cultural and organic rhythms and patterns, to the individual's unique sense of the passage of time.

Hear the brutality and constraints in the words and phrases we use to describe how we view time: *Deadline. Target date. Time limit. Cutoff date. A devil of a time. No time to breathe. Time is money. Doing time. Running out of time.*

> I'm running out of time,
> I dash out the door
> I forget my coffee cup, my vitamins, my goodbye kiss
> out of time
> I run off the road,
> off the field.
> I forfeit the game,
> concede.
> I don't even know
> what game
> we're playing—
> what game *you're* playing at.
> You, legs
> criss-crossed applesauce,
> hold up the black fig plucked
> from the tree in your
> backyard garden,
> heft it in the palm
> of your hand.
> What are you weighing?
> You turn the fruit, looking at it
> like the goddamn fruit inspector,
> intent before
> your teeth puncture the skin,
> and you lick the juice
> (Is it bitter? Or is it sweet?)
> as if you had
> all the time
> in the world.

I don't know this game—
and have no time to learn.
I run—
have a train to catch!
That will take me somewhere …
else,
a train moving fast
so time can't get away from me.

Time cannot be contained or tamed, regimented or parsed out sparingly—no matter how we try to corral it or how we try to hold onto the days and years. Quantum theory proposes that time is the Universe into which we are born and within which we dwell.[12] No matter how hungry corporate systems attempt to take time from us or homogenize it, there is no denying or escaping the gods of time.

Because constructs of time shape the lives and stories in a culture, dismissing or penalizing diverse experiences of time dismisses or penalizes those who identify with those cultures. For example, for Australian Aborigines time is multidimensional and phenomenologically horizontal, as described by Edmund Husserl.[13] To stand fully in the present moment is to have knowledge of a "temporal horizon,"[14] to know infinity backward and forward; it is to be in an enlivened state of being. Aborigines seem to experience time in concentric circles, thus they stand in the center with access to this temporal horizon.

The narratives of Aboriginal lives move through circles toward and away from the center where the person and his or her lifestory is situated.[15] The event that holds more weight sits closer to the center. The day a mother dies or the moment the long-awaited child is born is soonest—closest, even if it happened years ago in chronological time. Imagine forcing such a narrative into a more linear form. What then happens to the child's grief and the mother's joy?

There is "no word for an absolute time which measures the universe from outside of it"[16] in many of the American Algonquin language groups. Time is "relative and elusive in nature" for the Algonquin peoples.[17] Concepts of time are embodiments of and twined with the natural world. Without time as an absolute, everything in the past and future is integral to the present; the ancestors and those to come are part of the lived story today. For time to be divided into segments is unimaginable because the world then is torn apart. The ubiquitous wristwatch becomes, literally in this context, a time bomb. Banishing these "alternative temporalities" subsequently banishes historical memory[18] and cultural identities.

I imagine these experiences of time are like dreams or poems. As if I might see all things at once and move *into* them. I am a participant and witness. I enter poetry, the meandering route from experience to words to body to words to experience, recursive, lyrical, patterned, and oftentimes deviant. Poetry creates the space for the temporal oscillations among Chronos, Kairos, Mnemosyne, and Fortuna. Tempus embodies poetry and life. He is heartbeat, drumbeat, and breath. Poetry makes room for the other divinities of time, a social justice movement that honors alternative temporalities so perhaps we can "become whole in time."[19]

I cannot refuse this invitation to step into the timeless center. I cannot refuse to enter into the myths, the world. I cannot refuse to witness birds, wind, or the light. I cannot refuse to witness Spring—

> This immediacy of light
>   caught by
>   the shy curve of the narcissus,
>   her pale neck greening to April.
> Old perfumes rise as
> seedlings cling to the tomb,
>   a tentative greeting.

> This burdened soil
>   and fragile fragrance evince
>   ballads,
>   black curls shaped on tender shoulders,
>   a deft hand
>   sketching irises
>   and wintered landscapes.

> Do not refuse to witness
>   shadows
>   of webbed threads in early
>   evening phloxed light,
>   courtyards flanked by sentinel plums
>   and brooding stones, maidens
>   embracing the slim
>   hips of lovers.

> Do not refuse to witness,
>   for spring is not a season
>   but a moment.

Over the course of Western history, we proceeded from telling time by the movement of the sun, moon, and seasons, to the faces and hands of

the clocks in the town centers, to the ever-present ticking of the clocks in
our kitchens, to the most profane timekeepers of all, the digital clock—no
longer round, no longer can we *see* the cyclical nature of time. Clocks are
enigmatic entanglements, an apt description of the essential connection
between human culture and the cosmos.[20] With the digital clock, it feels
like the cosmos has been whittled away to mere digits. We suffer when we
sever our relationships with the enigmatic entanglements of time and the
nature of cycles, seasons, sunsets, and moonrises. Our world suffers.

As a psychotherapist and former educator, I have experienced and
witnessed firsthand the suffering caused by the attempts to maximize
productivity and profit and to "mathematically manage"[21] the soul in the
behavioral health and education systems, where organic rhythm and
poetic reverie are rarely considered, much less valued. For example, the
DSM-5, used for diagnosing mental health disorders, gives clients only so
long to grieve or to come to grips with unbearable and unimaginable
horror before they are given the stamp of pathology. Thus, the insurance
companies will not cover therapy for some conditions until the person has
suffered for an arbitrarily determined length of time, or will foreshorten
the therapy according to the diagnostic timeline, a corporate timestamp
on pathos. But for those of us who know, grief gets woven into our beings,
and trauma is that which lives in the timeless center, the otherworldly
place of suffering that has no beginning and no end.

> It must mean something, your small dream …
> A spider sits on the casement window
> anxious to be gone.
> Only mists behind her, the world
> disappeared.
>
> This is a dream poem. Hugo wrote a few.
> Lorca lived in one, saw fish
> swim on the moon,
> heard a nun's evensong
> in the pomegranate.
>
> Spider bides time, suspended
> with cold impatience
> on the edges of things.
> A boy eats ghosts,
> hunts on the autumn hillside
> for what is long gone and lost.
> What was buried has one name and more.
> He will spend his life trying to fill

the belly with what haunts
at him.

On the edge of the hedge rose
the Orb Weaver lives
a quick cold life.
Nothing stays buried forever.
November comes with wind. Windows
crack open. The world tilts
out of whack.

Pomegranate seeds are some kind of key.
Keening notes lift brown petal shavings,
and everything eddies and whorls.
The wind takes up the tattered threads
of web, the mandala catching
only ghosts.

As a teacher at an urban alternative high school, I saw the profanity of rigid corporatized time[22] imposed on students who needed to meander. There was, for instance, the student who danced:

At the end of the day the beautiful dancer, who has been sitting alone in the schoolroom for the last hour, instructed to work on math, has not been working on math. She is looking at images of her home city on the computer, trying to decide on the perfect image to decorate the front of her binder. She has been pondering, searching, and re-searching for several days now for this perfect image. I ask her if she has trouble with the math, if she needs help. She replies that she doesn't. I ask her if she is taking her meds. Are things okay at home with mom and dad? Is there fighting? No. No more than usual. It is nothing she can put her finger on.
"I am just feeling … weird. Funky."
She interweaves the search for the image with solitary, silent dancing in the middle of the room; her eyes focused on something far off in the distance or deep within, something the rest of us cannot see. Before she leaves for the day, she says, "I think it's the change in the weather. I can feel it, I think."
Autumn comes. Darkness is descending. She feels it—in her body. She feels *weird, wyrd, Word, wyrm, the worm,* the dragon of winter, the halls of darkness. *Weird.* The dancer knows her body. She cannot do math. She can only dance, can only seek

the perfect image, search for the perfect place to be, the perfect place to dance in this cold, gray city.[23]

We can assume that the Dancer encounters the normal unfoldings and challenges of maturation that a teen faces. Here, however, she tells me that something else is alive within her, something beyond family, friends, school, work, her future, and her past. She attempts to articulate something more, something else that courses through her body, a feeling that awakens with the change in the weather and the way the light falls because the earth continuously turns on its axis. Like a wild animal, her psychic skin is thin, and she feels the earth's subtle shifts. The change in the seasons awakens a yearning within her, a desire, something she cannot name, a melancholy that seems familiar and yet ancient. She can only turn to images, to movement, to a circumambulation around language and words. She requires room and time to follow her body and the images that beckon. In these moments when she dances I am grateful she can meander and follow at will. She is not working on her math assignment. She is seemingly not even making a halfhearted attempt.

I can choose to relate only to the behavior of the student in this moment, to redirect, coerce, or threaten. I can insist on the directives of mandated timelines, the urgencies of the cookie-cutter K-12 programs that tell both of us that we have a schedule to which we must adhere or face the consequences. I can choose to ignore this other energy that moves both of us, deny that it exists, and push on and through to what must be done. Or I can remain here in this moment and listen to what is coming forth, this Other who is speaking through her movements and words ... *feel* ... *weird* ... *funky* ... *the weather* ... words that circle round and round, a nebula that causes her to search and to dance.

Who and what gets shunned and shamed under the dogmatic march of linear, corporate time? Who and what gets disappeared and erased in the meaningless progression of the hours? The corporatization of time excludes the diverse ways of learning, working, being in a relationship, and suffering. There is an "erasure of other ways of knowing."[24] Time is a social justice issue when the indigenous, ethnic minorities, differently abled, the elderly, those suffering from mental illness are pathologized when they will not or cannot kneel before the Clock King, the "taskmaster who brooks no deviation."[25]

So let us calendar our lives by marking stone, bone, and antler.[26]
Let us not forget the old horologia
shadow clock sundial astrolabe—
the one that catches the heavenly bodies.

Let us move into once upon a time
into the savor of the moment
the dusky prayers of vespers
and song praises of matins.

Let us pause. Let us breathe
and stop killing time
deadlining our vocations
splitting seconds like atoms.

Let us invite Memory to the table
along with Fortune and Occasion.
Let Sweet Thallo and Carpo
usher in Spring and Autumn
and bring flowers and food.

Let us sit early or late
all in good time
and remember how to
be in time
as if we had
all the time in the world
as if time were the world.

Notes

1. The upper case spelling of Time indicates its mythic nature, and the more mundane nature of time is indicated with the lower case spelling.

2. Kerényi, *The Gods of the Greeks*, 114.

3. Yiassemides, "Editor's Foreword," xvi.

4. "Cronus," *New World Encyclopedia*.

5. Swan, "Motion, Measurement, and Mechanization," 142.

6. Mayes, "Teaching and Time," 146.

7. Mayes, "Teaching and Time," 143.

8. Yiassemides, "Editor's Foreword," xiii.

9. Connolly, "Broken Time," 8.

10. Harris, "Beating Time Blindness."

11. Regalado, "Super-Fast-Growing GM Plants."

12. "Physics Suggest That the Future Is Already Set in Stone."

13. "This world now present to me, and in every waking 'now' obviously so, has its temporal horizon, infinite in both directions, its known and unknown, its intimately alive and its unalive past and future." Husserl, "The Thesis of the Natural Standpoint," 70.

14. Husserl, "The Thesis of the Natural Standpoint," 70.

15. Janca and Bullen, "The Aboriginal Concept of Time."

16. Pritchard, *No Word for Time*, 11.

17. Pritchard, *No Word for Time*, 11.

18. Mayes, "Teaching and Time," 151.

19. Swan, "Motion, Measurement, and Mechanization," 108.

20. Frank, *About Time*, 10.

21. Mayes, "Teaching and Time," 143.

22. Mayes, "Teaching and Time," (corporatized time).

23. Author's personal journal.

24. Mayes, "Teaching and Time," 145.

25. Mayes, "Teaching and Time," 150.

26. Swan, "Motion, Measurement, and Mechanization," 134.

Bibliography

Connolly, Angela. "Broken Time: Disturbances in Temporality in Analysis." In *Time and The Psyche: Jungian Perspectives*, 3-19. Edited by Angeliki Yiassemides. New York: Routledge, 2017.

"Cronus." *New World Encyclopedia.* http://www.newworldencyclopedia.org/entry/Cronus.

Frank, Adam. *About Time: Cosmology and Culture at the Twilight of the Big Bang.* New York: Simon and Schuster, 2011.

Harris, Zara. "Beating Time Blindness." CHADD The National Resource on ADHD. October 2015. http://www.chadd.org/AttentionPDFs/ATTN_10_15_BeatingTimeBlindness.pdf.

Husserl, Edmund. "The Thesis of the Natural Standpoint and Its Suspension." In *Phenomenology: The Philosophy of Edmund Husserl and Its Interpretation*, 68–79. Edited by J. J. Kockelmans. Garden City, NY: Doubleday, 1967.

Janca, Aleksandar, and Clothilde Bullen. "The Aboriginal Concept of Time and its Mental Health Implications." *Australasian Psychiatry* 11, no. 1, suppl. (October 2003). doi:10.1046/j.1038-5282.2003.02009.x

Kerényi, Karl. *The Gods of the Greeks.* London: Thames and Hudson, 2006

Mayes, Clifford. "Teaching and Time: Foundations of a Temporal Pedagogy." *Teacher Education Quarterly* 32, no. 2 (Spring 2005).

"Physics Suggest That the Future Is Already Set in Stone." *BBC-Earth*. February 6, 2017.

Pritchard, Evan. *No Word for Time: The Way of the Algonquin People*. San Francisco: Council Oak Books, 1997

Regalado, Antonio. "Super-Fast-Growing GM Plants Could Yield the Next Green Revolution," *MIT Technology Review*. November 17, 2016. https://www.technologyreview.com/s/602932/super-fast-growing-gm-plants-could-yield-the-next-green-revolution/.

Swan, J. A. "Motion, Measurement, and Mechanization: The Sacred-Secular in Temporal Relics, Objects, and Possessions." in *Time and The Psyche: Jungian Perspectives*, 106-146. Edited by Angeliki Yiassemides. New York: Routledge, 2017.

Yiassemides, Angeliki. "Editor's Foreword," in *Time and The Psyche: Jungian Perspectives*, xii-xx1. Edited by Angeliki Yiassemides. New York, Routledge, 2017.

11.

Poetry as Incantation

Kimberly Dark,
California State University San Marcos

Language is a proxy for meaning, for truths deeply held, for manipulation. Poetry, which arranges the breath, offers more frequent line breaks and spaces for the body to enter the text through breath. This is part of why poetry has a long history as incantation. The body, the breath, and the word put together have power. As social scientists, our interest in the co-construction of meaning should naturally lead us to poetry and poetic understanding—both as a topic of social analysis and a method for disseminating scholarship and calls to action. The two poems I offer here illustrate a) the involvement of dreaming (and by extension, other ephemeral knowing) in the creation of meaning, standpoint, and assertion in a social action/response text and b) the communal, generative nature of poetic meaning-making. In the first instance, the untitled poem (which is titled at the end) includes dream imagery in making sense of a widespread social phenomenon often treated as a personal issue. In the second poem, "Ontological Reversal," I explore the ways in which meaning undulates through hope and oppression. This poem is also an example of collegial dialogue, as it was created based on offerings at the 2015 International Symposium on Poetic Inquiry and then shared at the 2017 meeting for further discussion.

Keywords: ontology, poetic inquiry, arts-based research, Bill Cosby, abuse, doublespeak, Orwell

Language is a proxy for meaning, for truths deeply held, for manipulation. Poetry, which arranges the breath, offers more frequent line breaks and spaces for the body to enter the text through breath. This is part of why poetry has a long history as incantation. The body, the breath, and the word put together have power. We cannot discuss poetic inquiry as social justice work without acknowledging the power of poetry as incantation—words that bring circumstances not just to light, but sometimes literally to being. As social scientists, our interest in the co-construction of meaning should naturally lead us to poetry and poetic understanding—both as a topic of social analysis and a method for disseminating scholarship and calls to action. There will naturally be many ways that poetry accomplishes this topical investigation and this prompting, calling, inciting.

The two poems I offer here illustrate a) the involvement of dreaming (and by extension, other ephemeral knowing) in the creation of meaning, standpoint, and assertion in a social action/response text and b) the communal, generative nature of poetic meaning-making. In the first instance, the untitled poem (which is titled at the end) includes dream imagery in making sense of a widespread social phenomenon often treated as a personal issue. In the second poem, "Ontological Reversal," I explore the ways in which meaning undulates through hope and oppression. This poem is also an example of collegial dialogue, as it was created based on offerings at the 2015 International Symposium on Poetic Inquiry and then shared at the 2017 meeting for further discussion.

> I am standing at the sink, drinking the poison.
> Sometimes one has to do something foolish
> in order to understand life.
>
> Violet is next to me, talking about how
> autopsy is a fiction and I am thinking
> *Yes, I know that, but keep talking.*
> *It comforts me.*
>
> Understanding something after death
> means it's still alive
> no death
> just re-arrange.
>
> She flails her arms akimbo, all elbows.
> I rotate mine at the wrist,
> hands like soft cups to indicate
> yes, yes, do go on.
>
> I am sipping the poison from the vial
> with the side of my mouth, the edge
> of my lips, as if maybe I can keep myself
> from knowing what I'm doing.
> Zoom Zoom, I say.
>
> I just want to speed things up, see what's next.

It's New Year's Day. Who are we kidding?
Nothing is *that* new.
Everything that matters is new all the time.

How did I ever learn to do such a good job
taking care of myself? I think, as I sip the poison.
My lips are burning.

The last man to marry my mother
was a mortician. He'd seen death
so many times, didn't want to
go himself, wanted more time,
day by one more day, not ready.
Everyone's life focused
on giving him one more day.

He marveled once at my mother and me
putting poison on our skin—acetone,
to remove nail polish.
When it's not being used for vanity,
it's handled with gloves, wearing a mask.
Don't inhale it, he'd say—cap the bottle.
No use admonishing the lack of gloves.
We were rubbing it right into the
little mouths of our fingers, cuticles dry and
choking, somehow reviving
to take the poison again every 3-4 days.

Autopsy is a fiction.
The very notion of cutting something up
after it's no longer living and moving
in order to find out what went wrong!

When it would've been quicker
(and more useful) to just ask, then listen.
Just   ask   then   listen
Ask then listen.
Ask then listen.
Ask then listen.

The title of this poem is:
Bill Cosby is on TV again, but he's not smiling
But that
is the end
of the story.

Ontological Reversal

In which the concept
becomes more important
than the thing itself.

In which children
in poor neighborhoods
are taught to love reading
without ever being
given a book.

In which learning
about photosynthesis
is a leaf-free endeavor.

Orwell warned us
that the language would
double back on itself
meaning-wise, but
did he see the pending
zeal for representations
that no longer conjure
origins? Live performance
becomes video just as
social media becomes
friendship.

Luckily, language conjures.
Put right in the mouth,
it always has. Lucky
things: poetry, picturing,
plays and prose
verbing all over
cannot be contained
by paper.

(I still long for paper,
a way to hold you when
your face won't move
with words.)

The child without the book
can still hold rhythm
in her body. Chapters
in the arms of sunrise,
soft of blanket, breath

of sister, the smiling
teacher, chapter, chapter,
chapter, day by day
a life becomes a
book and more.

Language conjures,
maybe not the leaf itself
but urge to leave the building.

A relation of pain can still
be a relation of affection
as children learn too often.
When consequence has
been recruited as cause,
language can both betray
and rescue.

An ontological reversal
can reverse again, be sure.
A snap is a movement
with a history—though
pressure on the twig is
harder to see than breakage.

Stories too have history,
show one can
break a promise
without making a promise,
reveal what others
are invested in not seeing.

Poetry is incantation.
Feel it in the soft tissue
of the body, how it
thumps on bone.
Just speak of walls
and walls come up
walls come down,
mortar cakes your
fingernails and all your
fences electrify.

When you tell someone
your story, you give them
a part of yourself. When you
see them again, you meet the you

that is in them.
They need not remember
the details, even
the very next day.

That's how we will re-form
a world that can hold
everyone. How we will do what
nature tells us (hopefully)
before it stops
speaking.

Notes

1. "Ontological Reversal" also appears in my poetry collection, *Love and Errors*. The other poem is previously unpublished.

12.

Stitching Inward:
Pausing Poetically Toward Connection,
Possibility, and Praxis

Sarah K. MacKenzie-Dawson,
Bucknell University

Within this poetic inquiry, I stitch together the poetic and visual to become present within the space of a particular pause—during a time when I could no longer predict or perform according to those expectations by which I had let myself be defined. I enter into the tactile/textile/textual space of layered identities, presence, and acceptance, attending to the shifting moments that shape my subjectivity—reimagining myself as teacher, artist, poet, scholar, mother, and citizen. The pause allows me the opportunity to gaze inwardly as I explore the complexities of experience and being. Through the poetic, the gaze is no longer solitary, but instead dialogic as stories, interpretations, and identifications fold into one another, facilitating social justice and love that creates a space allowing the fluid piecing together of perspectives, possibilities, and reflections. The pause becomes a place of attention and openings, a place of praxis.

Keywords: poetry, praxis, pause, breath, subjectivity

> To pause
> > *(I wait, breathing)*
> > > *(I take a seat and begin to stitch)*
> > *(silence)*
> It is uncomfortable, isn't it.
> We wait for the next word, action, motion.
> Body's shift, minds roaming

Across the vast landscape of nothingness
and everything
There might be a sudden or subtle awareness of physical discomfort
a sore back or tightness in the shoulders.
(I wait, breathing)

The poetic inquiry I share is a work in pieces—tattered edges of knowing and not knowing, doing and being, loss and grace, gratitude and growth, self and other. I am not the same woman I was ten years ago when I presented at the first International Symposium of Poetic Inquiry. In these past years, I have found love, known loss, gained sobriety, become a mother, sought to make sense of myself as a daughter, a teacher, a mother, a lover. I am not the same woman. When I entered the academy, I had visions of who I might become— soft etchings sketched out in the shape of my expectations. These etchings remain as beautiful fragments of the (im)possible motions of being human, those that tangle and fray across a living space of expectation, desire, and reality. As I write I join with you, a self still—a self always becoming. I am tired, away from my daughters for the first time; anxious, caught up in an ambivalent space of (un)knowing, a space of pause.

Life is a cacophony of doing
Shoulds, would, and musts
Echo across the cavernous space of doing
Bodies muffled with the expectation of
Othering
Beings without contact
with/out breath

Within a pause we breathe; despite anything else that might be going on, we breathe. We are connected in this breath, stitched together—fragments of our humanity and discomfort, and perhaps for the lucky few, peace. Yet even in this entanglement of humanity, we often feel alone. We may begin to hold our breath, seeking answers, an escape, some sense of certainty, an awareness of what is to come, what we might expect.

When discussing the nature of pedagogy and education and this quest for certainty, Sharon Todd poses the questions: "What if one begins from a slightly different place? What if one begins with the 'messy and ambiguous' nature of human reality? What if one reflects upon the failure and uncertainty of the demand for learning to become?"[1] I believe the pause creates the space to learn to breathe and be within the messy and ambiguous, to recognize that our spirits are stitched together in this space of uncertainty. When we return to the breath, becoming present within a pause, we have an opportunity to tap into something far greater than certainty, moving toward a spiritual connectedness, something perhaps beyond the human capacity for explanation. It is within such a space where social justice is cultivated, where we find ourselves moving beyond ego toward a way of being that is grounded in connection. We can no longer consider ourselves, our contexts, our actions to be exclusive. Rather, we become aware that we are threads within the larger social fabric of humanity—our breath, our beings, our becoming—our lives are shared. We enter into praxis, knowing that we are shaped by and shape, weave in and out of, the experiences of others. Irigaray suggests that we have forgotten the connection with the breath and the spiritual, noting that "often we confuse cultivation with the learning of words, of knowledge, of competencies, of abilities. We live without breath, without remembering that to be cultivated amounts to being able to breathe, not only in order to survive, but in order to become breath, spirit."[2] The pause allows us the opportunity to (re)learn what it means to breathe, to be connected, while at the same time unattached.

Poetry too, suggests the possibility of the pause. "A poem is a portrait of consciousness. It's a recording of the motions of a mind in time, a mind communicating to others the experience of its own consciousness."[3] Through poetry, we may linger in moments of connection and ambivalence, within those open spaces where we see our reflections in someone else's verse. Yet even within those reflections, there is often discomfort, an absence of answers as the language breathes, but the certainty remains intangible. To be within poetry, we must touch the breath, opening the threads of ourselves to the possibilities of be(com)ing.

I use stitching and the breath as metaphors throughout the space of this poetic interaction, as a means to reflect my own understanding of pause—that which is both grounded in something greater than ourselves and the moment, fluid and evolving, but also something that is always partially fixed, shaped by past movements and stories. The breath gives us life, yet we often find ourselves caught, holding onto the breath, holding onto experience. When we let go, our breath deepens, opening us up to life, to possibility, to connection. The stitch represents a long history of companionship and force, love and loss, as Thomas Hood shares in his 1843 poem, *Song of the Shirt*:

> Sewing at once, with a double thread.
> A shroud as well as a shirt.[4]

We are both with and without, doing and being, free and entrenched. The breath and the stitch reflect an ambiguity that allows us to reimagine through the messiness of our own logic, the meaning of our motions and the possibility of stillness. They are practices of continuity and life, always (in)complete, while at the same time stabilizing. As Irigaray suggests, "no theory or practice is ever completed. Both are always evolving. The task is to try to connect the here and now of today, this present moment of our life, to the reality of yesterday and that of tomorrow."[5] We are temporal beings, existing in connection to something greater than ourselves, even if that connection might simply be to one another.

When I set out to prepare this piece, I was eager for the possibility of further exploring and finding meaning through pause. I had recently become a part of a group of women artists who had decided to gather monthly and share in our lives through the practice of stitching. There were no guidelines, simply motion and presence. I made the commitment to myself to show up, to make time for this important space, this opportunity for connection and a brief reprieve from the day-to-day monotony of doing professor, mother, wife. It was an opportunity for pause. We met once; it was a lovely evening of getting to know one another, our stories, our craft. Despite our desire to make time to be present through the motion of our hands, there were other responsibilities, meetings, lists that overpowered the echoes of our own longing to pause, even if only for an hour or two a month. As the days and months went by, I began to forget about the pause, the importance of connection, of simply taking the time to be. Instead, I found myself racing through papers and class plans, sitting on committees, and losing time. I wanted to be home with my daughters and partner, to nurture and love them, to share my time—my being with them. Even in those moments, my mind raced; I had to make dinner, get the girls to bed, keep our home clean, I had to get everyone where they needed to be on time. When everyone drifted off to sleep, I returned to the papers, papers and planning and grading. There was no stopping as my body and mind moved with a hurried sense of action and anticipation. I was caught within the frays of expectation.

I hesitate when I say was, because even as I share with you, my mind is not fully present. It is advising week. I am away from my two-year-old, who has decided that she is not yet ready to stop nursing. I am teaching two new classes—classes I quickly discovered I was unprepared for. Most mornings I rush my daughters out the door to make sure they are not late for preschool: "Come on, we are going to be late, hurry, hurry," I shout to them, no laughter in my voice, simply anxious frustration. Once I drop them off I do not stop; instead, I am overwhelmed by a sense of failure and expectation. I long to pause, to relish presence, but so often I still find myself caught up in the sharp tangles of doing.

She can't sit still anymore
Blinded by the looming
    Reality she creates
Shapes of expectation
A web she cannot escape

Returning to inquiry, to the stitched poetic tapestry of living, knowing and (un)knowing, I find myself thinking about the messages I must send to those I love when I can't pause, when I can't simply enjoy being, because my mind is so focused on everything else that must be done. A dear friend of mine always says, "We have a choice, do we want to be the human doing or the human being?" I have spent a lot of time doing, but sometimes I forget how to be.

Breathing
there is work to be done
body and mind
breathing
the tension
is felt
upon the line
    that shapes the fabric of my consciousness.
Breathing
I begin
    to loosen
to become aware
        outside expectation
toward being
    body and breath
self and other
woven together
through the constance of unencumbered motion
breathing
the textual
        textile
    webs across my consciousness
        leave openings
for tactile grace
of being and creating
        through
the soft motion of pause.

Through the poetry I share with you, I seek to acknowledge a cacophony of contradictions as my thoughts thread both carefully and unwittingly across the (un)conscious landscape of my psyche. Pause, yes I do believe it is a good thing. It is something I want to do more often, yet I have become all too good at holding my breath. In this moment, upon this page I seek to move toward praxis and presence, breath and connection, embracing the pausibilities of poetry.

> I find myself
> In that space
> In between (be)longing
> Where the strands of the past, present, and future
> Move like protons, neutrons, and electrons across
> The atomic expanse of shoulds,
>   There is no answer in this space
> A body, mind
> Caught in stillness and movement
> Yearning for the (un)known, (un)named
> Moment
>   Of settling in
> Of becoming
> Okay
> With living
> In between the fibers of limbo

The summer I was twenty, I found myself one warm evening sitting in front of the television. I had been struggling. My parents had just separated, I was in love for the first time, and I was just beginning to fall into the deep clutches of alcoholism and depression. Yet for a moment as the evening embraced my senses, I found myself connected, feeling a sense of peace with the earth and my being. On the television, there was a program about a nun working with refugees. I don't remember the entire story, but the one phrase that stuck with me was: once a refugee always a refugee. In our current political climate, in a world where so many individuals are fleeing from significant violence and oppression, I find myself hesitant to even associate my experience with that of a refugee. I have not known the kinds of struggles so many individuals and groups must live with. However, something about that statement, "once a refugee always a refugee," stuck with me, a resonation of the personal.

When I was young
I dreamt
   of fireflies
and laughter amidst a lonesome story
love lived in this space
bonded lessons
stitched upon the psyche
with/in disconnect
An ignition of future that did not quite
turn over
in the old Volvo
with its tattered turquoise upholstery
the fireflies beside me
driving
driving away
no dreams of a present
presence
instead a body, mind
doing escape
Picking at the layers of fabric I sat upon
The skin on my fingers
I dreamt of driving
Away
   Peace within
Loss
   Caught up in woven ideals
of the possibility of escape.

I am intimately acquainted with the seductive beckoning of escape; perhaps in some ways, it is what I have always known best, myself in some strange way a refugee. Today, I am situated—a mother, one who is needed, who at times feels lost within need, a thread unraveling without option of escape.

A thread traveling with/in, upon and through knowing, "from nature to grace" a body, mind, self, connected through the soft etchings of divinity. "The instructions given ... remain a testimony of someone else's experience and way; they cannot substitute my own path. The teachings received from someone else can neither withdraw me from breathing nor paralyse my breath, my soul, without separating me from the divine.[6]

I find myself stitching
Old wounds upon
Constructions of the moment
A connecting of stories
Between the space
Of who
    I thought I knew
A self
  In motion
Kinesthetic gesticulations of possibility
And performance
Each motion of my mind
Intricately thought
out,
etched upon the space
so carefully the motions
in and out
in and out
a twirl of the line
    some consider this improvisation
presence
    the motion
in and out
in and out
    each destination of breath and thread
an articulation
      of expectation.

"For the world we feel, the world we remember, is also the world we make up. The place that is familiar can be the place where we are most lost."[7]

Symbiotic inscriptions
of worth outnumbered by longing
the tears of my child
who knows now
      the power of the stream upon her cheeks
how each drop screams upon my thoughts
the comfort of my breast
her need
my failure
    to want
within the soft fractures
of the textual

tactile,
pieced together story
where desire lives within
the comforting lines
of nurture

Most mornings and afternoons I walk through the grove on my way between home and my office. It is a beautiful space of trees and light. It is also the space where my thoughts begin to settle, where the strands of who I am begin to flutter across my consciousness and I am overcome with momentary senses of gratitude and panic as a struggle to comprehend the nature and worth of my own existence. The strands of these thoughts often come together through poetry; poetry that allows for solace, creates space for exploration, and moves me toward social justice as I enter into connection with the world around me. Poetry motions me beyond self, toward a way of being that is grounded in loving praxis. Through poetry, I begin to pause, to be, to recognize my being as a thread across the textile landscape of (one)selves—ourselves living, within this world of ambiguous truths, identifications, and responsibilities.

The leaves have scattered
ashes upon the sacredness
of purpose
each crunch echoes
possibility and disdain
    and the aching tendency of my heart
to lay upon the cold ground
waiting
    for the acknowledgement
of worth
even within awareness
failing calls out to me
    I see you
Know you
You are
Me and I
You
    the ground cannot
hold our becoming
one
    scattered
with/out

"The language of poetry is the means by which one human consciousness speaks most intimately, directly, and precisely to others. Yet it is also an empty mirror ... To me, the pleasure of the poem lies in its disquieting perspective, which enacts the self-dissolving,"[8] becoming one with the breath and those quiet open spaces of divine unity, carefully woven upon our hopes.

> She stitches
> mind unraveling
> through the beckoning
> layers
> of ambiguous
> unbecoming
>   when the inward
> motions of graceful escape
> take step
> upon the messy fabric of duality
> a child speaks
> and for a moment there is peace
> until the next motion of thought begins to weave its way
> upon her consciousness
> a story of completion
>   a tapestry to cloak
> the enormity of
>   of the tangles
> that linger
> tightening upon
> the body
> mind
>   self
> she and myself
>   we stretch out stitches
> in and outward
> the motions of yearning
> beyond our human capacity to know or
> be
>   known
> Stitches
> Etches of memory and reality
> those imagined possibilities
> that trace across the consciousness
> of a breath

>   released
>   in this moment
>   with/in
>   this
>   pause

Notes

1. Todd, *Learning from the Other*, 28.

2. Irigary, *Between East and West*, 76.

3. Twichell. "Toys in the Attic," 21.

4. Neff, 131-132, in Sharff, "Talk of Sewing Circles."

5. Irigary, *Between East and West*, 21.

6. Irigary, *Key Writings*, 165.

7. Grumet, *Bitter Milk*, 65.

8. Twichell, "Toys in the Attic," 26.

Bibliography

Grumet, Madeleine, R. *Bitter Milk: Women and Teaching.* Amherst: University of Massachusetts Press, 1998.

Irigaray, Luce. *Key Writings.* New York: Continuum, 2004.

Irigaray, Luce. *Between East and West: From Singularity to Community.* New York: Columbia University Press, 2002.

Todd, Sharon. *Learning from the Other: Levinas, Psychoanalysis, and Ethical Possibilities in Education.* Albany: State University of New York Press, 2003.

Twichell, Chase. "Toys in the Attic: An Ars Poetica Under the Influence." In *Unholy Ghost: Writer's on Depression,* 21-28. Edited by Nell Casey. New York: Perrenial, 2002.

Scharff, Valerie, J. "Talk of Sewing Circles and Sweatshops." In *Technology and Women's Voices,* 113-12. Edited by Cheris Kramarae. London: Routledge, 1998.

13.

Toward a Poetics of Graceful Pedagogy: Interspecies Encounter and a Certain Silence

Robert Christopher Nellis,
Red Deer College School of Education

What does it mean to live and act in ways consistent with social justice? Who is included within the scope of that project? Who does one imagine as being part of the *socius*? This chapter suggests the more inclusively one imagines such a circle to be, the richer the understanding and practices of social justice that may arise. This essay offers stories, poems, and reflections around these questions, and opens toward the inclusion in the *socius* of beings named as animals. This work proceeds from the author's journeys in trying to act responsibly toward more-than-human friends, companions, and co-inhabitants of this planet. Conclusions draw upon Patricia MacCormack's notion of gracious pedagogy and open toward Lori Gruen's characterization of human-animal relations as always already entangled empathy, to evoke a poetics of being, breathing, becoming—not as a matter of animals *over* humans, or of animals *or* humans, but of *both/and.*

Keywords: poetic inquiry, social justice, human-animal connection, life writing, veganism

What does it mean to live and act in ways consistent with social justice? Who is included within the scope of that project? Who does one imagine as being part of the *socius*? The more inclusive one imagines such a circle to be, the richer the understanding and practices of social justice that may arise. In this essay, I will share some stories, poems, and reflections around these questions, and open toward the inclusion in the *socius* of beings named as animals. This work proceeds from my journeys in trying to act responsibly toward my more-than-human friends, companions, and co-inhabitants of this planet. My conclusions will draw upon Patricia MacCormack's notion of gracious pedagogy[1] and open toward Lori Gruen's characterization of human-animal relations as always already entangled empathy,[2] to evoke a poetics of being, breathing, becoming. I share stories not thinking of social justice as a matter of animals *over* humans, or of animals *or* humans, but of *both/and*, a conception drawing whisperingly from one's existing integration with the natural world—the awareness of which becomes ruthlessly expunged through processes of material, ideological, and spiritual colonization.

In the summer of 2016, I was fortunate enough to receive an Extended Funding Grant from Red Deer College's Professional Development Committee. The funding allowed me to take two courses at Cambridge University in the UK, in its Summer Program in Creative Writing: "Writing Lives" and "People and Places" with British biographer Midge Gillies. My purpose was to learn more about the craft and art of life writing in hopes of clarifying and illuminating my own lived experiences in curriculum and curriculum living and working.

As with many of the writing topics teachers share with student colleagues, the prompts can seem somewhat mundane—at least if only considered on the surface. Perhaps the wisdom I have acquired now allows me to encounter them as doorways through which to walk, rather than as destinations. And walking emerges as an important image in the following piece I produced in the course:

A Short Piece on a Pair of Shoes

I can't tell you how much I love the little guy.

If you can believe it, I'm talking about my dog Charlie. A pair of shoes? I'm coming to that ...

A few years ago, I came home from a conference and found that my partner of twenty-three years, Joyce, had brought home a puppy; we named him Charlie. I'd never had a pet as an adult, and I don't think I counted on what a huge difference he was going to make in our lives.

Something I really value is the walks Charlie and I take. Have you ever seen the films of Terrence Malick? Movies like *Badlands, Days of Heaven,* and *The New World*? He's really into bringing his viewers into a kind of space of being, in which his characters walk dreamily through windswept faded fields, their hands gliding over the tops of wheat, grasses blowing whisperingly—calling one, if I may borrow from Orson Welles, from somewhere ever on the other side of the wind. You know, I feel that I have those kinds of experiences when we're out walking together. I watch him—so darn happy—and I feel myself pulled into a kind of phenomenological immediacy, with him, but through him as well into the broader natural world, redolence hanging so thick in the air I can almost see it.

I woke up one Friday morning and opened my eyes to a thought: how can I love Charlie so much and justify continuing to eat animals like him? I announced to Joyce, "That's it, I'm becoming a vegan!" So, I (and within a few days, Joyce too) didn't eat anything from animals, use anything tested on animals (as much as possible), or wear anything from animals.

So, I don't wear leather shoes. This brings me to the ones I'm wearing presently. They're not expensive or anything, but they are animal-free.

Now, this is just my thing, and I hope I don't proselytize. These are my shoes, and this is why.

People ask me, "What's the biggest thing you miss being a vegan?" Honestly, I have to say nothing—because I know why I am doing it. What's the line, "When you know the why, the how takes care of itself"? These are my shoes, and it is these and ones like them I intend to walk in for the rest of my days ...

And so, this is the way I continue to walk and in such shoes as those. My journey toward awareness of the relation between humans and their more-than-human co-dwellers as one of global vastness, paradigmatic significance, and epochal reach thus began in the space of immediacy, particularity, intimacy—in the space of a love revealed to me through a specific relation with a specific being.

How do I understand my vegan journey? What stories do I tell myself, whispering in my own ear to keep my eyes open on the path? These stories might sound blunt to those not within vegan conversations: that I do not partake in murder, torture, or cruelty in order to feed and clothe myself. I feel as though once I have seen the animal food industry as such, become aware of it, I cannot unsee it, not be aware of it. In fact, I see it and become aware of it almost everywhere I look.

I work in the beautiful country in and around Central Alberta in Western Canada. One of the blessings of my work there is that I frequently travel out of the region. Now, I don't mean this as a joke (but that traveling is the blessing, not leaving the place per se). What I mean is when I'm there, my head down, doing my day-to-day work, I don't see the place—I am, in a way, blind to it. But when I leave and subsequently return, I'm privileged to become reacquainted with its beauty all over again. I experienced this recently: catching a taxi in downtown Chicago at lunchtime and stepping out of the Edmonton International Airport by late afternoon, where I am immediately hit by the cool air, its pockets redolent with fecundity. I exit the service road from the airport out to the highway, and I notice the skies darted with cranes—not the beautiful birds but the tall red and white structures standing in service of construction and industry. I careen down the highway with my attention drawn to the rich fields of golden prairie on either side, bordered by thickets of trees—little clumps of pine sheltering farmhouses and crops. These trees were planted as part of a federal government program in the 1940s to create shelterbelts and protect agricultural land from the exposed rawness of the unfettered winds after the original trees had been stripped bare in colonizing cruelty and zeal to "develop" the land.

I would like to share a poem arising from my encounters in this landscape, inspired by the experience of a woman, to whom the piece is dedicated:

Purity
For Anita Krajnc

Riding in a bus on the highway,
I wind up alongside a truck for hauling animals.

It's empty,

but the corrugated steel trailer,
despite its last pressure wash,
cannot hide mysterious brown stains fanning outward
from the round, machine punched holes,
presumably for air—
large enough for poor creatures to breathe
before being taken to their deaths,
but not so large as to show their eyes.

Screaming, tripping,
shoved in and jammed as
many bodies will fit, some

facing frontward, backward, to the side—it doesn't matter
to the abattoir.

The first time I heard that word, I thought it sounded sophisticated,
like a cologne.

"Slaughterhouse" is a little more descriptive for me.
At least it admits what humans do there.

But the most incisive term might also be the cleanest sounding:
"meat processing plant"—
no murder or death to be heard here, just
processing commodities. Should
they survive the transport, anyone who was living,
breathing,
thinking,
loving,
nursing,
smelling,
seeing,
sleeping,
waking,
dreaming, and

then violently killed
is scrubbed from that name.

It has a kind of sanitation to it, cleanliness, politeness,

 purity,

and purity,
if such a thing exists,
is ever forged by excision, exclusion, ruthless removal, denial,

 murder.

Purity needs to be presented in
just the right way
so as not to reveal the ropes,
pulleys,
props,
costumes,
that only the hands backstage see.

Did you know they charged a woman in Burlington, Ontario, for giving water to pigs on the way to their deaths in one of these trucks?

She had to go to court and everything.

The industry representative said it was a matter of protecting food safety.

I've had people ask me, "Why did you call the poem 'Purity'?—I don't get that." Well, to put a fine point on it, it is to invoke fascism—cruelty, violence, and murder with some notion of purity as an animating, "justifying" nightmare. And nightmares can be global, panhistorical, and also haunt the slumber of individual minds. Sleep seems to be the necessary condition for accepting or participating in these nightmares. In moments between REM cycles, as it were, when my eyes may fleetingly open, I see something very troubling in the relations between humans and others, turning on a curiously self-denying chauvinism.

When I try to determine what I believe to be wrong with human/more-than-human relations, I don't need to look far. In fact, I can look within myself. I feel haunted by an always already relationality. I feel a kind of emptiness and pain, visceral and dwelling in my body during the moments prior to conscious thought. However, it's not that I am able to understand this trouble solely by looking inward, which would arguably be solipsistic.

I feel as though I am not discovering something out in the world as much as I am happening upon a river running within and between us as beings who inhabit it. Though we may seem to be separate along the bank, we are splashed by the same waves, feel the same wetness. Or perhaps it is as though we are walking on opposite sides of a hill and still feeling the touch of the same grasses.

Hillside

Hillside
and wind
above long grasses,
some resting
in tamped
down
clearings
as though still
warm

from
curled coyotes

or some ghost
choosing
to show
where
they sit
unless preferring
to
hide,

blowing

        through

             fields

my voice

I believe this matter of voice is of crucial importance. What I read in the poem above is a sense of voice as not being singular, crudely circumscribable, or reductive. I speak in my voice, but that voice is never merely the expression of some integrated, complete, Cartesian ego somehow firewalled off from others, including others of the past and of the present. It is a voice that acknowledges its contextualization within the natural world. My voice is haunted by others in ways that the "I" need not necessarily comprehensively understand. I speak my voice, but it also speaks me through its relationships—of which the "I" might not be completely aware. Others speak through me even though I might only hear them later.

Hearing is also an urgent matter in consideration of ethical dwelling alongside others. A colleague told me a story once of animal researchers cutting the vocal cords of creatures in the lab so that the researchers could not hear their screams. I feel the need to hear my more-than-human friends, even and especially in their moments of greatest pain. At the same time, though, I wish to remain aware of the space between us, that membrane of interconnectivity.

In this spirit and opening toward a kind of social justice, I so appreciate Patricia MacCormack's notion of gracious pedagogy—a leaving be, not attempting to give voice to the presumably voiceless, but just stopping and letting be, hearing as is. She writes of leaning "Toward a non-anthropocentric pedagogical ethics ... which is the unthinking of man simultaneous with the leaving be of the nonhuman-teaching ways to unthink the self in order to open up the thought of the world." [3] She writes of grace as a letting go of demands, "learning how to unthink our parasitic selves and teaching the grace of leaving be as an opening out, without recognition, evaluation, qualification," allowing "the non-human to be in its inaccessible way, without our demands."[4] I read this as being about simply allowing beings other than human to exist, rather than trying to force them into categories of human understanding—allowing every other to be wholly other, *tout autre est tout autre*.[5] Human connections with animals are already with us. We don't need to add new explanations to feel them. If anything, the spirit of "gracious pedagogy" hints that good relations among beings would benefit from fewer explanations. A short poem …

Being with
This very moment,
space as vast
as forgetting
will allow

Indeed, thinking such as MacCormack's calls one toward *being with* animals. Obviously, this is a vast improvement over outright murder and cruelty, as well as over mindless complicity—grabbing fast food burgers, chicken wraps, and McNuggets without a thought of their factory-farmed sources. This thinking opens toward a realization of human-animal interconnectedness and the ways of *being with* that such interconnection calls for.

In further defining this kind of interaction, I draw inspiration from *Entangled Empathy: An Alternative Ethic for Our Relationships with Animals* by Lori Gruen. I value her articulation of a way of thinking about ethical being between humans and more-than-humans not as a top-down deductivity, of individual cases standing in hierarchical subordination to general principles, but as authentic *in situ* being with. She draws upon the Feminist Care Tradition in Animal Ethics as described by Carol J. Adams and Josephine Donovan, sharing her ironic observation that this work has not received the attention it warrants, especially given the importance of "attention" to the approach, with it being "directed to individual animals of course, but also to the differences between animals, as well as to the larger structural forces that separate and maintain distance between us and them."[6]

I value her articulation of particular relations between particular beings. Assumptions of differences between humans and animals generally proceed at the level of species ontology—assuming that any human is different from all animals, and the level of responsibility affordable to any animal is set prior to any particular face-to-face encounter. Insistence upon attention to individual animals in specific relations with humans opens a space for authentic responsibility and affirms the worth, value, and dignity of individual beings rather than automatically assigning them subordinate status based upon categorical prejudgment.

In the summer of 2015, I took a course at Oxford University entitled "Wild Mind: EcoLiteracy and Reconnecting with Nature in the 21st Century," which drew from sources such as Joanna Macy and Molly Young Brown's *Coming Back to Life: An Updated Guide to the Work That Reconnects* and David Abram's *Becoming Animal: An Earthly Cosmology.* What I took away from the course was the urgency of creating a space where people can become mindful of the immediacy of their connections with the natural world, because this is, among many other things, a pathway to inspiring action in the face of climate change. Change does not occur on a macro level but through the individual experiences of people interacting with their environment. Gruen hints at this individual spirit in her ethics of entangled empathy.[7] She invites us to think about human-animal relations not as a macro, species-to-species interaction, but as embodied, situational encounters between specific creatures so named as humans and animals. My encounter and relationship with Charlie has opened such a pathway for me.

This insight spurred an evolution in my own thinking that continued even through the process of preparing this essay. At the outset, I knew I wanted to write with, around, and through poetry in order to consider human-animal relations. What I first proposed, somewhat immodestly, was that I wanted to seek, to uncover a language, as it were, through which to meet my animal friends. This is no longer my objective, and even if it were by some lingering, residual trace, my interest would no longer exclusively be language—at least not as I usually think of it. Now, I am interested in the intuited interconnection and an idea of both/and that lends meaning to all life, human and animal. Along these lines, I love the closing of Gruen's book: "My beloved [animal] companion Maggie was dying as I completed this book. Her strength and devotion and her mindful, empathetic attention shaped me and thus my ideas. She is a sort of coauthor of this book. Our entanglement continues in these pages and beyond. My debt and gratitude to her cannot be expressed in words."[8]

Notes

1. MacCormack, "Gracious Pedagogy."

2. Gruen, *Entangled Empathy.*

3. MacCormack, "Gracious Pedagogy," 13.

4. MacCormack, "Gracious Pedagogy," 16-17.

5. Derrida, *The Gift of Death*.

6. Gruen, *Entangled Empathy*, 30.

7. Gruen, *Entangled Empathy*.

8. Gruen, *Entangled Empathy*, 114.

Bibliography

Abram, David. *Becoming Animal: An Earthly Cosmology*. New York: Vintage Books, 2010.

Derrida, Jacques. *The Gift of Death*. Translated by D. Wills. Chicago: University of Chicago Press, 1995.

Gruen, Lori. 2015. *Entangled Empathy: An Alternative Ethic for Our Relationships with Animals*. Brooklyn, NY: Lantern Books, 2015.

MacCormack, Patricia. "Gracious Pedagogy." *Journal of Curriculum and Pedagogy*, 10, no. 1 (2013): 13–17.

Macy, Joanna, and Molly Young Brown. *Coming Back to Life: An Updated Guide to the Work that Reconnects*. Gabriola Island, BC: New Society Publishers, 2014.

14.

Love and Bones Continued: Finding Dialogue about Histories Shared and Diverse through Poetic Inquiry in a Time of Discord

Bonnie Nish,
*Pandora's Collective Outreach Society;
University of British Columbia*

Community-based poetry projects, such as *Word Whips in the Gallery*, a monthly reading event at the gallery in the Jewish Community, can change what we think of as a community. Poets are invited in to respond to artwork and then are featured. This kind of poetic inquiry allows us to enter into these histories and words, which are not ours. It is how we can see the possibility for change. Intertwined among poetry written about my own family and the Holocaust is my response to a poet writing about her own experience growing up Jewish and my realization that we need to begin poetic discussions between Palestinians and Jews that could bring change. This poet agreed to be one of the readers in this discussion. What started out as a monthly reading event at the gallery in the Jewish Community Centre would end up as a global discussion.

Keywords: community-based inquiry, poetic inquiry, social justice, ekphrastic, Jewish, Palestinian, art

Beginnings

As Executive Director of Pandora's Collective Outreach Society, a charitable organization in the literary arts in Vancouver, British Columbia, I am responsible for the organization and implementation of Pandora's many literary events. One of these monthly events is called *Word Whips in the Gallery*. Word Whips is an event we started in 2004, which is now run in five different locations. We give participants, who are community members, writing prompts and a chance to share their work. In the event in the gallery they are asked to write to the artwork. The idea behind this event is to get people writing and thinking in different ways about life and words. In this version of the event, which is the version I focus on in this paper, we brought in featured poets to respond to the art in the Sidney and Gertrude Zack Gallery in the Jewish Community Centre in Vancouver.

Over the years I have heard powerful poems written in this gallery space during *Word Whips*. With each new exhibit, featured poets typically have two to three weeks to prepare their response, and the audience is invited to write and read their poetic reactions during the opening as well. There seems to be something about the gallery, the art, and the writing that brings out deep, profound work. They are pieces about love, war, or marriage, which touch people on a very personal level. In this paper, I will explore how listening to one woman's poem in the gallery allowed me to see an opening by which we could address and begin a dialogue between Jews and Palestinians through the use of poetry. Word Whips is a way to use poetry for social justice and the power of community poetry. These stories and dialogue are important as they help us to see others' views and move toward the possibility of change. As Carl Leggo states, "Writing does not enable the writer to hammer down secure truth; writing enables the writer to explore possibilities of meaning."[1] This is what poetry can do and why we continue to write and share.

Extending Outward

This year the gallery's annual fundraiser was based on another event happening at the Community Centre, Festival Ha'Rikud with the theme of Israeli Music Through the Years. Over fifty artists each created a twelve by twelve piece of artwork related to the theme that was auctioned in support of the gallery. Poets were asked to use the Israeli Music theme loosely as they responded to the visual art. I was one of the poets responding, so I googled Israeli music. During this time (April 2018), there was an outbreak of violence in the Middle East because of the American Embassy's relocation to Jerusalem. Many protesters were killed, and I found myself trying to understand my position and how it fit into my own history; this is an ongoing theme for me as I examine my family history and the Holocaust.

The following poems about my family and the Holocaust became the basis for both my thesis and my first published book of poetry, *Love and Bones*. My mother told me repeatedly how lucky my great-grandparents were because they died together when their gas stove leaked. This robbed the Nazis of the chance to split them up and send them to the gas chambers. My Uncle Henry's family was not so lucky, as they all perished at the hands of the Nazis. While this is just one story, it shows the weight of what we carry. Poetic inquiry allows us to enter into these histories and words, which are not ours. When we feel vulnerable, we are revealing a piece of ourselves that is genuine. We liberate ourselves from the confines of our past, and in so doing allow movement to a shared experience. Through trust in this process there is a deepening of empathy and a connection to others' stories. Again, as Carl Leggo tells us, "Poetry acknowledges how the heart and imagination are always integral parts of the human knowing. Poetry seeks the truth about the human experience."[2]

Fathers Change the World
For Naomi Shihab Nye

A Jew sits at a computer screen
wearing a hat, listening to rain.
An Arab poet she has never met
recites poetry, her stories,
the missing of the homeland
held on the page
for her aching Palestinian father,
who plants fig trees in a Texas yard.

We both wear masks
to hide the horror of displacement,
the dust of our narrations
circling through our blood.
She is caught between worlds
and I am a Jew who doesn't know
the complexity of the history
that has landed us here.

My father, like hers, was hated
not for the color of his skin
but for his name, like hers, his faith.
My father, like hers, planted,
his love sprouting words and children,

he listened to the storms
that approached with fear.

Fathers on the other side of the world
sing for their children,
as the poet and I sing for our fathers.
Not all men carry guns, bring terror.
It is only the mad warrior
who carries the bomb.
A poet's heart can change
his identity, give him a flowerbed
to lie in with his lover.

The poet has signed off
I hold her worry and love.
Tonight a Palestinian and a Jew
held conference.
It is only a matter of time
before we begin to believe
what is written,
what is said,
what is heard.

Devotion

Her eyes have followed
his devotion for over 45 years,
some prayer shawls aren't as long suffering.
He pats her hand as she clears the table
for Sabbath dinner.
He sees the pain of her bones
when she moves,
has watched it travel through her
with time.
She never complains
but he knows,
hears the whimpers at night
when she shifts in dreams.
He holds her close as a sand dollar
found on a winter beach,
intricate designs on a breaking shell
needing to be protected.

In the ghetto they sit across the table
from one another,
the gray sky drops warnings
into the mud below their broken window.
They miss the children, grandchildren,
that have left for new countries, new prosperity,
and the ones left behind
who live in fear staying
in a place where they are invisible, hated,
the drone of war growing stronger every day.

He says a prayer for calm seas,
she sings a lullaby to babies
now grown.
He closes his holy book,
kisses its corner,
takes her hand
and they go to bed.
His arm around her loosely
so that she feels no pain.

In the middle of the night
when the world is silent
the fumes of an ancient stove
fill their tiny home
and they take their final breath.
In the sunlight their bones intertwined
are at peace, final and resting,
how wonderful they will never know
the terror of a world exploding
where they would have been ripped apart
into the death showers of gas chambers.
He is smiling,
she is free of pain.

Kaddish
A Prayer of Mourning

May He establish His kingdom in your lifetime
and during your days

At night I wake in cold sweats
a fever of fear runs through the room

as though the darkness has created it.
I cannot see but hear the voices still
that call out in dreams
distant and alone.
My bones creak the memory
of stories etched into walls cracking
from the weight.
Uncle Henry's tattooed wrists turning
the Yiddish paper,
sits on the sill of my mind.

Uncle Henry,
shorter than my teenage brother,
salami and smoked herring wrapped
in brown crumpled paper
carried carefully under his arm,
permeates the Sunday air, as he arrives
straight from his butcher shop
to argue, tell stories, complain.
His dark eyes laugh
while jokes hide bleak memories
that travel not far behind him,
stories that last a lifetime,
seep into bones
without his saying a word.

In my dreams there are guns,
men with no faces
peering through windows.
Nazi uniforms march in unison
up the middle of our street
while I hide shaking behind the sofa,
wait for my father to find me,
the smell of something burning
always just a little off center
pulling at me
as if from another world.
When I wake I find safety
beneath the covers,
calm breathing pushes me
to fall into a pleasanter sleep.

Uncle Henry,
cross-legged

stiff arms around his chest,
jumps up, touches the air above my head
to make a point, I laugh.
His eyes bounce around the room
as everyone watches
his enormous gestures filling space.
The fireplace hidden
behind the TV console crackles,
the momentary smell of smoke
and uncle Henry stops,
frozen in midair, his vision
sinks him back into his chair,
to silence.
I can see his mind is full of images,
the ones I have only seen in magazines,
real pictures of blue gray bones
piled as high as our garage,
carcasses rotting in the sun
and his mother lying exposed on a summer day
at the top or at the bottom, no one knows.

Sometimes, at night
I think I hear them,
voices calling words
I don't understand
above my dreams.
Some call out my Jewish name
"Bayaliba, Bayaliba"
haunting cries
over a low steady roar,
as skin falls away
to bones
I taste the ash in my mouth
and all that is left is fire
and a name on the wind's breath.

May His great name be blessed forever and to all eternity.
He who creates peace in His celestial heights, may
He create peace for us and for all Israel; and say, Amen.

As I stood in the gallery and listened to the featured Pandora's Collective readers' responses, I found Ingrid Rose's story particularly resonated with my own. Ingrid Rose grew up in England, the daughter of Jews. Like me,

Ingrid was a secular and cultural Jew, rather than a religious one. She explained how she struggled with the topic of Israeli music because of the weekly headlines, but she found a deeper understanding and sympathy for the Jewish people—her people—and herself through this medium.

As I listened to Ingrid talk and then read her beautiful, long narrative poem, my mind swirled with thoughts of my own childhood filled with Jewish stories and songs. As I listened, I realized there was something more we needed. We needed a dialogue about who we all are, what we each bring to the table with our different languages, customs, and histories. At the end of the evening, I approached Ingrid, who is a well-known and respected writer herself, and asked her if she would consider being in poetic dialogue with a Palestinian poet. My thinking was that I could arrange an opportunity for more of this kind of dialogue. Poetic dialogue where two voices sing back and forth in verse. One giving their life story, their ideas and view of the world, while the other responds with their own experience. The words of poets take us from an ordinary way of looking at things and bring us to a place where we can see things differently, to a place of understanding and reflexivity. As Carl Leggo informs us, "I write autobiographically about experiences in order to understand who I am in relation to others, in order to understand my connection to communities and to the earth."[3]

She immediately agreed. What started out as a monthly reading event at the gallery could end up as a global discussion. Community-based poetry projects, such as *Word Whips at the Gallery*, can change what we think of as a community. This is what needs to happen and this is how the power of poetry works. We listen, respond, and come into dialogue with one another through our work. We become engaged, while our most personal sides are brought forward. We touch on the most delicate of matters, such as war, race, and inequality, in the most profound ways, reaching our inner core, reminding us we are not in this alone. It is then we can see the possibility for change. As Robert Carroll tells us, "It is in times of extremity that we long to find words or hear another human voice letting us know we are not alone."[4] We all want to be heard and understood. In times when world relations seem so tenuous, it is important for all of us to remember how easy it is to forget and to repeat what should never be repeated or forgotten. If we wipe the Holocaust, the genocide in Rwanda, the invasion of Syria from our memories, we can never collectively heal. Worse yet, we might allow authoritarian figures to dictate our history. Poetry is a vehicle by which we can remember. When asked in an article "*This Is Not Who We Are*" by I. Gomez-Vega, after 9/11, why people continue to turn to poetry for answers, Naomi Shihab Nye responded, "As a direct line to human feeling, emphatic experience, genuine language, and detail, poetry is everything that headline news is not."[5] My response to her thoughts are naturally poetic.

Love and Bones was written ten years ago. Since then my poetry has shifted to where I look outward to the world around me. These poems were first performed in word and dance with my colleague and dancer, Lorraine White-Wilkinson, in the same gallery where Ingrid Rose read her work and I conceived the idea of poetic dialogue. I believe that our poetic dialogues contribute to shifting the stories that need changing and allow us to see and hear one another's stories in a significant way, providing empathy and promoting transformation. It is through the sharing of our stories that we find, as Clara Estes states, "that at least one soul remains who can tell the story, and that by the recounting of the tale, the greater forces of love, mercy, generosity, and strength are continuously called into being in the world."[6]

As my stories weave through the history of my family from before the Holocaust to present day, I discover that, while history can repeat itself, it can also be changed. If we share, listen closely enough to each other and then shift our perspective, we are not hearing and seeing only our stories but those around us as well. These poems can be in dialogue with our communities. We must keep writing our stories. We must keep sharing. We must keep dialoguing. This is what we strive for every month in Word Whips. This is what we have created by opening space in a gallery in a Jewish Community Centre for many voices. This is what we will continue to do with Pandora's.

Of Love and Bones

Pulling bones, pounding veins into powder,
my mother's blue twisted hands
wrapped around fish dough,
sizzle of ball after ball
dropping into water.
Her triangular body
dances between counter and stove,
blood red hair
bobbing over steaming pot,
she screams to Aunt Betty
for salt, to stir, more salt,
as I lie under the gray metallic table,
listen to life being crushed
into Passover dinner.

Fish guts and sweat fill my nostrils,
blankets me as I doze in the comfort
of the hustle and bustle
of the afternoon.

At night, my mother exhausted,
body clumped into the sofa,
knees pulled up to sagging breasts,
a fish ball crumbling.
The stench of death still wrapped
around her praying hands,
as closed eyes rummage
through a turbulent history
bubbling deep inside her.
She moves from one end
of a bad dream to another,
the death camps,
family carcasses piled against
a wall of stories told over time
pull at her frail bones,
memories burned into each family ritual
fall below the mind's surface,
as in the dark she reaches into thin air,
twisted blue hands searching,
desperately trying to wake up.

Notes

1. Leggo, "End of the Line," 72.

2. Leggo, *Autobiography and Identity*, 165.

3. Leggo, *Autobiography and Identity*, 115.

4. Carroll, "Finding the Words," 164.

5. Gomez-Vega, "Extreme Realities," 86.

6. Estes, *The Gift of Story*, 3.

Bibliography

Carroll, R. "Finding the Words to Say It: The Healing Power of Poetry." *Evid Based Complement Alternat Med* 2, no. 2 (2005): 161–172.

Estes, C. P. *The Gift of Story: A Wise Tale About What Is Enough.* New York: Ballantine Books, 1993.

Gomez-Vega, I. "Extreme Realities: Naomi Shihab Nye's Essays and Poems." *Alif: Journal of Comparative Poetics.* No. 30, Trauma and Memory / الفجيعة والذاكرة (2010).

Leggo, C. *Autobiography and Identity: Six Speculations. Vitae Scholastica* Caddo Gap Press, 2005.

Leggo, C. "End of the Line: A Poet's Postmodern Musings on Writing." *English Teaching: Practice and Critique* 5, no. 2 (2006): 69-92.

Leggo, C. "Astonishing Silence, Knowing in Poetry." In *Handbook of the Arts in Qualitative Research,* 165-174. Edited by J. G. Knowles and A. L. Cole. Thousand Oaks, CA: Sage Publications, 2008.

IV: Poetic Inquiry as Political Response

Poetry's strength lies in exposing realities and demanding visibility.
—Natalie Honein

In the final section, the authors show us how poetic inquiry is a response, a call to action, and a method to address political injustices in our world. Maya T. Borhani reiterates the performance in poetry in the chapter "Poetry through Song: Sounds of Resistance." When we perform our poetry, even singing it, we reinforce the praxis of poetry as performative. We can perform how we want our worlds to be as Borhani writes: "I sing poetry as a pushback against all those forces trying to deaden the world and its people, its landscapes, its sacred traditions, an anthem for the world and each other." Sandra L. Faulkner and Sheila Squillante present the script for a video and poetry collage they created in response to the 2016 U.S. Presidential election. "Nasty Women Join the Hive: A NastyWomanifesto Invitation for White Feminists" is a call to action for White feminists, in particular, around issues of race, gender, and social justice. The call is for an intersectional feminism that includes ALL concerns and a political stance of listening.

The poet-authors in this section address specific, often violent injustices, past and present. Poetry is an appeal for recognition of injustice and an awareness of how inaction as "spectators" is part of the problem. Sandra Filippelli writes poetry as a form of witness in media reports of violence against children in "Peace (Ahimsa) Pact." Poetry as a form of witness is also present in other chapters. Natalie Honein uses poetic inquiry to address and reflect on the refugees of the war in Syria. Honein's poetry "opens space for dialogue" in "Spectators in a Tragedy." In "War and the Lyric Voice: An Intergenerational Narrative," Gisela Ruebsaat and Heather McLeod show us how going back into our past and our family's past is a path toward navigating through our personal and political injustices we encounter.

Sean Wiebe and Pauline Sameshima also offer us a method for engaging in social justice work in their chapter, "Reframing and Reflaming Social

Justice through Poetry:" They use "existentialism as a theoretical position" and poetry that "reframes and reflames social justice through love." All call for both hearing and giving voice through poetry as means to ignite social change.

15.

Poetry through Song: Sounds of Resistance

Maya T. Borhani,
University of Victoria in British Columbia

This chapter describes singing poems as a vehicle for self-rejuvenation, connection with others, and the advancement of public political concerns. Singing poetry offers a pushback against conditions counterproductive to flourishing creative lives, expressing political dissent, and nurturing, inwardly, that which ennobles us. Singing poems enhances poetry's innate abilities to nourish the heart and replenish the spirit; singing, like metaphor, soothes. A good poem, enriched through music, can be a natural mechanism for self-calming and balancing; through the power of rhythmic, melodic, and harmonic entrainment, modulation of heart and breathing rates, and the development of elocutionary skill, singing poems becomes a powerful, meditative practice. Referencing poems by Frost, Lorca, Patchen, and myself, this essay explores the art of lifting words off the page through breath and voice, as we nurture ourselves, mend the heart of the world, and forge a way toward reconciliation, one note, one word, at a time.

Keywords: singing poetry, social justice advocacy, poetry as resistance, poetic inquiry, poetic performativity

I was first introduced to the wonder of singing poetry by Rex Richardson, self-styled guitarist with Flamenco influences, composer and songwriter setting new and classic poems to his original music. Through Rex's artful compositions, I discovered Opal Whiteley's[1] childlike voice and perceptive wisdom, and tasted the emotional grit of Robert Frost's contemplative night ride in "Stopping by Woods on A Snowy Evening."[2] Delicate stairstep rhythms in Gary Snyder's "Villanelle of the Wandering Lapps"[3] mirror the hunter's stealthy stalk, as "we seek the hidden lair / of the honey-footed bear;"[4] or feel our horse's lilting pace beneath us in "All in green went my love riding."[5] Rex's dark, brooding chords and rolling arpeggios suited Lorca's intense, surrealistic language perfectly, aural butterflies pouring from the singer's throat, as words sprang to life in ways never imagined from a mere page.

Within an intimate community of artists, poets, and writers living deep in the mountains of northern California, we shared these songs; inside warm cabin walls, we'd sing and sway, raising our voices in a joyful chorus. In weekly steam baths, hunched around a small wood stove draped with blanketed walls, we'd sing to open lungs and pores, for the gift of life flowing through our bodies, pounding blood and pulsing breath, rousing rounds of traditional folk tunes, ritual chants, and these old poems reimagined in song.

One night, dressing in the dark after a final cold water plunge to complete our ritual steam, I heard strains of a jaunty melody, bursting with quiet joy, wafting from Rex and Sarah's tiny cabin. Incredulously, I realized Rex was singing "Blue Horse,"[6] one of several poems I'd shared with him recently. As I heard my poem rendered as a song, its intrinsic musicality emerged as melody, cadence, and intonation. College classes had dissected poetry sufficiently to teach such important concepts; but *hearing* my poem set to music, its words sung, its melody and rhythms tenderly brought to life through the power of the human voice, this grabbed my heart and made the lesson real; my equivalent of *Letters to a Young Poet.*[7] Rex's musical interpretation embodied and expressed my poem's essence note-by-note, word-by-word.

Blue Horse
(After *Blue Horses*, Franz Marc, 1911)[8]

What's a blue horse?

The creature that's jumped
Over the rainbow
So many times
She wears the royal mantle
All the time now.
Even in darkness
Even in darkness,
All the time now.

She's the laughing and the
Dying in me
Nose to the ground or head
Flung back in gallop,
All the time now.
Even in darkness
Even in darkness,
All the time now.

She carries the world
Alight on her back
Sets her feet to dancing
Far across the sky,
Lithesome runner.
Even in darkness
Even in darkness,
Spirit a song.

A blue horse
Always comes
To find me
When I am sinking,
No matter the time now.
Even in darkness,
Even in darkness,
All the time now.[9]

What tune do *you* hear for these galloping words? One trick is simply to sing the words the way you imagine them, and hear what comes out: make a joyful noise, Friends,[10] and come into the Presence with singing.

Richardson's poetic-musical explorations have become wayfinding tools and teaching strategies, helping reveal a poem's essence, structures, and meaning in surprising ways. I find myself singing his poem-songs to myself over and over again, committing words to memory as voice brings them to life. Singing poems under my breath on a crowded street, full volume in a raging storm, or with friends in a sauna becomes poetic praxis; a deeper, more mythic connection to the words grows the longer I roll them around on my tongue and listen to their echoes inside me. The very act of singing—modulated breathing, exchanging air for words, the exhilaration of lifting one's voice—creates a more primal connection with the poems in their most ancient form, as oral tradition.

My experiences with singing poetry reiterate the idea and praxis of poetry as performative. Bob Dylan's 2016 Nobel Prize in literature "for having created new poetic expressions within the great American song tradition"[11] underscored poetry's penchant for performance and lyrical expression through song. The two genres, poetry and song, were officially sanctioned together as one. In the shock, many felt at Dylan's receipt of this award lie links between the worlds of high-art (or classical) poetry, and folk traditions of (protest) poetry and song. My advocacy for singing poetry builds on these links, seeking to reunite poetry with its roots as an oral storytelling tradition expressive of cultural concerns within the body politic. I imagine Bob Dylan and Will Shakespeare wiling away many an hour at the local pub, witty exchanges laced with bursts of song. I wish to see more of us singing poems and stories like ancient bards, weaving melody and lyricism, disseminating to each other, our "huddled masses,"[12] the poetical and political through song.

I sing poetry as a pushback against all those forces trying to deaden the world and its people, its landscapes, its sacred traditions, an anthem for the world and each other. I sing poetry as a pushback against all those who deny poetry's charms, its necessity and power as amulet, protest, and rallying cry. I sing poetry to remind the world of poetry's musicality, its voice aching to be sung, its siren as living performance art. I also sing poetry because of its unique and wonderful ability to express social justice mores through words, tone, rhythm, and melody, "these songs of freedom … redemption songs."[13]

I advocate for the singing of poetry, in service to/as/in/for social justice as a way to access inner well-being: a root source within everyone's possession to tune into harmonic sonic and sensorial vibrations that soothe the heart and calm the mind. As a form of protest in dark times, singing poetry conveys provocative expressions of inequity and oppression turned to justice and collaboration. Singing poetry helps us better understand poetry through the universal medium of music, and offers invaluable literacy instruction. Singing aids memorization; poetry, already full of mnemonic devices (like alliteration, repetition, and rhyme) especially resonates when sung. Just like we "never forget a tune," singing creates an additional mnemonic cue for recalling a poem's words through pacing, rhythm, and melody. Birds of a feather, singing and poetry go together.

Whether "just for fun" or as serious performance, singing poetry connects us to one another, creating camaraderie and community. Singing poetry extends a compelling lyrical advancement of social-justice-pedagogical concerns in and out of classrooms: at marches, rallies, and presentations, around a campfire with friends, discussing another round of disheartening headlines. Singing powerful poems, like this one by Kenneth Patchen, we're reminded what we're fighting for, and why we resist.

Instructions for Angels

Take the useful events
For your tall.
Red mouth.
Blue weather.
To hell with power and hate and war.

The mouth of a pretty girl …
The weather in the highest soul …
Put the tips of your fingers
On a baby man;
Teach him to be beautiful.
To hell with power and hate and war.

Tell God that we like
The rain, and snow, and flowers,
And trees, and all things gentle and clean
That have growth on the earth.
White winds. Golden fields.
To hell with power and hate and war.[14]

In the joy of raising our voices in song, *we resist*: our voices become gentle shields against strife and worry, our words poetic swords—wands, lightsabers—to forge through thickets of psychic darkness and fear.

Without the human voice, words don't quicken the same way. Long ago, bards and minstrels didn't merely recite poems like Homer's *Odyssey*, they *sang* and performed these stories of heroic journeys and epic battles, often accompanied by a lyre and other singers. Just as Richardson's *duende* infuses his musical interpretations with a voice the poem demands, Bagby describes how "The subtle flexibility of modal song is especially suitable as a vehicle for a narrative,"[15] wherein

> the vocalist makes use of a seemingly simple matrix of tones to support an infinitely complex textual structure, so that all elements—tone, text and performer—merge into one organic process which functions uniquely in the service of the story.[16]

When we sing poems, we embody and give greater voice to their stories. Fenoglio, the old storyteller in the *Inkheart* trilogy,[17] describes stories in books as "sound pressed between … pages [that] only a voice can bring …

back to life! Then they throw off sparks ... they go free as birds flying out into the world."[18]

Similarly, Heidegger extols, "To be a poet in a destitute time means: to attend, singing, to the trace of the fugitive gods. This is why the poet in the time of the world's night utters the holy."[19] Can we take "attend, singing" to mean exactly what it says—to sing as an act of attention? Can we utter the holy more sincerely than through song? How does such attention serve us, and the world? Singing poetry pushes back against conditions counterproductive to flourishing lives, illuminating the world's night, nourishing the heart and the holy. Singing begets retrieval of a wilder self that models joy in the face of oppression, claims personal sovereignty, defends territory, and reminds us how to be in relation to the world around us. Singing poetry as a form of resistance, we can choose poems that nurture joy, talk back to oppression, revere kindness and compassion, and actively resist current political agendas. When the sanctity and beauty of life are challenged every day by powers seemingly bent on destruction, stopping to appreciate poetry, let alone sing it out, becomes a radical act of resistance. Fostering corporeal and emotional release and rejuvenation, such resistance nurtures a rarified approach to social justice advocacy.

Federico García Lorca's *casida* and *gacela* poems are "free adaptations" of short, structured, rhymed forms in Arabic poetry,[20] excellent examples of what Robert Bly calls "leaping poetry,"[21] unexpected metaphoric leaps that inspire grand imaginative leaps, in turn. Such poems lend themselves to the social-justice singer's repertoire with their often startling, expansive imagery and unusual juxtapositions, shaking up the mind's static corners; new worlds appear, possibilities flower. Singing such lyrics suggests imaginative alternatives to a politic often stuck in linear thinking, forgetful of the dance, the inner music of poems, sunlight, and rivers. In "Gacela of the Flight," we hear mystery, and risk: death wrapped up in life; newborn babes, the smiles of unknown people; that which "consumes us" in its beauty. This poem rails, metaphorically, against Franco's boot heel crushing Lorca's beloved Spain.

Gacela of the Flight

I have lost myself in the sea many times
With my ears full of freshly cut flowers.
With my tongue full of love and agony
I have lost myself in the sea many times,
As I lose myself in the heart of certain children.

Because the rose must search in the forehead
For a hard landscape of bone.
And the hands of man have no other purpose
Than to imitate the roots below the earth.

There is no one who in giving a kiss
Does not feel the smile of faceless people.
And no one who in touching a newborn child
Forgets the motionless skulls of horses.

As I lose myself in the heart of certain children,
I have lost myself in the sea many times.
Ignorant of the waters I go seeking
A death full of light to consume me.[22]

Similarly, we must speak up and sing out against the crushing boots of our own time: pipelines approved despite clear dissent from Indigenous peoples whose lands they impact; climate change deniers on all continents; Faustian governance from a celebrity-culture president in the United States; neo-conservative factions grappling for power around the globe. A disheartening pall is cast over our efforts at resilient resistance.

Yet singing helps build the very spiritual endurance we need to disperse these shadows, offering grounded well-being and strong self-care along the way. Song becomes a valuable form of personal and political currency: we sing hard-hitting and lyrical poems to distract the forces of domination, to diffuse conflict, to ease a friend's mind, to entrain our own hearts and minds in harmonium. By lifting words off the page, through breath and voice, we embody and exude powerful possibilities for change: songs are our ancient-new tools *to speak up and speak out,* answering Ferlinghetti's charge: "Now is the time for you to speak / O silent majority."[23]

As we speak up, we continue to revere and promote values that nurture all life. We must continue to teach the critical feeling and thinking that poets and singers have long embodied, putting everyday words to wise, clear defense of all things beautiful and free. Richardson encourages this brave necessity: "Like you, I experience the politic and spirit of [Lorca's] poems. Lorca is a martyr murdered by the very motives that are yet punishing the sensitive and vulnerable. To educate with poetry and song can provide a deep awakening and seamless connection with everyday language so often co-opted by our somewhat sinister social order."[24] So we sing and carry on, bringing Lorca's commitment forward into a new day, his legacy now our own.

How do we find our voices in song? How do we listen for the poem's voice? Jim Watt, Butler University professor emeritus, teaches a revelatory, personal approach to poet William Blake that, among other praxis, invites *attention* through singing Blake's poems.[25]

Envisioning the study of poems alongside illustration practices similar to Blake's, Watt planned for his students to carve linoleum print blocks in response to the poems. When one of his "brightest students" comes to register for the class, Watt notes that "Anne" is blind, and tries to "explain to her that [they'll] be focusing on the interplay of image, or design, and text; something unfortunately inaccessible to her."[26] Much to Watt's surprise, "she turns those blind eyes to [him] and smiles as she says, 'But I can sing.'"[27] So Watt agrees to accept Anne's singing in lieu of design:

> though I have no idea what this will mean. And just like that ... my ignorance ... was ... transformed into a genuine revelation. For all of us in the class quickly grasped [that] what Anne was doing was *exactly* parallel to what Blake [had been] doing in his melding of word and image, design and text ... And so we began to learn another way into the apprehension of reality, an ancient way—and one central to story. And we did it together, not individually, reasoning away in a carrel deep in the bowels of the library, but together in a room that opened out with every voice into the whole story of who and what and where we are.[28]

For students shy to expose their voices, Watt shares a simple truth: *let the heart of the poem lead you into its tune.* The tune is already there: in phrasing, resonance of vowels, rhythm of consonants. Singing simply brings out a poem's innate features, its bones firm and structured, its fluid skin, its expectant voice. Every poem has its own internal music; if we listen carefully, and let ourselves explore and experiment unself-consciously, the poem will lead us to the tune that is right for *our* voice. Everyone's song will be different; that's part of the beauty of finding a poem's music.

> What Blake knew, what any true singer knows, is that singing is the art of blending your voice with your audience and with the song's innate direction, which is a matter of the heart and inspiration, not one of abstraction and reasoning. It is this mysterious "hidden direction" that also makes harmony possible when a group sings together. Indeed, we are "hardwired" to blend our voices, naturally and easily, with the chorus. Musicians call it, for very good reason, "playing (or singing) by ear."[29]

Keep experimenting until you find something that "fits." Let the words of the poem guide you. Trust yourself.

Sometimes, it's just about the joy. Robert Frost's "In a Glass of Cider,"[30] a poem with exemplary rhyming and metered structure, makes singing nearly effortless. A simple poem, offering simple joys—a cold glass of cider! Yet, the poem also decants the wisdom of the world, from the mire of material existence (sediment), a body and spirit (bubbles, rising on air), to the intertwining truth of the two, always bound, one with the other. As social justice advocates, we understand this philosophy swimming in a pint of cider, the constant process of waiting to "catch another bubble" in ascent, never giving up, remembering the joy: the thing is to get now and then elated.

In a Glass of Cider

It seemed I was a mite of sediment
That waited for the bottom to ferment
So I could catch a bubble in ascent.
I rode up on one till the bubble burst,
And when that left me to sink back reversed
I was no worse off than I was at first.
I'd catch another bubble if I waited.
The thing was to get now and then elated.

Notes

1. Whiteley, *Opal*.

2. Frost, "Stopping by Woods," 224.

3. Snyder, "Villanelle of the Wandering Lapps," 181.

4. Snyder, 181.

5. Cummings, "All in green went my love riding," 14.

6. Borhani, "Blue Horse."

7. Rilke, *Letters to a Young Poet*.

8. *Encyclopedia Britannica Online*, "Franz Marc: German Artist." https://www.britannica.com/biography/Franz-Marc#ref252630.

9. Borhani, "Blue Horse."

10. Barks, *Soul Fury*. Referring to Rumi's relationship with his teacher, Shams of Tabriz, and their spiritual relationship with what they called the "Friend"; anyone, in theory, is such a friend on the soul's path.

11. "The Nobel Prize in Literature 2016."

12. Lazarus, "The New Colossus."

13. Marley, "Redemption Song."

14. Patchen, "Instructions for Angels," 316.

15. Bagby, "*Beowulf* and the Performance of Medieval Epic."

16. Ibid.

17. Funke, *Inkheart.*

18. Funke, "Violante," 250-251.

19. Heidegger, *Poetry, Language, Thought,* 94.

20. Lorca, *The Selected Poems*

21. Bly, *Leaping Poetry.*

22. Lorca, *The Selected Poems,* 167.

23. Wolf, "Lawrence Ferlinghetti Poem."

24. Rex Richardson, e-mail message to author, October 31, 2017.

25. Jim Watt, e-mail message to author, October 3, 2017

26. Ibid.

27. Ibid.

28. Ibid.

29. Frost, 468.

30. Ibid.

Bibliography

Barks, Coleman. *Rumi: Soul Fury: Rumi and Shams Tabriz on Friendship.* New York: HarperOne, 2014.

Bagby, Benjamin. "*Beowulf* and the Performance of Medieval Epic." *Beowulf: The Epic in Performance.* https://www.bagbybeowulf.com/background/medieval_epic.html.

Bly, Robert. *Leaping Poetry: An Idea with Poems and Translations.* Pittsburgh: University of Pittsburgh Press, 1975.

Bob Marley and the Wailers. "Redemption song," *Uprising.* Island 602547276285, 2015, 33 1/3 rpm. Originally released in 1980.

Borhani, Maya Tracy. "Blue horse." Unpublished manuscript, 1984. Microsoft Word file.

Cummings, Edward Estlin. "All in green went my love riding." In *Tulips and Chimneys,* 14. New York: Liveright, 1996.

Encyclopedia Britannica Online, "Franz Marc: German Artist," accessed October 3, 2017, https://www.britannica.com/biography/Franz-Marc#ref252630.

Frost, Robert. "Stopping by Woods on a Snowy Evening." In *The Poetry of Robert Frost: The Collected Poems, Complete and Unabridged,* 224. Edited by Edward Connery Lathem. New York: Henry Holt and Company, 1979.

Frost, Robert. "In a Glass of Cider." In *The Poetry of Robert Frost: The Collected Poems, Complete and Unabridged,* 458. Edited by Edward Connery Lathem. New York: Henry Holt and Company, 1979.

Funke, Cornelia. *Inkheart.* Translated by Anthea Bell. New York: The Chicken House (Scholastic), 2003.

Funke, Cornelia. "Violante." In *Inkspell,* translated by Anthea Bell, 246-261. New York: The Chicken House (Scholastic), 2005.

Heidegger, Martin. *Poetry, Language, Thought.* Translated by A. Hofstadter. New York: Harper and Row, 1971.

Lazarus, Emma. "The New Colossus." Academy of American Poets/Poets.org. https://www.poets.org/poetsorg/poem/newcolossus?gclid=CjwKCAjwm ufZBRBJEiwAPJ3LpoIjwZ5Ja_nr6UXCXSdz5AyJusohiVG57jVFqvJcBkvCft KzUJSCxBoCNo8QAvD_BwE.

Lorca, Federico García. "Gacela of the Flight." In *The Selected Poems of Federico García Lorca,* 167. Edited by Federico García Lorca and Donald Allen. New York: New Directions, 2005.

Patchen, Kenneth. "Instructions for Angels." In *The Collected Poems of Kenneth Patchen,* 316. New York: New Directions, 1968.

Rilke, Rainer Maria. *Letters to a Young Poet.* Translated by Joan M. Burnham. Novato: New World Library, 2000.

Snyder, Gary. "Villanelle of the Wandering Lapps." In *Left Out in the Rain: New Poems 1947-1985,* 181. New York: North Point Press, 1986.

"The Nobel Prize in Literature 2016." Nobelprize.org. http://www.nobelprize.org/nobel_prizes/literature/laureates/2016/.

Whiteley, Opal. *Opal.* Arranged and adapted by Jane Boulton. New York: Macmillan, 1976.

Wolf, Rowan. "Lawrence Ferlinghetti Poem." *Uncommon Thought* (blog), February 25, 2003. https://www.uncommonthought.com/mtblog/archives/2003/02/25/law rence-ferlin.php.

16.

Nasty Women Join the Hive:
A NastyWomanifesto Invitation
for White Feminists

Sandra L. Faulkner,
Bowling Green State University

Sheila Squillante,
Chatham University

Squillante and Faulkner remix an intersectional approach to feminism and feminist identity through a *womanifesta* that uses poetic collage (video, images, and poetry). They wrote collaborative poetry in response to the 2016 U.S. presidential election. Faulkner shared a poem about the inauguration. Squillante responded with a poem. They marched in their local Women's Marches.™ They played a game of exquisite corpse with themes of a Trump presidency: rape culture, misogyny, locker room talk, feminist response. The poets reflected on their own ignorance about the symbolism of pink pussy hats and how race was ignored in local and national iterations of the Women's Marches.™ They then composed a *womanifesta* with text, images, and sound considering how an intersectional feminism can be realized with a hive metaphor. They hope to appeal to White feminists to decenter White women in women's movements, to eradicate White feminism, to reject White fragility, and to "just listen."

Keywords: exquisite corpse, intersectional feminism, poetic collage, White feminism, *womanifesta*

Artist Statement

In this work, we emphasize how local and national Women's Marches™ were too centered on White women's experiences, ignoring trans women and women of color with a singular focus on reproductive justice symbolized in pink pussy hats. Current feminist theory and practice call for inclusive feminism and the importance of being intersectional in our feminist work.

> We not only ask about gender—
> - What about race?
> - What about sexuality?
> - What about ableism?
> - What about socioeconomic inequities?
> - How do these conditions and positions work together or against one another?[2]

In what follows, we describe and present our experiences, conversations, and reflection on our participation in Women's Marches™ in Pittsburgh, PA, and Ann Arbor, MI. We move from depictions of binaries between race and class, and us versus them, to a womanifesta that asks White feminists, in particular, to listen to calls for an inclusive feminism so that our movements become focused on a WE.

The Problem (Call): Sheila

After the election, I felt such urgency. I wanted to be surrounded, or, I knew I ought to seek out people in similar distress. Actual, embodied persons. Flesh and sinew and respiratory systems rather than icons, avatars, profile pics. The echo chamber of righteous indignation. I'd never marched before, and the idea of a crowd, a mass, a throng felt terrifying, even depleting. There is a reason some of us retreat to the safety of a blue text box on a screen.

(For some of us, safety is a given.)

And yet, it felt like time. My daughter, 9, and my son, 11—we're trying hard to raise them with feminist principles. I felt swept by the energy and momentum of the marches I knew were forming all over the country (I didn't understand it would end up being the world). I imagined a wound, a body charred by fire—we all felt blown to bits—but cracking itself open into a new, pink healing.

(But already we have a problem. I do. I'm looking at that sentence just above, wherein I figure myself blown to bits, charred, a body, a wound. Mine is metaphorical maiming. My body remains intact. But there are others, elsewhere and certainly in Pittsburgh, for whom this image is both metaphorical and literal. **Pink. Bodies. Bits.**)

Pittsburgh planned a women's march to connect to the weaving web of Women's Marches™ that began in D.C. and sprang up everywhere, everywhere. We'll go, I told my daughter, as I clicked to purchase our pink pussy hats. Light pink for her, bright pink for me. I would rather have asked my friend Sandra to knit them for us, but there would be no time. She was already knitting for so many others. $20 a pop felt (I'll admit) steep for this unknown-to-me vendor, for this thing I'd don once. But it's a symbol, right? An important artifact, a representation of unity (support women-owned business!) we can be proud to wear and carefully keep.

(Who gets to be included? Who's been traditionally left out?)

Then, in the blue text box on the screen, I begin to see an unraveling. I quietly follow a thread in which women of color document problems with the way the Pittsburgh Women's March™ machinations are developing. They say they have not been invited to be a meaningful part of the planning. They describe a meeting in a suburban chain restaurant where White women have taken the lead, making them feel unwanted, un-listened-to. They want to be part of the We.

(Blue box. Pink hat. White suburb.)

In the box I read comments, carefully. I try to understand. To listen. It sounds reasonable, what they are saying. They want a de-centering of White Feminism. (I am a White Feminist.) They want an acknowledgment of the intersectional issues that have plagued Pittsburgh (everywhere, everywhere). They want the voices of women of color and femmes to fill the room, for once.

(But again there's a problem. In the paragraph above, the one I just wrote, I'm wondering how best to arrange sentences so that my (white) voice doesn't come last. I teach my students the power of the final word in a line/stanza of poetry. And yet, even as I'm writing this, I see the deep irony in this parenthetical aside.)

Someone criticizes the planning of the Pittsburgh Women's March ™ with respect to the above. **(Just listen!)** Someone defends it, says any slights were unintentional, not racist. Someone says "erasure." Someone says "diminishing." Someone says this is not a new phenomenon, Pittsburgh. Get your shit right.

To say that a fracture then happened would be both literal and metaphorical. A new march, planned and led by seasoned activists—***black women and femmes***—rose up in East Liberty, a historically important neighborhood for Black people in the city. An embodied throng my family chose to join instead of the downtown masses. We stood in the dirt and grass in front of Penn Plaza apartments, a site that had been threatened by plans to build a Whole Foods Market, its residents displaced in a textbook gentrification move. They called their march "*Our Feminism Must Be Intersectional.*" They asked us to listen to their history and help them move toward *real* equality. They asked us to think about the commodification of feminism and social justice. To prioritize intersectionality. To question our motives and our complicity.

(I teach this to my memoir students. You have to be willing to show your whole ass.)

They asked us to *pick up our signs* and **leave our pink pussy hats home**. The overwhelming critique of the marches is that they were too white,[3] too nice, too homogenous,[4] too vagina-centric,[5] too unfocused,[6] too stereotypically feminine.[7]

My daughter was disappointed but I did my best to explain. It's still a symbol of something important, but now it's richer, more complicated. More complex. She put hers in a box at the top of her closet.

We took our places near the back of the crowd by the fence.

(I want to keep learning.)

Behind us, a halted construction site.

In front of us, black women and femmes on stage with a microphone. Electric possibility, defiant and embodied, claiming their home.

Can you be a White Feminist without embracing White Feminism? *(Response)*: Sandra

Sheila and I have been friends, collaborative partners, and writing buddies for quite a few years. The morning after the election, we checked in on instant messenger, as we do, typing slowly.

What are we going to do? Sheila typed.

I am going to do what I know how to do, what I can do. Make art. Write poetry. Teach. Community Service, I typed. I am a White woman, and a (White) feminist. I am the director of Women's, Gender, and Sexuality Studies at Bowling Green State University. I am a feminist ethnographer, competitive knitter, runner, and poet. I have to do something. I do what I know how to do. Educate. Write. Knit. Talk.

In January 2017, someone sent me a link to a pattern for a pussy hat. Women contacted me via email and over Facebook asking if I could possibly knit them or their partners a hat. I knit pink hat after pink hat for friends and friends of friends. I knit pink hats during meetings, knit over coffee with friends and colleagues who will attend the Women's March™ in DC and other places. I knit. I knit and write. I call my representatives. I talk with students. I talk with my Brownie Girl Scouts.

I knit twelve pussy hats. I write about my (White) feminist, middle-aged rage. I decide to take my daughter and partner to the march in Ann Arbor, because it is close. We host a sign-making party for students and friends who will march with us. I am thrilled when my daughter makes her own sign after we explain why we will march: "Girls Choose Rights!" I knit a hat for myself and my daughter. At the march, we shout about immigrant rights, reproductive rights, but I see many White faces—White bodies and White women's bodies holding space and marching freely, unmolested by police violence.[8]

And I don't hear the other voices at first. The critique of pussy hats as equating women's rights to white, cis-gendered, able-bodied women's vaginas;[9] pussy hats as representing White privilege;[10] White women wearing pink hats and not acknowledging racism or body essentialism, and not listening to people of color, disabled people, and trans rights activists.[11]

I didn't consider that placing White in the parenthetical is part of the problem.

Sheila and I decide to write collaborative poetry in response. I share a poem about the inauguration. She responds with a poem. We play a game of exquisite corpse with themes of a Trump presidency: rape culture, misogyny, locker room talk, feminist response. We write a womanifesta with text, images, and sound. We consider how an intersectional feminism can be realized with the hive metaphor: we remix an intersectional approach through an appeal to White feminists.

Sheila and I keep talking. She tells me how things in the Pittsburgh march fell apart because of White women. There would be another march where White women were not centered, where pussy hats would not be visible.

We think about being White women. We think about being White feminists. We ask how we can be White Feminists without White Feminism. Fifty-three percent of Trump's vote was White women. This is our audience.

We ask. We start to listen. We invite other White feminists to listen. Then to act.

Nasty Women Join the Hive (Script)

Calling Nasty Women (Call and Response)
who dress like women, and, nevertheless, persist

On Inauguration Day we leave our pink pussy hats home

Drape yourself in unmet resolutions,

strap on your yak feet
and cleat the ice scattered on sidewalk:
Resolve to rush into the wind's season.

Run where the trees have thrown off
their bothersome fall clothes,
hear the groan of bark on bark:
Resolve to love with hot consent.

Take the baby and throw him out
with your dirty obligations,
the dust balls and grit of unmopped floors:
Use your resolve like a steel to sharpen

the needles of your feminist rage,
knit the revolution in all hues of pink,
wrap and turn the crooked stitches:
Call a senator with bitchy resolve.

Lick the cat clean with impatience
as you drip cream cold from the carton
into cheap, black coffee that tastes like work:
resolutely step in your community walk.

Always wash your ibuprofen down
with two glasses of flat champagne
to taste the disappointment of stuck bubbles:
Resolve to remember middle-class aches.

Throw an alcohol-free New Year's party
with too many balloons and stray kids,
belch your affections into your apple cider,
you will need to be sober with resolve.

Let your food cake face and fingers
like this is your death meal,
eat without wiping your mouth:
Resolve to be a nasty woman every hour this year.

despite **Locker Room Talk**

Fifth grade. Gym class. Changing in the toilet stall. They found your diary at the sleepover. Read it. Threatened to pass it to the boys.

Summer of eighth grade. The sweat of band practice in Georgia heat. They stare at my breasts that grew two cup sizes in two months. The taunt, "You grew boobs!"
Returned with, "Too bad you didn't grow a penis."

Same year, Suzanne R. grew to encompass the doorway (out), pushed her new breasts (out) at me and said the boys all know now. I slapped her across the face. **My first personal violence.**

One year, I tried to fuck like a man.

despite **Rape Culture**

I had to stop listening to Billy Joel
and Jane's Addiction—sex is violent?!
In the 90s, my first conscious act of political resistance: I'm only listening to women sing.
"Your feminism has ruined you," they said.

What are new feminist metaphors?

Let's say grapefruit, thick skin peeled by a sharp thumbnail.
An onion, too. Tears of anger shed in righteous rings.
Cumin if we're staying with sustenance. The heat of it. Taste. The warm, living funk.
If feminism is food, and food is life, eat with dirty abandon, you nasty women.
Make honey from the sting of politics. Be Queen Bees.

"When we place ourselves with people aware of their oppression, we begin to see how we are implicated, to wrangle with the connections between privilege and oppression."[12]

(Who gets to be included? Who's been traditionally left out?)

Call and Response

"We build alliances to link our lives together, to transmit power, and potentially for the purpose of transforming power."[13]

What if?

What if instead of a wave?

What if instead of a wave of hegemonic staid understanding?

What if we create a feminist alliance like a HIVE? Think about this moment.

"Our Feminism Must Be Intersectional."

What if we see alliances like hives of bees?

For some of us, safety is a given.

Just listen!

Pink. Bodies. Bits.   (Blue box. Pink hat. White suburb.)

a de-centering of White Feminism. (I am a White Feminist.)

leave our pink pussy hats home

They want an acknowledgment of the intersectional issues that have plagued Pittsburgh (everywhere, everywhere). They want the voices of women of color and femmes to fill the room, for once.

"In other words, rather than going in search of a set of themes or watershed periods that have been argued to characterize a particular wave, we may well be better served by explaining why moments emerge as meaningful and by what the initiating and connecting impulses are locally, globally, and regionally."[14]

What if we make honey from the sting of politics?

What if we leave our pink pussy hats home?

    What if we listen?

        What if we keep learning?

        What if we

- recognize our role in allyship as one of active listening and educating our peers[15]
- decenter White women
- consider different women's experiences
- acknowledge various realities

"Eradicating white feminism is worth the growing pain."[16]

The Hive Responds

Friend, may I borrow your resolve?
I need it to feel more than frayed
and aching. My anger blooms but bruises

so easily. Spent and tender, it wilts
toward despair. I watch you
from my too-small space, hair

unwashed, face lit with flickering glow.
You scroll by, all muscle and motion
on my screen, your signs sure and pink

and beseeching. *Wake forever*
from this endless dull dumb sleep!
I know what crowds sound like,

metallic thrum of three million
bees in the hive. I've seen parades go by.
I've seen my daughter stride down the sidewalk

to the stop, angry with more than just
her mother's loving limits. The world
wants to pin her wings to the wall. Listen,

my hair is falling out; creases deepen every day

around the stuck-open scream of my mouth.
You can resist and resist and yet

still feel terror. You can weep while
you wield your best intentions, march
around your small city block. It's okay.

Grab your child by the hand and keep going.
Throw your fist in the air knowing it's just another
word for *watch what happens when I open my palm.*

Notes

1. This piece first appeared as a video in *Women & Language Online*, 40, no. 1 (2018). https://www.womenandlanguage.org/40-2womanifestos

2. Leavy and Harris, 2018, iv.

3. Kozol, "White Privilege."

4. Xiao, "The White Feminism."

5. Riddell, "Transgender Community."

6. Dvorak, "The Women's March."

7. Derr, "Pink Flag."

8. Ramanathan, "Was the Women's March?"

9. Compton, "Pink 'Pussyhat' Creator."

10. Kozol, "White Privilege."

11. Mosthof, "If You're Not Talking."

12. Rowe, "Belonging," 35.

13. Rowe, *Power Lines*, 1.

14. Rowley, "The Idea of Ancestry," 80.

15. Xiao, "The White Feminism."

16. Ibid.

Bibliography

Compton, Julie. "Pink 'Pussyhat' Creator Addresses Criticism over Name." *NBC OUT*. February 7, 2017. http://www.nbcnews.com/feature/nbc-out/pink-pussyhat-creator-addresses-criticism-over-name-n717886.
Derr, Holly. "Pink Flag: What Message Do 'Pussy Hats' Really Send?" *bitchmedia*. January 2017. https://www.bitchmedia.org/article/pink-flag-what-message-do-pussy-hats-really-send.

Dvorak, Petula. "The Women's March Needs Passion and Purpose, not Pink Pussycat Hats." *The Washington Post*. January 12, 2017. https://www.washingtonpost.com/local/the-womens-march-needs-passion-and-purpose-not-pink-pussycat-hats/2017/01/11/6d7e75be-d842-11e6-9a36-1d296534b31e_story.html?utm_term=.0e42e591841b.

Kozol, Wendy. "White Privilege and the Pussy Hat." *The New York Times, Reading the Pictures*. March 2, 2017. http://www.readingthepictures.org/2017/03/feminism-race-pussy-hat/.

Leavy, Patricia and Harris, Anne. *Contemporary Feminist Research from Theory to Practice*. New York: Guilford, 2018.

Mosthof, Mariella. "If You're Not Talking about the Criticism Surrounding the Women's March, Then You're Part of the Problem." *Bustle*. January 20, 2017. https://www.bustle.com/p/if-youre-not-talking-about-the-criticism-surrounding-the-womens-march-then-youre-part-of-the-problem-33491.

Ramanathan, Lavanya. "Was the Women's March Just Another Display of White Privilege? Some Think So." *The Washington Post*. January 24, 2017. https://www.washingtonpost.com/lifestyle/style/was-the-womens-march-just-another-display-of-white-privilege-some-think-so/2017/01/24/00bbdcca-e1a0-11e6-a547-5fb9411d332c_story.html?utm_term=.8c2fb6071b73.

Riddell, Kelly. "Transgender Community Says Women's March Made Them Feel Isolated." *The Washington Times*. January 24, 2017. http://www.washingtontimes.com/news/2017/jan/24/transgender-community-felt-isolated-womens-march/.

Rowe, Aimee Carrillo. "Belonging: Toward a Feminist Politics of Relation." *National Women's Studies Association Journal* 17 (2005): 1-35.

Rowe, Aimee Carillo. *Power Lines: On the Subject of Feminist Alliances*. Durham, NC: Duke University Press, 2008.

Rowley, M. V. "The Idea of Ancestry: Of Feminist Genealogies and Many Other Things." In *Feminist Theory Reader: Local and Global Perspectives*, 77-82. Edited by S. K. Kim and C. R. McCann. New York, NY: Routledge, 2013.

Xiao, Jessica. "The White Feminism of the Women's March Is Still on My Mind." *Everyday Feminism*. April 9, 2017. http://everydayfeminism.com/2017/04/white-feminism-womens-march/.

17.

Peace (Ahimsa) Pact

Sandra Filippelli,
University of British Columbia

In this poetic inquiry, I declare school violence and incarceration of children in detention centers that I have witnessed in the media a social justice issue, provoking a call for a poetry of protest and a poetic peace pact. Children in Thailand clean their homes and meditate for peace in temples and caves, while their American counterparts practice mindfulness, opening their world to joy and tranquility. Through peace practices, they transform a sense of displacement from home by cultivating a protective sanctuary of imagination, a mind of *ahimsa*, or inner disarmament. They may create literary and visual art to release embedded trauma and petition for social justice. In my own aspiration for the eradication of violence against children, I sculpt poetic images calling for the return of the stolen inner and outer child to the sanctuary of home.

Keywords: social justice, poetry of protest, school violence, detention, meditation, home, sanctuary, peace, *ahimsa*, non-violence

The escalation of violence against children has become a widespread media issue that merits investigation. The proliferation of school shootings and child migrant detention in the United States leaves me, as a Canadian consumer of news, shocked, wounded, and helpless. I find it painfully difficult to respond to the fractured and fragmented media reports of terrified, hurt children hurling down my Internet newsfeed. My reactions tend to take on a lyrical, poetic tone as I connect words with my own visual images of suffering children and my wish for alleviation of their pain.

If "one task of a publicly vibrant poetry is to challenge social, political, and moral orders,"[1] I turn to poetic inquiry as a call for action. In its own uniquely pedagogical way, "poetic inquiry is both a method and product of research activity…to effect social change."[2] Here, I offer poetry to reflect on the violence against children that I have witnessed in the media. When I interweave verse with social science research, it becomes a poetic inquiry into a human phenomenon that urgently needs a solution. When school children die in a shower of bullets or shiver uncontrollably on a cold migrant detention center floor, their plight becomes a social justice issue. I merge online news research with my own imaginings as a media witness to these events.

In the 2018 Marjory Stoneman Douglas High School shooting, a disturbed student opened fire on his classmates. In this poem, I imagine the chaotic scene in the classroom and call for poetic justice.

> A shower of bullets rains
> across the classroom, splatters
> blood on landscape drawings,
> fanning crimson blots
> onto sketch pads and children
> quaking under tables.
>
> A girl drags a boy into a closet,
> caresses his quivering back.
> A teenager films the room
> on his phone, holding his gun
> high with glee while children
> beg for mercy.
>
> Dear parents, we regret to inform
> you, art class is cancelled. The big
> box outlet had a gun sale. Let us
> know when your kids make it home.
> We'll tell you more about program
> cuts to art and music later.
>
> If they survive—
>
> Circulate a poetic
>   peace
>   pact.
>
> Protest
>   violence
>   against
>   children.

Every year, several hundred thousand children gather at the Phra Dhammakaya Temple in Thailand to participate in the annual V-Star Change the World outdoor meditation for peace and contemplate their role as world citizens. For three months prior to the event, they perform daily tasks, such as helping around the house, making their beds, and saving money. Then they go to the temple to chant and practice sitting meditation, a skill they can transfer to daily life. The organizers of this event believe that meditation has a transformative effect on self and, subsequently, society. As Phramaha Somchai Thanavuddho, the Buddhist monk interviewed, maintains, "if we are going to change the world, we need to have children change themselves first."[3] One girl asserts that fifteen minutes of daily meditation enhances her life and her studies. Here, I praise these students' parents for their children's wondrous mindfulness.

> Dear parents, your singing children
> illuminate the sky, sit, meditate,
> vibrate peace into the earth,
> a green channel of light.
> They birth
> joy, life.
> Breathe.

Across the world in a Baltimore elementary school, distressed children, who in traditional contexts might endure stringent punishment, can access the decorative and interactive Mindful Moment Room, where they drink herbal tea, meditate, engage in focussed breathing practices, and discuss what transpired.[4] They experience more relief there than they would in silent, spartan detention rooms. Baltimore students begin and end the school day centering themselves through mindfulness and attending "to the stillness."[5] They achieve mental clarity through refreshing "belly breath," inhaling into their lungs then expelling out "all the ruminating thoughts and clearing [the] mind."[6] High school students lead meditations, following the Holistic Life Foundation's "reciprocal teaching model,"[7] then take the practices into their homes and neighborhoods, where they guide their parents and others in mindfulness. Inspired by their teachers, who engage in group practices while at school, these young people open their world to peace, joy, and calm, a protective home of imagination. Here, I merge my recollections of rolling across the moistened morning lawn during childhood with an illuminating moment of mindful awareness.

Take a breath,
exhale,
sprawl under blue
sky, sapphire
sun.
If you're still breathing
come morning,
somersault on dewy
lawns, laugh, sniff
lavender, watch honeybees
pollinate—dawn
of a new day.

The development of mindful, productive citizens should, indeed, start in the sanctuary of home. French philosopher Bachelard asserts that the "house shelters daydreaming, the house protects the dreamer, the house allows one to dream in peace."[8] Like a "large cradle,"[9] the house offers the secure and stable frame within which the "thoughts, memories, and dreams of mankind...[are bound by] the daydream"[10] and, thus, have a lasting impact on the individual, who might, otherwise, become a "dispersed being"[11] in society. For child migrants thrust into border town detention centers, home has become a caged enclosure where they sleep on the floor under flimsy blankets.[12] They weep with the acute anxiety of separation from their parents, their once secure and happy family homes now mere "memories of former dwelling-places...relived as daydreams."[13] For child survivors of school shootings, home should become their sanctuary but, if they relive the trauma in their dreams, they may no longer feel safe in the "cradle"[14] they once trusted. I ruminate here about how a mother might disconnect from the sanctuary of home when her child is abruptly and permanently torn away.

You left your lunch
on the table. I was going
to call you –

Last night, I heard
your footsteps
echo ...

I cleaned your room.
When—
you come home—

We'll—

In reflecting on the search for imaginative, fulfilling living, Greene cites Freire's assertion that the "'oppressed'...have to be aroused to a consciousness of how the real is constructed and...challenged to 'name' their lived worlds and, through the naming, to transform these worlds."[15] When they release themselves from silence, their renewed feeling of hope may enable them to commune with other people and develop wholesome lives. In finding hope, they may take confident, humane action to awaken their communities to imaginative ways of being in their worlds. Greene emphasizes the role of imagination in our desensitized "world of fearful moral uncertainty,"[16] in elevating our visual and auditory sense perceptions to higher frequencies as we channel our awareness of what has been repressed into art. In this way, we may "touch the ultimate poetic depth of the space of the house."[17]

I write this poem in honor of Marjory Stoneman Douglas High School shooting survivor Emma Gonzalez, who bravely spoke out for a judicious end to school gun violence.

> "'6 minutes and 20 seconds."[18]
> The time it took for Emma
> Gonzalez to name
> her lived world,
>
> to voice
>   an incantation.
>
> "'We call B.S.'"[19]
>
> "'6 minutes and 20 seconds.'"[20]
> Seventeen bullet-ridden
> students left the earth—
> bedrooms empty.
>
>
> And now the people
> abandon their homes
> and march.
>
> Break the silence.
>   Chant—
>
> "'Never again! Never again!'"[21]
>
> Rant
>   resistance
>   poetry.

Gandhi asserts that "[n]onviolence...has no cause for fear."[22] The trick to alleviating violence lies in projecting compassion onto our enemies: "It is nonviolence only when we love those that hate us."[23] In the home of aesthetic imagination, we may dwell in the space of *ahimsa,* or nonviolence, abandoning *himsa* by putting down our physical and emotional weapons and cultivating inner disarmament. Gandhi states that he can control his feelings of anger, attaining an indescribable awareness of "peace and a meaning of the mysteries of nature."[24] Like Gandhi, adherents of nonviolence continually practice peace, for they know the struggle to change the world begins within themselves in abandoning fear of others and releasing imagined adversaries.

When I witnessed the March 24, 2018, Seattle "March for Our Lives" protest, I saw demonstrators holding banners proclaiming, "Guns are not school supplies."[25] Here, I reflect on the incongruous correlation between school gun violence preparedness, student writing implements, and the weapons themselves, a powerful one being a tranquil mind.

> No more shooting drills! Pens
> aren't semiautomatics. Running
> drills belong in PE class. Up
> the track. Rest 30 seconds. Race
> back down. Hit a home run. Hurl
> your bodies onto home plate,
> not the floor under your desks,
> not a table in the morgue.
>
> Meditate twenty minutes
> before morning class.
> Listen to the singing birds,
> inhale lilies and tulips,
> the brilliant yellow sun
> a pigment in blue skies.

When captured in a poetic narrative, the poignant visual images of Syrian children running from their bombed homes or their American counterparts marching for gun control in Washington give rise to a powerful voice. Gandhi's concept of *ahimsa* resonates in contemplative poetry and art, where we can relocate our displaced space of home and daydream in a call for our children to reclaim it. We can take inspiration from Friedl Dicker-Brandeis's teaching of aesthetic art to children in concentration camps, a pedagogy which "created a psychological space of empowerment and meaning in the midst of oppression and horror."[26] Following the Bauhaus art school's aesthetic practice of "externalizing...inner experiences of things...to render...the outer physical appearances of such things,"[27] she taught the children contemplative visual techniques to hone their subjects' essence, whether the image of another person or a plant. In this way, they could connect "the self and the other, including things of the natural world."[28] When her students drew pictures of their enjoyments and dreams, they were "'transported'"[29] to worlds far away from the concentration camp. Dicker-Brandeis claimed that she harnessed the children's energetic spirit of creativity "'to stimulate fantasy and imagination and strengthen [their] ability to judge, appreciate, observe, [and] endure.'"[30] Even if the children perished in the camp, their artwork empowered them to reflect intuitively and perceptively on their own inner and outer worlds and, thus, cope with their dark, chaotic external reality. Their example suggests that children, as well as adults, who create contemplative art reflecting difficult childhood experiences may release their own embedded trauma and begin to envision a template for a more ideal world. Survivors of detention centers and school shootings may find art a therapeutic practice for processing traumatic memory.

Dicker-Brandeis's courageous teaching of art to prisoners has inspired me to reflect on the therapeutic value of drawing trauma.

> Rifle pointed, silhouette
> of a boy crouching,
> sparrows twitter on tree
> branches.

> Sketch of a shadow—
> seen in a dream or
> a courtyard. Artist
> unknown.

> Could he be your
> brother, classmate,
> imaginary friend?
> Draw to paint
> away nightmares.

The poetry of protest, accompanied by visual images, offers writers an opportunity to draw out their inner outrage at violent abuse of children in school shootings, bombings, domestic disputes, and other vehement acts, including natural disasters. Lorie Shaull's installation of 7000 pairs of shoes on Washington's Capitol Hill lawn,[31] representing children who have died in shootings since the Sandy Hook incident, projects a shocking, aesthetically poignant image of protest. I imagine the faces of the children and the feet that once inhabited the shoes, while recalling media photographs of tiny shoes strewn in street rubble in war-torn countries. The haunting beauty of this photograph conveys a chilling message to me as the perceiver.

Shaull's poignant photo of pairs of shoes lining the Capitol Hill lawn moves me to ruminate on the empty shoes of children who lost their lives in civil violence, where bombs that supersede guns decimate the social infrastructure.

> Only shoes remain
> in the bombed-out market.
> Tiny x-sizes.
> A tattered shred of cloth
> hangs on the wall,
> final remnants of a life.
> Perhaps a genius,
> or aspiring mom.
>
> Lost love. Aborted dreams.
> No final resting place,
> just memories.
>
> Shoes now artifacts
> of strafed museums.

Images like Lynn Hershman Leeson's Tillie, the Telerobotic Doll 1995-1998,[32] draw our attention to the use of children for surveillance and acts of terrorism. Visitors to the 2018 Art in the Age of the Internet, 1989 to Today exhibit at The Institute of Contemporary Art/Boston[33] could look through Tillie's penetrating camera eyes by clicking an online link and viewing, on their phones and tablets, the external environment from her perspective. To me, her blank yet penetrating stare reflects the mental state of a witness scarred by inhumanities inflicted by adults, governments, accidents, or even whimsical acts of nature. I wonder if her vacant expression would match that of a child cooped up in a detention center, a survivor of a school shooting, a young refugee, or the Thai soccer players trapped in a flooded cave for eighteen days.[34]

Media images of sleeping children wrapped in foil blankets on American detention center floors and in the flooded cave in Thailand sadden me as I reflect on how much they must miss their warm, cozy bedrooms in homes so far away, even long gone. How they must cry themselves to sleep!

Toddlers crawl on chilly concrete
floors, cuddle sisters, foil space
blankets wound around bony
ribs, sleep inside a metal cage, a
haunting, cries for mama shivering
echoes on spartan detention walls,
dreams of warm bedrooms grown
cold, home a memory fading with
the evening light—

while miles away, thirteen boys
huddle in a cave, rushing waters
graze bare legs, fester skin gashes,
time a waning moon, cries for mama
vanish into rock, dinner a dry protein
bar and stalactite water,[35] spirits whisper
love poems into quivering ears,
dreams of cozy beds a mirage
like the long swim home.

Child witnesses of war, floods,
earthquakes stare into cameras,
photos shot by dogged journalists.
Their telerobotic eyes document
time, date, location of indignities
to ripening minds and bodies.

Cry, children, cry, embrace
your stolen child. Crawl
out of the cave. Cut
the cage wires. Rush
into a fresh breeze.

Demand the stalking bear
depart from your dreams.

Children in detention centers cry for parents they don't know whether they will see again, a "cry...from deep in [their] hearts...from the wounded child within,"[36] that shakes the cells of their sprouting bodies. Later in life, they may hear this hurt inner child calling to them. They may take their child on a mountain trek or forest bathing and see that the people who hurt them once suffered harm to themselves. Their revelations may enable them to generate self-compassion then compassion for others as they relocate their displaced space of home and daydreaming in a call to reclaim it.

I conclude with a call for an Ahimsa Pact, an awakening, a signing of a declaration on nonviolence, for the illumination of a light at the end of a dark, enclosed tunnel.

> Practice cave
> meditation.
> Swim out
> its narrow
> chambers.
> Walk
> in peace.

> Scrawl ahimsa
> poetry
> on school
> walls.

Notes

1. Fisher, "Outside the Republic," 977.

2. Faulkner, "Poetic Inquiry," 210.

3. "One Million Children."

4. Haupt, "Mindfulness in Schools."

5. Ibid.

6. Ibid.

7. Ibid.

8. Bachelard, *The Poetics of Space*, 6.

9. Ibid., 7.

10. Ibid., 6.

11. Ibid., 7.

12. Raff, "Kids Describe the Fear."

13. Bachelard, *Poetics*, 6.

14. Ibid., 7.

15. Greene, *Releasing the Imagination*, 24.

16. Ibid., 122.

17. Bachelard, *Poetics*, 6.

18. "Emma Gonzalez's POWERFUL March."

19. Mead, "Joan of Arc."

20. "Emma Gonzalez's POWERFUL March."

21. Ibid.

22. Gandhi, *All Men Are Brothers*, 89.

23. Ibid., 90.

24. Ibid. 90.

25. Cornwell, "How It Unfolded."

26. Wix, "Aesthetic Empathy," 152.

27. Ibid., 153.

28. Ibid., 153.

29. Ibid., 154.

30. Ibid., 154.

31. Shaull, "Capitol Lawn Covered."

32. Hershman Leeson, "Tillie."

33. ICA, "Art in the Age."

34. Flynn, "Miracle."

35. Ibid. 36. Nhat Hanh, "Healing the Child."

Bibliography

Bachelard, Gaston. *The Poetics of Space*. Translated by Maria Jolas. Presses Universitaires de France, 1958. Reprint Boston: Beacon Press, 1994.

Cornwell, Paige. "How It Unfolded: Seattle's March For Our Lives." *The Seattle Times*, March 24, 2018, https://www.seattletimes.com/seattle-news/seattle-march-for-our-lives-against-gun-violence-today/

"Emma Gonzalez's POWERFUL March for Our Lives Speech." YouTube video, 6:45. Posted by "Reflect," March 24, 2018. https://www.youtube.com/watch?v=l_RB_3Oqk7c.

Faulkner, Sandra. "Poetic Inquiry: Poetry as/in/for Social Research." In *Handbook of Arts-Based Research*, edited by Patricia Leavy, 208-30. New York: Guildford Press, 2018.

Fisher, Thomas. "Outside the Republic: A Visionary Political Poetics." *Textual Practice* 23, no. 6 (2009): 975-86. doi: 10.1080/09502360903361600.

Flynn, Sean. "Miracle at Tham Luang." *GQ*, December 3, 2018. https://www.gq.com/story/thai-cave-rescue-miracle-at-tham-luang.

Gandhi, Mohandas Karamchand. *All Men Are Brothers: Autobiographical Reflections*. 1958. Reprint, London: Bloomsbury, 2013.

Greene, Maxine. *Releasing the Imagination: Essays on Education, the Arts, and Social Change.* San Francisco: Jossey-Bass, 1995.

Haupt, Angela. "Mindfulness in Schools: When Meditation Replaces Detention: Why Breathing and Movement Exercises—and Quiet Time—Belong in the Classroom." *U.S. News & World Report,* December 8, 2016. https://health.usnews.com/wellness/mind/articles/2016-12-08/mindfulness-in-schools-when-meditation-replaces-detention.

Hershman, Leeson, Lynn. "Tillie, the Telerobotic Doll." Accessed March 31, 2019. http://www.lynnhershman.com/tillie/.

ICA Institute of Contemporary Art/Boston. *Tillie the Telerobotic Doll, 1995-1998 Art in the Age of the Internet, 1989 to Today.* (2019) February 7-May 18, 2018. Available at: https://www.icaboston.org/exhibitions/art-age-internet-1989-today. [Accessed 30 March 2019].

Mead, Rebecca. "Joan of Arc and the Passion of Emma González." *The New Yorker,* March 26, 2018. https://www.newyorker.com/culture/cultural-comment/the-passion-of-emma-gonzalez.

Nhat Hanh, Thich. "Thich Nhat Hanh on Healing the Child Within." *Lion's Roar: Buddhist Wisdom for Our Time,* December 24, 2018. https://www.lionsroar.com/healing-the-child-within/.

"'One Million Children' Join Buddhist Meditation Event.'" *BBC News Asia.* Posted by Aggarat Bansong, January 15, 2013. https://www.bbc.com/news/av/world-asia-21016612/one-million-children-join-buddhist-meditation-event.

Raff, Jeremy. "Kids Describe the Fear of Separation At The Border." *The Atlantic,* June 30, 2018. https://www.theatlantic.com/politics/archive/2018/06/kids-describe-the-fear-of-separation-at-the-border/564227/?utm_campaign=the-atlantic&utm_source=facebook&utm_medium=social&utm_term=2018-06-30T19%.

Shaull, Lorie. "Capitol Lawn Covered in 7000 Pairs of Shoes, One for Every Child Killed Since Sandy Hook, Washington DC." Photograph. 2018. https://www.flickr.com/photos/number7cloud/40082169354/in/photolist-244VAvq-H21JV3-H21Lv7-H21Mm5.

Wix, Lanney. "Aesthetic Empathy in Teaching Art to Children: The Work of Friedl Dicker-Brandeis in Terezin." *Art Therapy: Journal of the American Art Therapy Association* 26, no. 4 (2009): 152-58. doi: 10.1080/07421656.2009.10129612.

18.

Spectators in a Tragedy

Natalie Honein

Poetry often embodies colorful musings of a poet's self and ruminations of her world. Yet poetry must also provoke the reader, raise consciousness, invoke compassion, and inflame. In this poetic inquiry, Honein reflects on the injustices of war that we, as detached observers, woefully witness on television screens and proceed to neglect. She considers the fate of refugees in crisis, particularly victims of the protracted war in Syria. The hardship of refugees has become recurrent, ordinary news, overshadowed by more compelling world headlines that come as welcome distractions from the shock of atrocities on the ground. In her poetry, Honein calls on spectators, each of us, to be attuned to the persistent injustices being committed toward refugees, and to be especially mindful of our inaction. It is in such moments of political turmoil and humanitarian vacuity that we need the power of poetry to remind us of the humanity of the "other."

Keywords: refugee, Syria, Aleppo, war, poetry, poetic inquiry

Poetry embodies colorful musings on our *selves* and ruminations on our world. In the face of injustice, poetry has a remarkable ability to raise consciousness and invoke compassion. By inquiring poetically into social injustice, we are better able to question our existing realities, raise doubts, and expose our vulnerabilities.[1] Poetic inquiry is thus particularly concerned with how a poem evolves,[2] and how meaning is made in the writing of the poem, or what Chase calls "retrospective meaning-making."[3]

In attempting to make meaning of the social injustice of war, this poetic inquiry addresses a prevailing reaction to, and perception of, refugees of the war in Syria that began in 2011. It considers the fate of refugees we woefully witness on television screens and then proceed to neglect. At the receiving end of oppression, refugees struggle against power, discrimination, and humanitarian and social injustice. The fate of these living casualties has become recurrent, mundane news, overshadowed by incessant headlines and intermissions that come as welcome distractions from the shock of atrocities on the ground. This poetic inquiry examines the role that we play as detached observers, spectators, waiting as an audience does, for the horror show to end.

Poetry has been written from a place of social and political activism across time and cultures. Much of contemporary western activist poetry has dealt with issues of victimization, oppression, and social injustice, particularly, issues concerning slavery, racial violence, women's rights, and more recently sexual identity. Such poetry is expressed powerfully by Maya Angelou:[4]

> Did you want to see me broken?
> Bowed head and lowered eyes?
> Shoulders falling down like teardrops,
> Weakened by my soulful cries.
>
> ...
>
> Out of the huts of history's shame
> I rise.
> Up from a past that's rooted in pain
> I rise.

Angelou's poetry on injustice echoes the writings of earlier poets, such as Chilean writer and activist Pablo Neruda. Neruda understood the power of poetry to effect political change, and articulated it in his verses. His poetry on action and social change epitomized resistance poetry.[5] Barbara Harlow called attention to resistance literature and poetry from Africa, the Middle East, and Latin America. She brought together writings that represented non-Western, national liberation movements, reminding us of the voice of the "other." Similarly, the eloquence and wealth of Arab poetry has been employed in writing about social injustice, emigration, and exile: notably, Abu Al-Qasim Al-Shabbi's poetry on the Tunisian revolution (later used during the Arab Spring uprisings); Kahlil Gibran's poetry on Arab national awakening in the face of the Ottoman Empire; and Mahmoud Darwish's poetry on Palestinian loss of home and identity:[6]

> To our land, and it is a prize of war,
> the freedom to die from longing and burning
> and our land, in its bloodied night,
> is a jewel that glimmers for the far upon the far
> and illuminates what's outside it...
> As for us, inside,
> we suffocate more!

Darwish's poetry on exile rings true of the current state of Syrian refugees. In a tragedy such as the displacement of a population, poetic inquiry enables us to ask, who are the victims? The families fleeing persecution or those who have been trespassed upon? The ones forced to escape, or the ones forced to be hospitable? And if we are witnesses to the oppression of refugees, are we also victims? James states, "the further an inquiry goes, the more surprises we encounter."[7] Each line of this poetic inquiry led to a story, a new perspective, as the words were landing on the page. It allowed for recognition and articulation of different manifestations of pain—the undeniable suffering of refugees, but also the struggles of those forced to be hospitable, and even the guilt-ridden spectators compelled to act. Inquiring poetically into this humanitarian crisis gives us permission to articulate many facets of collateral damage, many facets of suffering.

A slaughtered soul

What's Aleppo?
he asked
as the city went down in flames
as millions fled their homes
as he ran for elections

We mocked him
pointed the finger at his ignorance
but he wasn't alone

What *is* Aleppo?
Do any of us remember
the oldest city in the world
the embrace of Christianity and Islam
home of centuries of civilizations
where art flourished
and architecture found its name?

Aleppo's soul
is the antithesis of extremism
and yet it fell
or for that,
it fell

Where *is* Aleppo?
Do any of us know?
How many of us have seen it
    witnessed
    experienced the horror
but on a screen?

Spectators

We sit
in comfortable living rooms
watching news
long enough to say we've seen it

We're told
the following report contains disturbing images
Unmindfully,
TV remote in hand
we change the channel
Thank god for warnings

We may feel guilty
helpless
we try to imagine the pain
shake our head in disbelief
we try hard to feel empathy
we try real hard
but it's not easy
when we see only
difference
scarves on heads
beards on faces
difference
brown
dark
angry
unwashed
difference

We don't recognize
we can't empathize
with men, women, children
escaping bombs
abandoning homes
crossing borders
their most valuable belongings
in one bag

Clutching existence

Ever wonder what's in that *one* bag?
What might *you* put in one bag?
your passport?
if you have one
if it's not expired?
your birth certificate?
your wallet, your cash?
How about the little brown teddy bear
your daughter can't sleep without?
her diapers,
a change of clothes
but how many?

What will go in your bag?
Your son's two EpiPens?
because you should never leave home with only one?
Sweaters to keep him warm,
hats, gloves for the winter looming?

How much more can you fit in that bag?

Maybe the photo albums you spent years creating?
for each child
perfectly labeled
on the shelf
And the only picture of your grandmother
who looks just like you,
will that go in your bag?

How about your cat?
the brown and white stray that adopted *you*
Who will feed her
keep her safe
listen to her purrs?
Will there be room for her
in that one bag?

Would you take the keys to your front door
hoping to return home?
Will the house stay standing,
will it still be yours?
You remember the Palestinians
still holding on
to the keys of their homes

no longer their homes
their land
no longer their land

It's safe to say you'll leave your father's old watch behind

Broken dignity

Where would you go
with one bag over your shoulder?
Suppose you cross the border
to an unwelcoming neighbor
scared small hands gripping your elbow

Too proud for tears of fear
weakness your own secret
you hope someone will open their door
you beg for your dignity to remain unbroken
you've made the passage
you've become a refugee

Pride is a peculiar thing

And pride breeds blame
blame the politicians
the terrorists
the ignorant
blame him
his regime
his injustice
blame society
those who profit
who believe in the wrong god
blame the *other*
always the *other*

Back in the living room
you ignore
you avoid
you deny
Aleppo
you wait for the tragedy to end
you wait
TV remote in hand

Numbness of defeat

Urged by conscience
or in search of purpose
the Lebanese-Syrian border
was closer than you expected
School diplomas in small hands
dressed in finest hand-me-downs
mismatched hair clips
outgrown princess crowns
piercing blue eyes
tanned faces
untouched by sunscreen

Urged by conscience
or eager to display humility
you reach out to her
almost invisible
taking up little space
"Where are you from?"
I don't know
barely a whisper

You ask again
"Are you Syrian or Lebanese?"
Syrian
numbness in her mannerism
traces of defeat in her eyes
"Where in Syria are you from?"
I'm from the Salem Refugee Camp
now, the only home she knows

Watching closely
her father sees your pity
We didn't ask for this
we came seeking refuge
we worked the land
never been hungry
we're artists and teachers
engineers and doctors
proud of our civilization
we don't need your pity
spare us that look on your face

Pride is a peculiar thing

Urged by conscience
or desperate to display empathy
you nod in agreement
slightly shamed

Varieties of pain

In the back seat
pondering guilt, privilege, injustice
you're interrupted with perfect English
the taxi driver speaks unsolicited
expecting the nod of agreement
when discussing *them*

I went to college, my friend
managed a warehouse for twenty years
We all lost our jobs
to those refugees
they're paid half our salary
they get stipends for school
housing for their family
while we're left in the dirt
in our own country

Recalling the traces of defeat in her eyes
you protest
"But they've lost their homes,
forced out of their land
whole families in one tent
They're artists, engineers, doctors
proud as we are
They've not chosen this path"

Have we?
they're a quarter of our population
a high price to pay for opening our borders
a high price to pay for their war
What does my family get in return?
I lose my job and my dignity

Eager to display empathy
to yet another audience
you nod in agreement
recognizing the many varieties of pride
the many varieties of suffering

Cleared by conscience
attempt executed
a gentle pat on the back
the brown and white stray
purring on your lap
you watch
as new horror shows unfold
Somalis, Libyans
Yazidis, Rohingyas
perpetual journeys of social injustice
perpetual journeys of bags
crossing
borders

Mindfully,
you wait
for the tragedies to end
you wait
TV remote in hand
you're reminded
the following report contains disturbing images
Thank god for warnings

Poetry's strength lies in exposing realities and demanding visibility. The reality of the war in Syria has not been limited to its borders, but has leaked into, or rather flooded, its bordering countries with millions of displaced families. What began as a refugee tragedy on the Syrian stage soon drew in its audience of neighbors, unwilling hosts, as well as sofa spectators to take part in the performance—all experiencing pain in one form or another. Spectators *of* the tragedy became spectators *in* the tragedy. Through poetic inquiry, we are able to reflect on such a reality and be reminded of our blindness to the humanity of the "other." It allows us to recognize the challenges faced by living casualties of war, and the inaction of those of us witnessing developments from a distance. In these moments, as Lorde has stated, poetry becomes not a luxury, but a necessity.[8] It becomes a choice between changing the channel, heeding news warnings, or facing the reality and seeing, with eyes open, the existing fate of refugees and the sweeping consequences of such a tragedy.

Notes

1. Prendergast, Leggo, & Sameshima, *Poetic Inquiry.*

2. Richardson, "Musings on Experiences," 242.

3. Chase, "Narrative Inquiry," 656.

4. Angelou, "Still I Rise," 41-42.

5. Eisner, *The Essential Neruda.*

6. Darwish, "To our land," 203.

7. James, "what lovely words," 23.

8. Lorde, *Sister Outsider*, 37.

Bibliography

Angelou, Maya. "Still I Rise." *And Still I Rise: A Book of Poems.* New York: Random House, 1978.

Bushrui, Suheil and Malarkey, James, Eds. *Desert Songs of the Night: 1500 Years of Arabic Literature.* London: Saki Books, 2015.

Chase, Susan. "Narrative Inquiry: Multiple Lenses, Approaches, Voices." In *The Sage Handbook of Qualitative Research*, 3rd ed, 651-679. Edited by Norman Denzin and Yvonna Lincoln. Thousand Oaks, CA: Sage Publications, 2005.

Darwish, Mahmoud. "To Our Land." *Butterfly's Burden.* Washington: Copper Canyon Press, 2007.

Eisner, Mark. *The Essential Neruda: Selected Poems.* San Francisco, CA: City Lights Books, 2004.

Gebran, Kahlil. *The Garden of the Prophet.* London: Heinemann, 1935.

Harlow, Barbara. *Resistance Literature.* London: Methuen Press, 1987.

James, Kedrick. "what lovely words might also mean." In *Poetic Inquiry III: Enchantments of Place*, 23-27. Edited by Pauline Sameshima, Alexandra Fidyk, Kedrick James, and Carl Leggo. Wilmington, DE: Vernon Press, 2017.

Lorde, Audre. *Sister Outsider: Essays and Speeches.* Berkeley, CA: Crossing Press, 1984.

Prendergast, Monica, Carl Leggo, and Pauline Sameshima, Eds. *Poetic Inquiry: Vibrant Voices in the Social Sciences.* Rotterdam: Sense Publishers, 2009.

Richardson, Pamela. "Musings on Experiences of Poetic Time." In *Poetic Inquiry III: Enchantments of Place*, 241-249. Edited by Pauline Sameshima, Alexandra Fidyk, Kedrick James, and Carl Leggo. Wilmington, DE: Vernon Press, 2017.

19.

War and the Lyric Voice:
An Intergenerational Narrative

Gisela Ruebsaat

Heather McLeod,
Memorial University in St. John's, Newfoundland

In this article, a found poem is used to explore the impact of war on two young people and to examine their efforts to come to terms with war-related propaganda. The poem is drawn from personal writings by the authors' parents during and shortly after WWII. By juxtaposing documentary excerpts and organizing them thematically, the intent is to illustrate how these two young people responded and resisted in different ways related to their gender, geographic location, and cultural position and to show that the tone of the language used to express their response was also filtered through the lenses of gender, geography and culture. This work is informed by emerging qualitative research methodologies including duoethnography and poetic inquiry as well as by historical literature regarding youth movements during WWII.

Keywords: youth and war, women in Nazi Germany, duoethnography, poetic inquiry, war narratives, intergenerational narratives

Informed by poetic inquiry and duoethnography, we are engaged in an ongoing project focused on poetic and aesthetic responses to our parents' deaths.[1] As young people, Gisela's mother and Heather's father each developed an artistic voice and sensibility in response to the dislocation they experienced due to the Second World War, poverty, and social exclusion (e.g., class, gender, geography, culture/language). In Ursula's (Gisela's mother) case she expressed herself through weaving, knitting, music-making, storytelling, and diary writing; in Donald's (Heather's father) case it was his poetry and other writings, which called for social justice. The writings of Maxine Greene frame our understanding that our parents' artistic expressions allowed them to transcend the confines of the historical moment in which they found themselves.[2] Their writings helped them come to terms with and navigate through the personal and political injustice they encountered. Our own voices have developed in part as a response to the historical forces of our generation, but our narratives have also been shaped by the proto-narratives inherited from our parents. It is this learning to see things differently that speaks to issues of social justice.

Poetic Inquiry

Poetic inquiry is an original and inventive research method because poetry is a particularly direct kind of research; poetry expresses everyday life in its lived language.[3] Boughn considers poetry as knowledge in a linguistic mode in which knowing is multitudinous, varied, vigorous, and stratified all at once.[4] Prendergast holds that poetic inquiries can be categorized according to the voice that is employed.[5] Our work combines two categories: 1. Vox Autobiographia/Autoethnographia: a researcher-voiced poem in which the data source consists of reflective / creative / autobiographical / autoethnographical writing (our writing about our parents) and, 2. Vox Participare: participant-voiced poems (the diary of Gisela's mother and the poem by Heather's father).

In this chapter, we use the vehicle of a found poem—"War Triptych: A Young Person's Primer"—to explore the impact of war on two young people. One is male and one female, one geographically and culturally removed from the violence and one in the thick of it. The found poem is distilled from two documents: excerpts from Heather's father's poem and excerpts from Gisela's mother's diary. We feel the found poem, "War Triptych," speaks to social justice issues in the following ways:

- The poem illustrates how both Ursula and Donald were impacted by and struggled to overcome war-related propaganda.
- It illustrates how they responded and resisted in different ways related to their gender, geographic location, and cultural positioning.
- It illustrates how the language they used to express their response was also filtered through the lens of their gender, geography, and culture.

Donald McLeod age 15—Poem Written in his mother tongue: English circa 1945	Ursula Schumacher —Diary Original 1941-45/ Translated into English by her daughter age 61— 2017/2018	Ursula Schumacher age 16 —Diary Written in her mothertongue—1941-45
Document Geography: North America	Document Geography: North America	Document Geography: Europe

Lying and Deceiving	June 22, 1941: We Made Them Sandwiches	22.6.41

Lying and Deceiving

By a foul treachery
Lying and deceiving
In 1933 he took power
of the Reich
Starting out the
world to conquer

And now the stage
for human misery set
He gave them work and
bread
The work this world
to conquer

First with the Jews
And then with
followers of Marx
These wretches he did
slay
For he wished a world
to conquer
And they stood in his
way
The concentration
sites
Of squalid hut and
barb wire
Were filled to
overflowing
With Blood, sweat and
tears and Rotten
flesh
The whole world yet
to conquer
And to the sound of
human cries
From camps and murder
chambers
The remaining world
was deaf
He had not yet them
conquered
They gave Him wire

**June 22, 1941:
We Made Them Sandwiches**

Then we went to Wurzburg and visited a military hospital for paratroopers. We made them sandwiches. Then they invited us to an evening variety show. It was lovely! I got to know Sepp. The paratroopers fought in Crete. We would have liked to stay a bit longer. This morning at 5am, war with Russia!
(June 22 1941 operation Barbarossa launched)

**March 19, 1944:
Political Seminars**

Now I have already been in the Third Reich Labour Force camp in Niederbrombach for 2 weeks! The landscape is nice but I don't like it here. I am always homesick. Mornings at 5:30 is reveille and physical training. At 7am, coffee. Subsequently, singing and then work begins at 8am and continues until 4pm in the afternoon. Then we have political seminars till lights out. There are 6 high school graduates in the camp. We joined a full contingent of workers. The girls are very nice but they are city girls.

22.6.41

Dann sind wir noch nach Würzburg gefahren. Wir haben dort ein Lazarett von Fallschirmjägern besucht und ihnen Brote geschmiert. Dann haben sie uns eingeladen abends zum Varieté. Es war prima! Ich hab da den Sepp kennen gelernt. Die Fallschirmjäger hatten auf Kreta mitgekämpft. Wir wären gerne noch länger da geblieben! Heute morgen um 5 Uhr Krieg mit Rußland

19.3.44

Nun bin ich schon 2 Wochen in Niederbrombach im R.A.D. Lager!! Die Landschaft ist ganz schön, aber es gefällt mir gar nicht. Ich hab immer Heimweh. Morgens um ½ 6 ist Wecken und Frühsport. Um 7 Uhr Kaffeetrinken. Anschließend Singen und um 8 Uhr beginnt die Arbeit bis mittags um 4 Uhr. Dann haben wir Schulungen bis zum Schlafengehen. Wir sind 6 Abiturientinnen hier im Lager. Wir kamen in eine volle Belegschaft herein. Die Mädel sind ganz nett, aber Großstadtmädel.

Donald McLeod age 15—Poem Written in his mother tongue: English circa 1945	Ursula Schumacher —Diary Original 1941-45/ Translated into English by her daughter age 61— 2017/2018	Ursula Schumacher age 16 —Diary Written in her mothertongue—1941-45
He gave them butter Which from his own he'd wrested Tools! He would them yet conquer. And then the devil thought that it befitting of his slaves To worship Him and he'd for them They follow him As sheep unto the slaughter They gave their thoughts, they gave their family They gave both son and daughter To that mad man who Was the world to conquer.	I would be happy if I could get out of here soon. This tightness in my chest makes me crazy. Am I a mother's baby? Why am I so homesick? What is going on?	Aber froh wäre ich, wenn ich bald wieder hier heraus käme. Dieser Knoten im Hals kann mich verrückt machen. Bin ich denn eigentlich so ein Mutterkindchen, daß ich so Heimweh habe, oder was macht das?
Slovakia, Poland, on to France Next in the plans Slovakia, Poland, on to France The Third Reich did advance They tried then the world to conquer Prague was given Warsaw did fall The Lowlands were swamped beneath the tide No ebb war yet, the tide rushed on	**January 17, 1943: At Some Point** Now it is once again still and lonely here. I am so sick of the war as never before. Hopefully, it will end soon. At some point it has to stop.	**17. 1. 43** Jetzt ist es wieder still und einsam hier. Ich bin den Krieg so satt. Wie noch nie! Hoffentlich ist er bald zu Ende. Einmal muß er ja aufhören!
	February 27, 1944: Love It is lovely when one is coddled and surrounded by love.	**27. 2. 44** Es ist so schön, wenn man so umhegt und mit Liebe umgeben wird.

Donald McLeod age 15—Poem Written in his mother tongue: English circa 1945	Ursula Schumacher —Diary Original 1941-45/ Translated into English by her daughter age 61— 2017/2018	Ursula Schumacher age 16 —Diary Written in her mothertongue—1941-45
The Vichy Came the Nazi Fuhrer to Hail France gave to defeat Paree was gone with all its gay existence The Vichy came The Nazi Fuhrer to hail Was he not the world conqueror!	**January 1944: When I Think of the Other Women** On New Year's we all felt a bit melancholy. As the clock struck midnight, the thing I most wanted to do was cry. I don't know why. On New Year's Day I again had that feeling of abandonment that I hadn't had for a long time. Helmut didn't come and I was alone. Leni came over at 3 and Helmut and Edi at 3:30. We sang and played. Towards evening I was happy again. Soon I will surely have to go back to the labour force camp. Maybe I will be lucky and be posted nearby.	**6. 1. 44** Auch waren sie alle ein klein bißchen wehmütig gestimmt. Als es 12 Uhr schlug hätte ich am liebsten geweint. Warum weiß ich nicht. Am Neujahrstag hatte ich seit langer Zeit das 1. Mal wieder so ein verlassenes Gefühl. Helmut kam nicht und ich war allein. Um 3 Uhr kam Leni und um ½ 4 Uhr Helmut und Edi. Wir haben gesungen und gespielt. Gegen Abend wurde ich wieder froh. Sicher, ich muß bald in den Arbeitsdienst: aber vielleicht habe ich Glück und komme nicht so weit fort.
	This time the parting was more difficult than ever before. But when I think of the other women who had to let their loved ones go to Russia, I see myself as very ungrateful.	Diesmal ist mir der Abschied so schwer geworden wie noch nie. Aber wenn ich dann an andere Frauen denke die ihre Liebsten nach Rußland gehen lassen müssen komme ich mir direkt undankbar vor.
It'll Only be Weeks Was not the Balkans gone Britain could alone not save the world With the Red Bear upon his perch Was all to go well, It'll be only weeks and all world he'll conquer. **The Bear He Would Bear** And then this fool on what was once a tool	**January 27, 1945: Well Well** The Russians are storming in from the east. Marienburg, Posen, etc. are being fought over. One could become despondent but strangely enough I have hope that everything will go well. Well, so many young men must also believe in this.	**27. 1. 45** Die Russen stürmen von Osten an. Marienburg, Posen usw. sind umkämpft. Man könnte mutlos werden. aber seltsamer Weise habe ich die Hoffnung daß alles gut geht. Nur müssen so viele junge Kerle daran glauben.

Donald McLeod age 15—Poem Written in his mother tongue: English circa 1945	Ursula Schumacher —Diary Original 1941-45/ Translated into English by her daughter age 61— 2017/2018	Ursula Schumacher age 16 —Diary Written in her mothertongue—1941-45
Started new offensives But ah the Bear he would bear To have his people murdered Ah no he would be the conqueror		
People Would not Admit Defeat Factories hummed planes soared Tanks battled and guns roared But these people would not admit defeat At Berlin he raged he swore His hands he wrung, his hair he tore Knew they not he was to win the war	**February 18, 1945: One is Not Permitted to Ask Why** Who knows whether I will ever get back to Rheinberg. The enemies are already in Kleve. I am so worried about my mother. Good thing that at least father is nearby. I could easily run away from here. Mail isn't coming. I don't even know what is happening to my loved ones. It could be that I will be left here totally alone. Can we withstand this attack or will we be displaced? I just can't believe it. What will become of us? What will become of the German men? I dare not think about it. Some type of resolution must come of this. God cannot completely abandon our poor people. Surely we are not any worse than the others.	**18.2.45** Wer weiß. ob ich überhaupt noch einmal nach Rheinberg komme. In Kleve sind die Feinde schon. Ich hab so Angst um Mutter. Gut daß Vater wenigstens in der Nähe ist. Ich könnte glatt davon laufen hier. Post kommt nicht. Ich weiß gar nicht. wie es meinen lieben geht. Es kommt noch. daß ich ganz allein da steh. Ob wir diesem Ansturm noch lange stand halten können u. sogar vertreiben? Ich kann es bald nicht mehr glauben. Aber was wird dann aus uns? Was wird mit den deutschen Männern? Ich darf gar nicht darüber nachdenken. Es muß irgendeine gute Lösung kommen. Gott kann unser armes Volk nicht ganz verlassen. Wir sind doch nicht schlechter als die anderen auch.
	One is not permitted to ask why. My father also did not know what to advise. I must go to the air defence. It can't last much longer. Will I become a German soldier.	Warum darf man gar nicht mehr fragen. Vater wußte auch keinen Rat. Ich geh zur Flak. lange kann es ja so nicht mehr fragen. Vater wusste auch keinen Rat. Ich gehe zur Flak. lange kann es ja so night mehr dauern. Werde ich deutscher Soldat.

Donald McLeod age 15—Poem Written in his mother tongue: English circa 1945	Ursula Schumacher —Diary Original 1941-45/ Translated into English by her daughter age 61— 2017/2018	Ursula Schumacher age 16 —Diary Written in her mothertongue—1941-45
They Burned Their Earth They smashed their barns They burned their earth so red They bled their wine and destroyed their bread Without which the conqueror cannot conquer When Winter came the Aryan froze or starved In a fertile land he had wrested From those who knew it's key Here was his world That which his might had conquered	**January 13, 1945: Familiar** Now I have suffered hunger for the first time. Yes, real hunger. Well yeah, I guess one has to experience everything at some point.	**13.1.45** *Jetzt habe ich das erste Mal Hunger gelitten. Ja, tatsächlich Hunger. Nun ja. Alles muß man mal kennenlernen.*
Many Lived to be Driven from Soil They fought, they died With the madness for to conquer Oh many died, relief from hellish misery But many lived to be driven from soil of honest men For now, the tide was turned.	**September 21, 1943: We are Simply Not Yet Complete People** Helmut and I have been having constant arguments. Over minor matters. Why? We are simply not yet fully formed people. Today the Brandenbusches were notified that Gunter is missing. It's terrible. One person after another is lost. All the lovely lads. The loss of Norbert hurt me the most. But they are not dead to me. They still live somewhere, they just won't ever come home again.	**21.9.43** *Helmut und ich hatten dauernd Streit. Über ganze Kleinigkeiten. Warum? Wir sind eben beide noch keine fertigen Menschen und müssen uns eben noch abschleifen. Heute bekamen Brandenbusch die Nachricht daß Günter vermißt ist. Es ist furchtbar. Einer nach dem andern bleibt draußen. Alle die lieben Kerle. Am meisten hat es mich bei Norbert geschmerzt. Aber sie sind für mich nicht tot. Sie leben irgendwo. kommen nur nicht mehr nach Hause.*

Gisela's Reflections

This chapter is part of an ongoing project exploring personal and social histories of our parents and how this has influenced our own trajectories as writers and researchers. My mother, Ursula Schumacher, was born in the Rhineland in 1925, the eldest of three girls. As a poet and researcher, I am interested in investigating the impact the war and the Nazi youth program had on the evolution of my mother's social and gender identity. Ursula's father, Herbert, was a math and physical education teacher at an all-boys school. He encouraged both academic excellence and physical prowess in his daughters. During the war years, Herbert was away serving as a soldier. The Schumacher household reconfigured as all-female. In the early 1940s, my mother was conscripted to work in the Arbeitsdienst (the Reich Labour Service). During this time period, young girls were removed from their home communities to provide free labor for the war effort.[6] They lived in camps and political "training" was an important component of camp life. In my poems, I have documented aspects of my mother's war experience and my relationship to it. The poems are based on interviews with Ursula before her death, as well as on anecdotes I heard as a child.[7] In this chapter, I focus on working more directly with my mother's written voice as expressed in her diary.

The Found Poem as Artifact. Rather than adopting an analytical approach, I wanted to investigate what my mother's personal voice might reveal about her burgeoning transformation from girl to woman and the social forces, including the Nazi youth propaganda machine, that influenced this process.[8] I worked with her diary, first through the filter of my translation from German to English. Then I sat with the text, rereading it often and in both languages to attune my ear not so much to the meaning of words but to an underlying lyrical refrain. I then excerpted text fragments that best captured the lyric voice. The fragments became a rudimentary found poem. Then in dialogue with my co-author, I reflected on the text in relation to her father's more didactic war poem written when he was a young man viewing the war from overseas. We identified both resonances and dissonances between the two poems. During this process, certain fragments within both poems were "shed" and others highlighted.

As the culmination of this exegesis and dialogue, I created the found poem: "War Triptych: A Young Person's Primer." A triptych consists of three artistic, musical, or literary works meant to be considered together. The three parts may be closely related or presented in contrast to one another.[9] The triptych does not dictate which voice is to be read first. Arguably in our case, this makes the filtering process more transparent, namely, the translation of the original German text and the juxtaposition of contrasting voices. The triptych poem acts as a visual artifact similar to a medieval altarpiece. In "War Triptych," different fonts remind the reader that the three different voices emerge from different times and places. The diary excerpts are presented thematically rather than chronologically. The piece is both a literary and visual puzzle, to be appreciated with a spirit of play and discovery.

Heather's Reflections

I explore my father's teenage poem that lay unread since his death from cancer at age forty-four in 1974. For him, writing poetry was an opportunity to chart the trials and tribulations of his experience.[10] He was born Donald Kenneth to working-class Scottish immigrants in Winnipeg in 1929. Within a few years my grandfather, an electrician, lost his job in the economic depression of the 1930s and the family was plunged into poverty. They moved to rural Manitoba to farm in a government-sponsored scheme; however, the effects of drought on a small plot of marginal land, combined with the fact that Donald's parents knew little about farming, meant that it was a hard living. Sometimes they went without food.

From his mother, Donald inherited a love of language and writing poetry as well as aspirations for social justice. He first attended a one-room, one-teacher, multi-grade school. When my grandfather got work in Victoria, BC, in the shipbuilding industry fueled by the Second World War, Donald was enthusiastic about his chance to attend a city school with subject-specialist teachers. At Esquimalt High School he was active in the school newspaper.

My grandparents couldn't afford a university education for Donald so after graduation he used his technical skills to find work. Working for the BC Telephone Company in isolated northern towns, Donald's voice was sidelined from the broader world of ideas for reasons of class, regional disparity, and conclusively by his early death. Nevertheless, throughout his life, he endeavored to reach beyond his restricted sphere by acquiring knowledge through wide reading. He was interested in the big questions and sought answers in poetry, philosophy, history, and religion.

Donald wrote often using anything that was at hand. After his death, our family kept my father's papers. We knew they were central to who he'd been. After four decades, a gem caught my eye as I shuffled through: penned in the 1940s, a teenage rhyming narrative about the evils of Hitler's armies and the sacrifices of youth in war.

Poetic Inquiry as Social Analysis

In conclusion, poems both evoke and contain knowledge. A poem is a vessel where concepts appear early and in an ambiguous form. The vessel can be opened by way of analysis and by maintaining a listening and embodied presence alongside the image. Poetic practice introduces an element of mystery, playfulness, and potentially a deeper, more receptive level of awareness and openness to the other. Our relationship to thought and our level of awareness changes when we work with an image-based, as opposed to a logic-based process. Poet Gary Snyder speaks about thought images that come into language at a certain point. He describes these as fundamental pre-linguistic thought processes that are image-based.[11]

Final Reflections from Gisela

On a simple reading of my mother's diary, my take was: "She hasn't said much about the war." It was only after I unpacked the text by reconfiguring it into poetic form, that a different voice or presence revealed itself. This lyric voice articulated a narrative of wartime loss and dislocation from the perspective of a young woman navigating her relationships with family, with camp life, and with soldiers not much older than herself. Ultimately, by juxtaposing Ursula's words alongside those of Donald's, I deepened my insight into youthful responses to war and how these responses are shaped by culture, gender, and geography. As Leggo writes: "poets remind, see, reveal, listen, remember, startle, imagine, tease, question, pray, hope, linger, love, and connect."[12]

Notes

1. Sawyer and Norris, *Duoethnography*, 1.

2. Greene, "Prologue to Art."

3. Brady, "Forward."

4. Boughn. "The New American Poetry Revisited."

5. Prendergast, "Introduction."

6. Stibbe, *Women in the Third Reich.*

7. Ruebsaat, *Heart Mechanic.*

8. Stibbe, *Women in the Third Reich.*

9. Merriam-Webster Dictionary, "Triptych"; Oxford Dictionary, "Triptych.

10. Soutar-Hynes, "Points of Articulation."

11. Snyder, *The Gary Snyder Reader*.

12. Carl Leggo, "What Is a Poem Good For?" 57.

Acknowledgement

Research and Development Funds, The Faculty of Education, Memorial University.

Bibliography

Boughn, Michael. "The New American Poetry Revisited—Again." *Dooneyscafe.com*. August 20, 2013. https://www. dooneyscafe. com/archives/3761

Brady, Ivan. "Forward." In *Poetic inquiry: Vibrant Voices in the Social Sciences*, 12-17. Edited by S. Thomas, A. Cole, and S. Stewart. Boston MA: Sense Publishers, 2009.

Greene, Maxine. "Prologue to Art, Social Imagination and Action." *Journal of Educational Controversy* 5, no.1 (2010): Article 2. http://cedar.wwu.edu/jec/vol5/iss1/2.

Leggo, Carl. "What Is a Poem Good For? *Journal of Artistic and Creative Education* 5, no. 1 (2011). http://jaceonline.com.au/issues/issue-title/

Leggo, Carl. "Living Language: What Is a Poem Good For? *Journal of the Canadian Association for Curriculum Studies* 10, no. 1 (2012). http://jcacs.journals.yorku.ca/index.php/jcacs/article/viewFile/36281/33003

Merriam-Webster Dictionary, s.v. "Triptych," June 2018, https://www.merriam-webster.com.

Oxford Dictionary, s.v. "Triptych," June 2018, https://en.oxforddictionaries.com/definition/triptych.

Prendergast, Monica. "Introduction: The Phenomena of Poetry in Research." In *Poetic Inquiry: Vibrant Voices in the Social Sciences*, 13-19. Edited by C. Leggo and P. Sameshima. Boston, MA: Sense Publishers, 2009.

Ruebsaat, Gisela. *Heart Mechanic*. Victoria BC: Quadra Books, 2016.

Sawyer, Richard and Joe Norris. *Duoethnography: Understanding Qualitative Research*. New York NY: Oxford University Press, 2013.

Snyder, Gary. *The Gary Snyder Reader*. Washington DC: Counterpoint, 1999.

Soutar-Hynes, Mary. "Points of Articulation: A Letting Go and a Reaching Towards—a Poet's Journey." In *The Art of Poetic Inquiry*, 427-445. Edited by S. Thomas, A. Cole and S. Stewart. Halifax, NS: Backalong Books, 2012.

Stibbe, Matthew. *Women in the Third Reich*. New York: Oxford University Press, 2003.

20.

Reframing and Reflaming
Social Justice through Poetry

Sean Wiebe,
University of Prince Edward Island

Pauline Sameshima,
Lakehead University

In Ron Kortege's poem, "Do you have any advice for those of us just starting out?" there is a moment when the tower of books collapses. It is hard not to wonder whether education is similarly under threat of collapse. Perhaps this is why so many have turned to George Orwell's (1949) *Nineteen Eighty-Four* for some kind of prophetic assurance. In a critical moment in this text, Julia, by all appearances a womanly representation of the party's ideal, stumbles in front of Winston and passes him a note. In the bathroom, later, Winston reads the note, which contains the most important words of his life to date, *I love you.* In our dark times the resurgence of Orwell's political text brings urgency to the question, what are we to make of the political act of love for making social justice? Assuming educators are the public intellectuals Gramsci invites them to be, in what ways might love offer educators a means to refuse token advocations of justice and take up instead poetic making to rethink our social relations? Taking existentialism as a theoretical position, the poems in this chapter will seek to reframe and reflame social justice.

Keywords: education, Gramsci, love, Orwell, social justice

In Ron Koertge's poem, "Do you have any advice for those of us just starting out?" there is a moment when the tower of books collapses.[1] It is hard not to wonder whether education is similarly under threat of collapse. Perhaps this is why so many have turned to George Orwell's

Nineteen Eighty-Four for some kind of prophetic assurance. In a critical moment in this text, Julia, by all appearances a womanly representation of the Party's ideal, stumbles in front of Winston and passes him a note. In the bathroom, later, Winston reads the note, which contains the most important words of his life to date, *I love you.*[2] In our dark times the resurgence of Orwell's political text brings urgency to the question, what are we to make of the political act of love for making social justice? Assuming educators are the public intellectuals Gramsci invites them to be,[3] in what ways might love offer educators a means to refuse token advocations of justice and take up instead poetic making to rethink our social relations? Taking existentialism as a theoretical position, the poems in this chapter seek to reframe and reflame social justice through love.

In Koertge's poem referenced above, Koertge writes: "Give up sitting dutifully at your desk. Leave / your house or apartment. Go out into the world."[4] We hear Koertge prompting us to leave our desks. We hear echoes of Pinar's *currere* pushing us out into the world,[5] and this means letting go of the desk, not as easy as it seems. The desk symbolizes a kind of professorial responsibility, even accomplishment that we might be doing something good or important. Thank you, Koertge, for puncturing that balloon, for pointing to that element of duty that keeps us inside, tied to the desk, voiceless, and mostly afraid. In letting go, in all that means, we enable regeneration and love to occur.

We are glad for what Koertge humorously points out as distractions: academics wearing turtlenecks, perhaps a sports coat with elbow patches.[6] Imagine that—that our creative and critical scholarly work might be a distraction. If it is, then what is Koertge pointing us to? Laughter? Joy, maybe? We think a clue is in the kind of reaction laughter provokes: frowning, shushing. Here is a starting point for this chapter: may there be those in the world who frown and want to shush us.

Love as Anti-Idealism

Language smooths words that practically shush themselves. Paul Beatty, in his Pulitzer Prize-winning novel, *The Sellout*, writes:

> Sitting here on the steps of the Supreme Court smoking weed, under the "Equal Justice Under Law" motto, staring into the stars, I've finally figured out what's wrong with Washington, D.C. It's that all the buildings are more or less the same height and there's absolutely no skyline, save for the Washington Monument touching the night sky like a giant middle finger to the world.[7]

Under United States President Donald Trump, it appears the Trump Administration is learning to use its middle finger. Whether it is undermining trade agreements with its allies, or obfuscating facts for its electorate, or pardoning friends and bigots, there is a newfound privilege and entitlement in Washington. Those with cultural capital and the media have been largely ineffective, offering apologies and little more than empty analysis of "how could he possibly say that?!" Trump's power of discourse draws from a social imaginary that America was great and could be great again. What is it about idealism that draws in the masses of support?

The inspiration for our first poem comes from work that Wiebe has been doing on the superhero effect in education.[8] In an essay called "Teacher as Silenced Superhero," he argues that teachers are given the token social status of superhero and that this obligates them to be expressions of our social ideals for education, and in doing so, this also silences them. To expand that work, in a co-authored paper, we critique the public intellectual's role in projecting educational idealism. Below is a selection.[9] Following Sameshima's Parallaxic Praxis Model as a methodology we used Viet Thanh Nguyen's *The Sympathizer*[10] as a play object to consider two critical questions for understanding social justice: 1. "What is more important than independence and freedom?" and 2. "What do those who struggle against power do when they seize power?"

If You Want Justice

The two most important days in your life
are the day you are born
and the day you find out why.
　　　—Anonymous

i.
"We wake, work, eat, and sleep
according to what the landlord,
the owner, the banker, the politician,
and the schoolmaster command …
but in truth [time] belongs to us."[11]

Awaken paper tiger
the rooster is calling
awaken public intellectuals
you conference goers, funding magnets
creatives lost in history
you need a respite from it

your own capital investments
stolen from your integrity
awaken bankrupt scholar
steal back your time
remember the pleasure
of a lawn chair, a book,
a circuitous walk, sword fern
shoulder high, a path overgrown
remember cherry blossom air
warmth through your feet
carrying firewood
arranging your words like kindling
first the twigs, fanning
the flames, poetry burning
bright symmetry
in the forests of the sky

The poem, "If You Want Justice," has ten sections and concludes with a denouement that insists that justice is impossible unless we generate an alternative future. We do this by making, by materializing something from nothing, by making/generating love. Beatty writes, "That's the problem with history, we like to think it's a book—that we can turn the page and move the fuck on. But history isn't the paper it's printed on. It's memory, and memory is time, emotions, and song. History is the things that stay with you."[12] Beatty writes in the face of Auden's insistence that poetry doesn't do a damn thing to change the world.[13] To some degree it is true, especially if we think history is just a book. But what if history were our making, our song, our pleasures set out, not to explain its mysteries, but to simply render it?

Love as a Political Act

We want to turn now to Orwell's contribution to our thinking, the advocation of love as a political act. In *Nineteen Eighty-Four*, when Winston reads the note, *I love you*, what is he thinking? I love you. What are we to make of these three words in our dark times? We don't think Orwell is suggesting we convert love-making to a politics. Instead, we align with the thinking of Barthes's *The Pleasure of the Text*, that pleasure-seeking and pleasure-making are their own form of protest.[14]

This contrast is borne out in how Julia and Winston differ in their understanding of love. Winston receives Julia's love and it motivates him to social action. Julia, by contrast, loves Winston because of the pleasure of it.

The assumption implicit in Orwell's presentation of Julia is that pleasure-seeking is not an egoist. Artists, says Huddleston, "best serve the general good through the exercise of the personal freedom."[15] While such a position has been critiqued from both the political right (on utilitarian or moral grounds) and the left (on ideological and idealist grounds), what such critiques fail to consider is the social phenomenon of the individual. It may seem an obvious assertion—but the individual is alive, takes up space, is located in time, is a node of connection to others—the materiality of the individual makes it a being in the world, a social phenomenon. What logically follows is that when practicing individual freedom, social freedom is also asserted. We change the world simply with who and how we are.

The Fragrance of Her Love

awake in the stillness
turning into the hush
lake of his full back
flames rise in the east
blood pressed
against her veins
their legs untangled
roots raw in the fecund
soil of them burning
the bed of her dreams

she rises, leaves
in the kitchen
she cooks, organizes, clears
surfaces, cleans, smooths

fragrance escapes
from her stove
her oven
and her slow cooker
the coffee drips

he will rise, leave,
and she will still bloom

Before the 2017 American Educational Research Association (AERA) conference that took place in San Antonio in April 2017, thousands of academics had signed an open letter to boycott U.S. conferences. This open letter was a response to Trump's order to bar entry to the U.S. by people from seven majority Muslim nations. The American Educational Research Association and the Canadian counterpart organization, The Canadian Society for the Study of Education (CSSE), both publicly expressed dismay at this discriminatory policy. At this time of unrest, as Canadian scholars, we, along with many others, felt unsafe in the United States.

In Canada, the Canadian Association of Curriculum Studies is the curriculum organization comparable to AERA's Division B—the Curriculum Studies Association. Like Division B, our Association is the biggest organized Association in Canadian Education. Working with Division B, our Canadian Association, and Sameshima's university, Wiebe and Sameshima sought to offer Lakehead University as a meeting ground for curriculum scholars planning to boycott AERA. The "Future Generation" conference was not designed to take away from our colleagues in AERA's Division B, but to offer scholars another location to promote international research in curriculum studies.

We were grateful the ban was lifted and ultimately the conference call did not go public. The reason the alternate space was created was based on our stance that boycotting is revolt on the oppressor's terms and while we stand in solidarity with others, we silence ourselves and our research, and concede to powerlessness. As we have been arguing in our poetic scholarship over the last few years,[16] love-making and awakeness to the material moment recognize that to seek refuge in an endangered space is futile. The political imagination must turn away from the source of resistance and contention emerging through fertile acts of creation to generate new networks and systems of social relationships. Research constructs our future. Relocating and presenting in Canada is what we consider "generation." Creating the alternative location for the conference is a making; it is a construction born out of relation, of love, and in the outcome, more relation and love are constructed.

I Am Not a Soldier Going off to War

I am not a soldier
going off to war
but incline time's axis
not a jot, and falling
back a century, how easy
it would be to put my hands
into his pockets
to search the photo
you have traded
for a safe return.

Sun low in the sky,
sideways shining,
bidding farewell
as I am, thankful
that regardless of how
I invent this metaphor
I am not a soldier
going off to war.

This flight reddens
its colors, ochre
then chili-pepper red,
as my cheeks, flushed,
a man of uniforms,
hesitant, shy, stuck
in his mouth unformed
what he needs to say
just in case, though
I am not a soldier
going off to war.

Perhaps he will say after all,
afraid love heart-hidden
is a prom dress
not worn, yards of crinoline
envious of fabric
that will be stained
with blood, though
I am not a soldier
going off to war.

Writing letters by night
sky huge and black,
dusted with the dead,
he talks to them,
tries out little romances
meant for you,
sometimes laments
he cannot put down,
yellowing with age
the paper cannot bear
some words.

Some die so others live,
every language
has words for this,
though not a soldier
going off to war,
mine are similitude,
so what happens
to his letters is the same
as what happens
in my poem,
the all he risks
against the nothing
bearing down is mine
as well, his promise
his return, all mine,
his breaking into a run,
flowers falling to free
hands that will never
let go, though I am
not a soldier
going off to war.

Love as Redirection

Believing in Worms

the earthworms
on my driveway
squirm hardheadedly
whenever
they want
out of the green
drowning melt
onto the stamped concrete
a vast gray desert with no
beginning and end
searching
how many hours
of contractions
and to what end?
to set my path?

In situations of interpersonal violence, we applaud the victims for leaving the relationship and creating new lives, and shun those who do not have the strength or courage to leave; yet in the political and educational environments, we continue to try to resist thinking outside the box, attempting to fix and reform with the language of the canon, or on the terms of the oppressor.

Hashtag #whyistayed is evidence of the reasons why many women don't leave domestic violent situations. Cravens, Whiting, and Aamar conducted a social media metadata analysis and found eight themes for why women do not leave. We encourage the reader to think about these reasons in parallel to reasons why we do not leave dysfunctional political or education paradigms: 1. distorted thoughts, 2. damaged self-worth, 3. fear, 4. wanting to be a savior, 5. children (We'd call this sunken investment), 6. family (or past) expectations and experiences, 7. financial constraints, and 8. isolation.[17]

We believe in the poetic creation of the not yet—as we think, imagine, and make, we construct a new social love and possibility. If we can turn away, and make something new, we can make love.

What Can Happen in Three Days

A man can receive word he has lung cancer,
stage IV, go home, phone his children scattered
round the world, and tell them he loves them,
or he can plant a tree in the garden, hope
that it becomes known as the one he planted
just before he died.

It doesn't have to be cancer, the rise and fall
of a stock portfolio can bring a man to his knees
in even less than three days. It could be
a mosquito bite, something viral, nuclear,
or as simple as train tracks and a well-timed jump.

In the spy novels I read the course of a war
is changed in three days. A man wearing
an indistinct overcoat opens a briefcase,
hands over a few papers. The rest is history,
and why shouldn't it be? History is always in the making
so by virtue of choosing one road
and not another, aren't we the makers?

When you asked me if three days was enough
to be sure, I realized that the things I know
to be true are unrelated to numerical convention.
A second, two, three sips of tea,
time is an empty cup, a prop
the actor pretends to drink from,
but it is what gives permission
to be there, what matters in creation
is not the number of days
but what comes into the void.

Love as a Political Act of Pleasure

The pursuit of something for the self is frowned upon. In this world of intense surveillance, every action—every thought—has a target outcome. It is the ultimate form of the Tyler Rationale—love, sex, raising children, work, play, pleasure, thinking itself is for the Party.[18] It is an educational ideal, that the entirety of human experience could be oriented toward an end goal. A normative moral structure says something like, "Take your eyes off yourself and make the world a better place." The trouble, as Rana's blog explains, is that "the biggest paradox we face when it comes to decision-making is that we are forced to make decisions now about something that doesn't exist."[19] Rana uses Jeffrey Bezos, CEO of Amazon, as the example to explain Bezos's simple rule to stay the course, to "Focus [your vision] on the things that won't change," then tinker and build.[20] Knowing that there are multiple ways of getting to a point is key. Immersed in the variables, not hoping for a fixedness, we play, knowing that the thing that doesn't change is love.

We submit that Orwell's argument is that love is dangerous because it enlivens us, gets inside us, re-orients our hearts toward experience. The existentialist maxim is appropriate here: existence before essence. In love, the physicality, the materiality, the sensuality of experience is in the making. Here, then, is a poem that celebrates the pleasure of love, a potent love, as a means of refuge in these dark times:

The Earth Hears Your Song

On your shoulders rests
a fragrance of gratitude,
so when you kneel
to plant, your hands
are home in grit and sediment,

your arms know rhythm, style,
motions for all of what exists.
The earth hears your song,
the ways you care, unbending
a too far leaning shoot,
grafting another to its source,
a reservoir of love
that never empties.

Still there is much to be done,
the Light of day calls you
to goodness, whether plucking
a sticky plum or pulling
a thorn from a little one's palm,
all is love, given over long ago
in your will to not live a life
without planting life,
your time and faithfulness
pressed into the ground.

The harvest is the children
and what is unfrozen in them
how they write to know
to trace the line of the petals
in their school books
their laughing
clusters of blossoms

and the windows are open—
They know you open windows
in reverse, to let the outside world
come in, the secret of your voice
is in their hearts, its slope
and waft unlocking shutters
to let in joy, they listen, and then
speak truly of their love for you
without needing a reason why.

Reflaming Truth

As Koertge advises, "give up sitting dutifully at your desk."[21] He reminds us that academic theorization needs action. We ask what we should make of the political act of love for making social justice. How do we rethink our social relations beyond token theorization? Can we imagine the future by looking back? Shakespeare's *Hamlet* was first performed in 1609. We see in that work, as Hamlet struggles to enact revenge, the perennial dilemma between duty and moral decisive action. Shakespeare suggests that "thinking too precisely on the event" offers only "one part wisdom" and "three parts coward."[22] Talk is thin morality. What if morality were directed at our own being? Our beingness or going out into the world is materialized action.

Grown from Koertge's poem, we write only our thinkings about age-old dilemmas, confrontations between ethics and moral duty as framed in social justice, theory and practice in terms of courage and fear. Our advice: turn away, make new, make love. Laugh, cry, let them say shush. Consider what you are willing to speak truthfully about.

James, I'm Sorry

Nancy writes

hot summer days
have slipped
out

> *Yes, I remember Nancy walking*
> *with me on the street*
> *late without our jackets*
> *the Thai restaurant playing*
> *music that reminds me of him*
> *wanting him back*
> *but I'm with you now*
> *the movie theatre quiet as we enter*
> *our lives silent and decades slipping by*

and we are back
to our west coast
rain

> *it has been raining here too*
> *inside all summer*

then thoughts of you
having tea, walking
your hair, your shoes
your red leather jacket
flash in front of me
how are you?

> *I want to go back*
> *to those still places, the way it was*
> *with him because now,*

when the reporters call
or when the galleries say yes
   it's a high profile show
I remember
I remember
   the old safety
     the room holding me
   the breeze not even
   coming in through the window
   or from the narrow pane in the kitchen
     his sheets smelling like mine
I want to go back
   even when I know
   he no longer loves me
   or knows me
I am waiting
   still waiting for him to find me
   come back to me
   to unbreak me
     to break me from you

You must be
busy with all
the wonders of life

   yes

     outside everyone sees a picture
     they think we're a wonderful couple
       perfect
And inside
   I am spinning down
   clockwise like my baby
     swirling down the toilet
And my other baby lying blue when I
   breathed into her tiny lips
     bringing her back from the dark
And the other is swaddled tight only her head exposed
and I hold her against me
   my eyes squeezed
   tight so I block out the image
   of her head cracking
     on the hard floor
     I do not let her go
And the blood pools in my hands

and I have nowhere to put it
sitting in his car on lambskin covers
And the neighbor with the cigarette
on his porch shouting
                    at the boyfriend to stop
                    kicking me
I don't feel it
And now you hold me
        always trying to make me safe
        and I am so sorry I STILL don't feel anything
        I don't know how to wait alone, hoping
for him, just him
                to come back
                and hold me

My summer this year
has been quite full
with fun and work
and lots of visitors
What about you?
                    the same

Notes

1. Koertge, "Do you have any advice."

2. Orwell, *Nineteen Eighty-Four.*

3. Gramsci, Hoare, and Nowell-Smith. *Selections.*

4. Koertge, "Do you have any advice."

5. Pinar, *What Is Curriculum Theory?*

6. Koertge, "Do you have any advice."

7. Beatty, *The Sellout*, 278.

8. Wiebe, "Teacher as Silenced Superhero."

9. Full work available at
https://journals.library.ualberta.ca/ari/index.php/ari/article/view/29243.

10. Nguyen, *The Sympathizer.*

11. Nguyen, *The Sympathizer*, 60.

12. Beatty, *The Sellout*, 115.

13. Huddleston, "Poetry Makes Nothing Happen."

14. Barthes, *The Pleasure of the Text.*

15. Huddleston, "Poetry Makes Nothing Happen," para. 1.

16. Wiebe and Sameshima, "Generating Self."

17. Cravens, Whiting, and Aamar, "Why I Stayed/Left."

18. Tyler, *Basic Principles.*

19. Rana, "The Jeff Bezos Way."

20. Ibid.

21. Koertge, "Do you have any advice."

22. Shakespeare, *Hamlet*, 85.

Bibliography

Barthes, Roland. *The Pleasure of the Text.* Trans. by R. Miller. New York, NY: The Noonday Press, 1973.

Beatty, Paul. *The Sellout.* New York, NY: Farrar, Straus and Giroux, 2015.

Cravens, Jaclyn D., Jason B. Whiting, and Rola Aamar. "Why I Stayed/Left: An Analysis of Voices of Intimate Partner Violence on Social Media." *Contemporary Family Therapy* 37, no. 4 (2015). doi: 10.1007/s10591-015-9360-8

Gramsci, Antonio, Quintin Hoare, and Geoffrey Nowell-Smith. *Selections from the Prison Notebooks of Antonio Gramsci.* New York: International Publishers, 1971.

Huddleston, Robert. "Poetry Makes Nothing Happen." *Boston Review: A Political and Literary Forum.* February 25, 2015.

Koertge, Ron. "Do you have any advice for those of us just starting out?" Poetry 180. https://www.loc.gov/poetry/180/007.html

Orwell, George. *Nineteen Eighty-Four.* London, UK: Penguin, 1949.

Pinar, William, F. *What Is Curriculum Theory?* Mahwah, New Jersey: Lawrence Erlbaum, 2004.

Nguyen, Viet Thanh. *The Sympathizer.* New York, NY: Grove Press, 2015.

Rana, Zat. "The Jeff Bezos Way: How to Design Your Ideal Future." *Medium.* May 13, 2018. https://medium.com/personal-growth/the-jeff-bezos-way-how-to-design-your-ideal-future-f1d0a3cc23c

Shakespeare, William. *Hamlet.* Mineola, NY: Dover, 1992.

Tyler, Ralph. *Basic Principles of Curriculum and Instruction.* Chicago: University of Chicago Press, 1949.

Wiebe, Sean. "Teacher as Silenced Superhero." *Learning Landscapes* 9, no 2 (2016), 535-550.

Wiebe, Sean and Pauline Sameshima. "Sympathizing with social justice, poetry of invitation and generation." *Art/Research International* 3, no. 1 (2018), 7-29.

Wiebe, Sean and Pauline Sameshima. "Generating Self: Catechizations in Poetry." *Revista VIS* 16, no. 2 (2017), 140-155.

Biographies

Laura Apol is an Associate Professor at Michigan State University. In addition to professional publications on children's literature and creative writing, she is the author of numerous collections of her own poems, including *Falling into Grace* (Dordt, 1998); *Crossing the Ladder of the Sun* (Michigan State University Press, 2003); *Requiem, Rwanda* (Michigan State University Press, 2015); and *With a Gift for Burning* (Finishing Line, 2018).

Robin Reynolds Barre, Ph.D. is a depth psychotherapist in private practice in the Pacific Northwest. She works mainly with adolescents and clients who have survived trauma. Barre earned her master's and doctorate from Pacifica Graduate Institute. Her doctoral dissertation was a poetic inquiry exploring mythology, poetry, the archetype of Adolescence, and the Unsayable Dimension of trauma. In addition to being a therapist, Barre is also, at heart, a teacher—though she was first, before anything, a writer.

Lee Beavington is an award-winning poet and ecologist. He is an SSHRC scholar and PhD candidate in Philosophy of Education at Simon Fraser University, and has taught a wide range of courses and labs at Kwantlen Polytechnic University, including Ecology, Genetics, Expressive Arts, and the Amazon Field School. His interdisciplinary research focuses on ecopoetics and using poetry to cultivate a connection to place. Find Beavington reflecting in the forest, mesmerized by ferns, and always following the river. Find more about him at www.leebeavington.com.

Maya T. Borhani, poet and wordsmith, is currently a doctoral student in Educational Studies at the University of Victoria in British Columbia, specializing in poetic inquiry and applied theatre; she holds a master's degree in Language and Literacy Education from the University of British Columbia, Vancouver. Her interest in poetic inquiry stems from a lifelong relationship with place-centered pedagogies, and poetry as voice, political currency, and personal salvation. When not studying, writing, or singing, Borhani enjoys attending to the small movements of the natural world in wild places, in cityscapes, and within the intricacies of the human emotional mind/land/scape.

Abigail Cloud is a poet and Senior Lecturer at Bowling Green State University. She is Editor-in-Chief of *Mid-American Review* and faculty advisor to *Prairie Margins*. Her first collection, *Sylph* (Pleiades, 2014), was a Lena-Miles Wever Todd Prize winner. Her research interests include Laban's effort principles as applied to language and mortality theory.

Kimberly Dark is a writer, professor, and raconteur, working to reveal the hidden architecture of everyday life one clever essay, poem, and story at a time. She has performed poetry and stories at hundreds of venues worldwide during the past twenty years. She teaches in the MA program in Sociological Practice at California State San Marcos. Learn more at www.kimberlydark.com.

Sandra L. Faulkner is Professor of Communication and Director of Women's, Gender, and Sexuality Studies at Bowling Green State University. Her interests include qualitative methodology, poetic inquiry, and the relationships among culture, identities, and sexualities in close relationships. Her poetry appears in places such as *Literary Mama* and *damselfly*. She authored three chapbooks, *Hello Kitty Goes to College* (dancing girl press, 2012), *Knit Four, Make One* (Kattywompus, 2015), and *Postkarten aus Deutschland* (http://liminalities.net/12-1/postkarten.html), and a memoir in poetry, *Knit Four, Frog One* (Sense, 2014). She was the recipient of the 2016 Norman K. Denzin Qualitative Research Award.

Alexandra Fidyk, PhD, is Associate Professor in the Department of Secondary Education, University of Alberta; Associate Editor of the *International Journal of Jungian Studies*; past President of the Jungian Society of Scholarly Studies; joint editor of *Poetic Inquiry: Enchantment of Place*; Certified Jungian Psychotherapist, Integrated Body Psychotherapist, Constellation & Family System therapist (inherited and transgenerational trauma); lover of horses, cats, and nature.

Sandra Filippelli's current explorations include peace, mindfulness, and happiness. Her research interests encompass arts-based research areas of poetic inquiry, creative writing, art education, and art research. She has published in *Art Research International, Poetic Inquiry: Enchantment of Place, Visual Inquiry: Learning & Teaching Art, EVENT Magazine, Joyland,* and *The Flat Earth Excavation Project*. She is a PhD candidate in the Department of Language and Literacy, University of British Columbia.

Amanda N. Gulla is an English Education professor and a published poet. Her poems and her research and writing on poetic inquiry and aesthetic education have appeared in many literary and academic journals. She is the coordinator of the English Education program at Lehman College of the City University of New York, a member of the Board of Directors of the Maxine Greene Institute for Aesthetic Education and the Social Imagination, and the Professional Development Liaison for the Maxine Greene High School for Imaginative Inquiry.

Natalie Honein is a writer, poet, educator, and parent. She holds a doctorate in Education from the University of Bristol, UK, and has taught academic writing at the American University of Beirut and the American University of Sharjah in the UAE. Her publications explore narrative research, gender issues, poetic inquiry, and Arab women activists. She is published in *Poetic Inquiries of Reflection and Renewal*, the *Canadian Journal of Education*, *Poetic Inquiry III: Enchantments of Place*, and *Narrative Works*. Honein currently works and writes in Dubai.

Sarah K. MacKenzie-Dawson spends her days negotiating among her identities as a mother, artist, poet, partner, teacher, scholar, and introvert. She relishes the rare moments of quiet, but also finds her spirit nourished by the beauty of watching her two young daughters discover the world or listening as her college students discover themselves beyond the definitions that may have been placed upon them by society. She is an Associate Professor of Education at Bucknell University, where she teaches courses related to literacy, arts-integration, holistic education, spirituality, gender, and social justice. Her research focuses on ideas of identity, connection, and isolation.

Mark McCarthy is a doctoral candidate in Teacher Education at Michigan State University. His research investigates teacher preparation, specifically as inquiry into his own teaching practice. Interests bridging his research and teaching include children's literature, literacy and discourse, and a pedagogy of creative interference.

Margaret McKeon is an outdoor educator, poet, and doctoral candidate in Language and Literacy Education at the University of British Columbia. A person of Euro-Settler ancestry, for her dissertation she is creating poetry and stories about land relationship, ancestral knowledges, and colonialism. This research builds on professional work coordinating an outdoor education program in Western Newfoundland as it transformed to also be a strong Mi'kmaw cultural education program, and master's studies that theorized on this weaving process of "indigenization."

Heather McLeod (Ph.D. University of Victoria) is Associate Professor (arts education) in the Faculty of Education at Memorial University in St. John's,

Newfoundland, Canada. She pursues a critical research agenda and is interested in arts-based research methods. Her funded research initiatives include a parents and poetry project, an examination of the process of becoming a researcher, an initiative to understand student experiential learning in an art museum, and an Open Studio project with immigrant and refugee youth. McLeod has won national and faculty awards for curriculum development and teaching. She currently serves as the Editor-in-Chief of the *Canadian Review of Art Education*.

Robert Christopher Nellis is a continuous faculty member in the Red Deer College School of Education. He is the author of *Haunting Inquiry: Classic NFB Documentary, Jacques Derrida, and the Curricular Otherwise* (Sense, 2009) and a former co-President of the Canadian Association for Curriculum Studies. He teaches courses in Educational Psychology, Family Studies, Educational Foundations, Curriculum Studies, and Media Education. Recent scholarship has taken up creative nonfiction and poetic inquiry to explore place, memory, and human-animal relations. He shares his life with both humans and animals yet laments that his gifts received shine far, far richer than those given.

Bonnie Nish is Executive Director of Pandora's Collective Outreach Society. She has a master's in Arts Education from Simon Fraser University and is pursuing a PhD in Language and Literacy Education at The University of British Columbia. Nish's research examines how poetry and life writing can help those recovering from trauma. Nish's book *Love and Bones* was published in 2013 (Karma Press). Her book *Concussion and Mild TBI: Not Just Another Headline* was published by Lash and Associates in 2016. Ekstasis Editions will release her next book of poetry, *Cantata in Two Voices*, co-written with Jude Neale, next fall.

Gisela Ruebsaat is a legal analyst, writer, and independent scholar whose work has appeared in literary and academic journals. In 2016, Ruebsaat was selected by the Canadian government as one of 150 woman leaders in Canada to support gender equality. Her poetry collection, *Heart Mechanic*, was published in 2016 by Quadra Books. Ruebsaat has performed her poems locally and internationally: She performed at the "Soulfood-Lesebuhne" in Marburg Germany; she presented at three International Symposia on Poetic Inquiry and also, in 2017, at Winter Wheat: The *Mid-American Review* Festival of Writing at Bowling Green State University. Most recently Ruebsaat worked as legal analyst for a feminist advocacy organization.

Pauline Sameshima is a Professor and Canada Research Chair in Arts Integrated Studies at Lakehead University. Her interests are in creativity, imagination, curriculum theory, and community health. Sameshima's interdisciplinary projects use the arts to catalyze innovation, generate wanderings, and provoke new dialogues. She is the Editor-in-Chief of *The Journal of the Canadian Association for Curriculum Studies* and curates the Lakehead Research Education Galleries. She is online at solspire.com.

Molly H. Sherman has taught EFL, English, and English Education on three continents with students at the elementary, middle, secondary, and post-secondary levels. She taught for ten years in the South Bronx and is currently an English teacher at Harvest Collegiate High School in New York City, a school founded to enact and promote social justice. She also facilitates professional development as a teacher consultant with the New York City Writing Project and teaches graduate students in the English Education Program at Lehman College. With Amanda N. Gulla, Sherman has been developing pedagogy that embodies the philosophy of Maxine Greene, guiding students through in-depth inquiries into works of art and fostering of voice through the act of writing poetry.

Sheila Squillante is Assistant Professor of English and Director of the MFA program in Creative Writing at Chatham University. She is the author of the poetry collection *Beautiful Nerve* (Tiny Hardcore, 2015). She has published poems and essays widely in print and online journals such as *Brevity, The Rumpus, Prairie Schooner, North Dakota Quarterly, River Teeth,* and elsewhere. She is Editor-in-Chief of *The Fourth River*, a literary journal of nature and place-based writing.

Sheila Stewart has two poetry collections, *The Shape of a Throat* (Signature Editions, 2012) and *A Hat to Stop a Train* (Wolsak and Wynn, 2003), as well as a co-edited anthology of essays and poetry, *The Art of Poetic Inquiry* (Backalong Book, 2012). Recognition for her poetry includes the gritLIT Contest, the Pottersfield Portfolio Short Poem Contest, and the Scarborough Arts Council Windows on Words Award. Recent work has appeared in *CV2* and *Art/Research International: A Transdisciplinary Journal*. She teaches at the New College Writing Centre, University of Toronto.

Anne McCrary Sullivan is Professor Emeritus at National Louis University. Her poems and essays have appeared in many literary and academic publications. She was a Fulbright Scholar at the University of Calabar 2012-2013. Her permanent home is in Florida.

244   *Biographies*

Professor Heidi van Rooyen is an Executive Director at the Human Sciences Research Council in South Africa. She leads a multidisciplinary research group interested in the development of individuals over the life course with a focus on how diversity relating to race, gender, sexuality, and disability impacts our ability to live our best lives. Her current research focuses on the influence of sexual orientation and gender identity as social determinants of health, and issues of race and identity. Van Rooyen is a certified life coach who balances the demands of leadership, publishing, and grant writing with a regular contemplative writing practice and poetry.

Sean Wiebe, an Associate Professor of Education at the University of Prince Edward Island, teaches courses in multiliteracies, curriculum theory, and critical pedagogy. He has been the principal investigator on four Canadian Social Sciences and Humanities Research Council funded projects exploring the intersections of creativity, the creative economy, language and literacies, and arts-informed inquiries.

John J. Guiney Yallop is a parent, a partner, and a poet. His doctoral dissertation is a poetic inquiry that explores identities, emotions, and communities. He has presented and written about growing up gay in a small, rural, Catholic community and being an out gay teacher in public schools. His poetry has been presented in local, national, and international venues, as well as being published in literary and peer-reviewed academic journals.

Index